S0-BAE-120

Frommer's®

P O R T A B L E

Charleston & Savannah

3rd Edition

by Darwin Porter & Danforth Prince

IDG Books Worldwide, Inc.
An International Data Group Company
Foster City, CA • Chicago, IL • Indianapolis, IN • New York, NY

ABOUT THE AUTHORS

A North Carolina native, Darwin Porter has lived in South Carolina and Georgia and explored extensively in the region's major cities and backwoods hamlets. He was a bureau chief of the *Miami Herald* at age 21 and has written numerous best-selling Frommer guides, notably to France, England, Italy, and the Caribbean. He is the co-author of Frommer's *The Carolinas & Georgia*, working with Danforth Prince, formerly of the Paris bureau of the *New York Times*. Dan has lived in Georgia and traveled extensively in the tristate area.

IDG BOOKS WORLDWIDE, INC.

An International Data Group Company
919 E. Hillsdale Blvd.
Suite 400
Foster City, CA 94404

Find us online at **www.frommers.com**

ISBN 0-02-863602-3
ISSN 1090-154X

Editor: Kelly Regan
Production Editor: Robyn Burnett
Design by Michele Laseau
Staff Cartographers: John Decamillis, Roberta Stockwell
Photo Editor: Richard Fox
Page Creation by Natalie Evans, Linda Quigley

SPECIAL SALES

For general information on IDG Books Worldwide's books in the U.S., please call our Consumer Customer Service department at 1-800-762-2974. For reseller information, including discounts, bulk sales, customized editions, and premium sales, please call our Reseller Customer Service department at 1-800-434-3422.

Manufactured in the United States of America

5 4 3 2 1

Contents

List of Maps

AN INVITATION TO THE READER

In researching this book, we discovered many wonderful places—hotels, restaurants, shops, and more. We're sure you'll find others. Please tell us about them, so we can share the information with your fellow travelers in upcoming editions. If you were disappointed with a recommendation, we'd love to know that, too. Please write to:

Frommer's Portable Charleston & Savannah, 3rd Edition
IDG Travel
1633 Broadway
New York, NY 10019

AN ADDITIONAL NOTE

Please be advised that travel information is subject to change at any time—and this is especially true of prices. The authors, editors, and publisher cannot be held responsible for the experiences of readers while traveling. Your safety is important to us, however, so we encourage you to stay alert and be aware of your surroundings. Keep a close eye on cameras, purses, and wallets, all favorite targets of thieves and pickpockets.

WHAT THE SYMBOLS MEAN
✪ Frommer's Favorites

Our favorite places and experiences—outstanding for quality, value, or both.

The following abbreviations are used for credit cards:

AE	American Express	EC	Eurocard
CB	Carte Blanche	JCB	Japan Credit Bank
DC	Diners Club	MC	MasterCard
DISC	Discover	V	Visa
ER	enRoute		

FIND FROMMER'S ONLINE

Arthur Frommer's Budget Travel Online (www.frommers.com) offers more than 6,000 pages of up-to-the-minute travel information—including the latest bargains and candid, personal articles updated daily by Arthur Frommer himself. No other Web site offers such comprehensive and timely coverage of the world of travel.

Planning a Trip to Charleston & Savannah

*T*his chapter is designed to provide most of the nuts-and-bolts travel information you'll need before setting off for South Carolina or Georgia. Browse through this section before you hit the road to en- sure that you've touched all the bases.

1 Visitor Information & Money

VISITOR INFORMATION

IN SOUTH CAROLINA   Before leaving home, you can get spe- cific information on South Carolina sports and sightseeing by con- tacting the **South Carolina Division of Tourism,** 1205 Pendleton St., P.O. Box 71, Columbia, SC 29202 (☎ **803/734-0122;** fax 803/734-0133). They can also furnish a copy of *South Carolina: Smiling Faces, Beautiful Places,* a detailed booklet with photos that covers each region of the state.

You can also contact the **Visitor Reception & Transportation Center (VRTC),** P.O. Box 975, Charleston, SC 29402 (☎ **803/ 853-8000**), for an advance copy of its comprehensive *Visitor's Guide* to Charleston.

When you get to South Carolina, look for one of the 10 **welcome centers** located on virtually every major highway near borders with neighboring states. All are open daily from 9:30am to 5pm (closed New Year's, Thanksgiving, and Christmas). For more information on these welcome centers and all South Carolina welcome programs, call the **South Carolina Visitors Service Section** at ☎ **803/ 734-0124.**

IN GEORGIA   For advance-planning information on Georgia, contact the **Division of Tourism,** Georgia Department of Indus- try, Trade & Tourism, P.O. Box 1776, Atlanta, GA 30301 (☎ **800/VISIT-GA** or 404/656-3590). Ask for information on spe- cific interests, as well as a calendar of events (Jan to June or July to Dec).

There are three **Georgia State Information Centers** near Savannah. The first is in **Garden City,** on I-95 South at the South Carolina border (☎ 912/964-5094), about 5 minutes north of Savannah; the second is in **Richmond Hill,** on I-95 and Hwy. 17 (☎ 912/756-2676), about 10 minutes west of Savannah; and the third is in **Brunswick,** on I-95 South between exits 8 and 9 (☎ 800/933-2627), about 30 minutes south of Savannah. They're all open Monday to Saturday from 9am to 6pm and Sunday from noon to 6pm.

INTERNET WEB SITES   If you have Internet access, check out the following sites: **CityNet (www.city.net)** provides links organized by location and then by category to hundreds of other sites. The **Charleston Convention and Visitors Bureau (www. charlestoncvb.com)** will keep you up-to-date on what's new in Charleston. At the **Charleston Connection (www.aesir.com/ charleston/welcome.html)** you can find details on dining, history, events, and more. And the **Charleston Tourism Index (http:// pages.prodigy.com/SC/familyhx/tourism1.html)** gives you access to all kinds of information on the city.

The **Savannah Area Convention & Visitors Bureau (www.savcvb.com)** will provide you with a variety of info about the city and environs. The **Ultimate Midnight Site (www. midnightinthegarden.com/)** is just what its name implies—you'll find just about everything you want to know about the book and the movie and the city of Savannah. Another choice is the **Midnight in the Garden of Good and Evil site (www. savannahnow.com/ goodandevil/),** sponsored by SavannahNOW and the *Savannah Morning News.*

For details on the Lady Chablis, the Grand Empress of Savannah, check out the Lady Chablis site (www.simonsays.com/titles/ 0671520946/chablis.html). The Grand Empress also offers the Lady's Tour (www.phorum.com/microsites/savannah/chablis/ chablis.htm), a multimedia tour of Savannah.

MONEY

It's becoming easier all the time to just bring along your ATM card and access your bank accounts while you're on the road. There are ATMs all over both Charleston and Savannah (even in supermarkets), but if you need help locating one, call ☎ **800/424-7787** for the **Cirrus** network or ☎ **800/843-7587** for the **Plus** system. On the Web, you can locate Cirrus ATMs at **www.mastercard.com**

and Plus ATMs at **www.visa.com.** Most ATMS will also make cash advances against MasterCard and Visa, but make sure that you've been assigned a PIN in advance.

Some people still prefer having the extra security associated with carrying traveler's checks. One major issuer is **American Express** (☎ **800/221-7282**).

2 When to Go

This is a mighty hot and steamy part of the country in summer—it's incredibly humid in July and August (sometimes in June and Sept as well). But temperatures are never extreme the rest of the year, as shown in the average highs and lows noted in the chart below. Winter temperatures seldom drop below freezing anywhere in the state. Spring and fall are the longest seasons, and the wettest months are December to April.

Spring, which usually begins in March, is just spectacular. Delicate pink and white dogwoods and azaleas in vivid shades burst into brilliant bloom. Both Savannah and Charleston are heaven for gardeners (or anyone who likes to stop and smell the roses), so March and April are memorable times to visit. During spring and Charleston's Spoleto Festival (see Calendar of Events, below), hotel prices rise and reservations are hard to come by.

Charleston's Average Temperatures (°F)

	Jan	Feb	Mar	Apr	May	June	July	Aug	Sept	Oct	Nov	Dec
Avg. High	59	61	68	76	83	87	89	89	85	77	69	61
Avg. Low	40	41	48	56	64	70	74	74	69	49	49	42

Savannah's Average Temperatures (°F)

	Jan	Feb	Mar	Apr	May	June	July	Aug	Sept	Oct	Nov	Dec
Avg. High	60	62	70	78	84	89	91	90	85	78	70	62
Avg. Low	38	41	48	55	63	69	72	72	68	57	57	41

CHARLESTON, HILTON HEAD & SAVANNAH
CALENDAR OF EVENTS

January
- **Low-Country Oyster Festival,** Charleston. Steamed buckets of oysters greet visitors to Boone Hall Plantation. Enjoy live music, oyster-shucking contests, children's events, and various other activities. For details, contact the Greater Charleston Restaurant

Association, 185 E. Bay St., Suite 206, Charleston, SC 29401
(☎ **803/577-4030**). Mid-January.

February

- **Wormsloe Celebrates the Founding of Georgia,** Savannah.
  Wormsloe was the Colonial fortified home of Noble Jones, one
  of Georgia's first colonists. Costumed staff demonstrate skills used
  by early settlers. Call ☎ **912/353-3023** for details. Early
  February.

- **Southeastern Wildlife Exposition,** Charleston. More than 150
  of the finest artists and more than 500 exhibitors participate at 13
  downtown locations. Enjoy carvings, sculpture, paintings, live
  animal exhibits, food, and much more. Call ☎ **803/723-1748**
  for details. Mid-February.

- **Savannah Irish Festival,** Savannah. This Irish heritage celebration, complete with traditional music, dancing, and food, promises fun for the entire family. Call ☎ **912/927-0331** for details.
  Mid-February.

March

- **Festival of Houses and Gardens,** Charleston. For nearly 50 years
  people have been enjoying some of Charleston's most historic
  neighborhoods and private gardens on this tour. For details,
  contact the Historic Charleston Foundation, P.O. Box 1120,
  Charleston, SC 29402 (☎ **803/723-1623**). Mid-March to
  mid-April.

- ✪ **St. Patrick's Day Celebration on the River,** Savannah. The
  river flows green, and so does the beer, in one of the largest celebrations held on River Street each year. Savannah's parade is the
  third largest in the States. Enjoy live entertainment, lots of food,
  and tons of fun. For details, call the Savannah Waterfront Association at ☎ **912/234-0295.** St. Patrick's Day weekend.

- ✪ **Family Circle Magazine Cup,** Hilton Head Island. This
  $750,000 tournament draws the world's best women tennis play-
  ers to the island. Call ☎ **803/363-3500** for details. Late March
  to early April.

April

- **MCI Classic,** Hilton Head. This $1.3 million tournament brings
  an outstanding field of PGA tour professionals each year. The
  weeklong tournament is held at Harbour Town Golf Links in Sea
  Pines Plantation. For details, contact Classic Sports, Inc.,
  71 Lighthouse Rd., Suite 414, Hilton Head, SC 29928 (☎ **803/
  671-2448**). Mid-April.

South Carolina

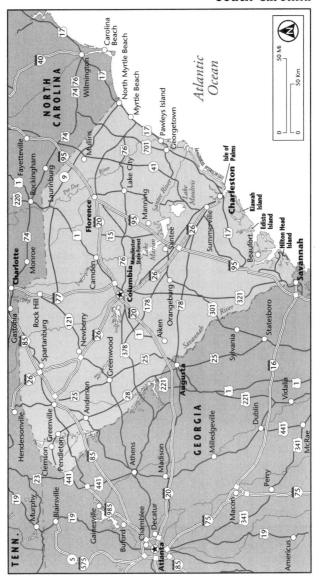

May

- **American Classic Tea Open House,** Charleston. America's only tea plantation welcomes the public for free tours—and don't forget to buy some superb blends when you leave. For details, contact the Charleston Tea Plantation, 6617 Maybank Hwy., Wadmalaw Island, SC 29487 (☎ **803/559-0383**). Early May.

- **Savannah Symphony Duck Race,** Savannah. Each year the Savannah Symphony Women's Guild plays host as a flock of rubber ducks hit the water to go with the flow of the tides along Savannah's historic River Street. There's a $5,000 grand prize for the winning ducky. For details, contact the Savannah Symphony Women's Guild at ☎ **912/238-0888.** Early May.

- **Memorial Day at Old Fort Jackson,** Savannah. A 21-cannon salute, a flag-raising ceremony, and a memorial service pay tribute to America's fallen troops. The S guard (honor guard) for the ceremony is made up of members of the 1st South Carolina Volunteers reenactment unit. For details, contact the Coastal Heritage Society at ☎ **912/238-1779.** Late May.

- ✪ **Spoleto Festival USA,** Charleston. This is the premier cultural event in the tristate area. This famous international festival, the American counterpart to the equally celebrated one in Spoleto, Italy, showcases world-renowned performers in drama, dance, music, and art. Performances and exhibits are held in various venues around Charleston. For details and this year's schedule, contact Spoleto Festival USA, P.O. Box 157, Charleston, SC 29402 (☎ **803/722-2764**). Late May to early June.

June

- **Juneteenth,** Savannah. This event highlights the contributions of more than 2,000 African Americans who fought for their freedom and the freedom of all future generations. For details, contact the Savannah Trade and Tourism Office at ☎ **912/944-0456.** Early June.

July

- **Thunderbolt Seafood Harvest Festival,** Savannah. A celebration of the harvest in a historic fishing village with food, fun, games, entertainment, arts and crafts, and a parade. For details, contact the Thunderbolt Seafood Harvest Festival Committee at ☎ **912/355-4422.** Late July.

August

- **Savannah Maritime Festival,** Savannah. This celebration of the sea is competitive, educational, and entertaining. Experience a

Midnight **Madness**

John Berendt's *Midnight in the Garden of Good and Evil* brought Savannah out of a long, self-induced slumber. The story—about an older gay antiques dealer named Jim Williams who shot a young hustler named Danny Hansford, and the colorful, eccentric characters that populated their world—isn't the type that usually appears on the best-seller list. Published to critical acclaim, *Midnight* landed a fairly permanent spot on the *New York Times* best-seller list. At press time, the book has sold some 1.5 million copies in the United States alone—and that's hardcover only; there are 19 foreign editions.

The wildly successful best-seller spawned a mediocre movie. When Hollywood came calling, Berendt turned down the screenwriting job, but he was lucky (unlucky?) enough to secure Clint Eastwood as the director of the film. While critics raved over Kevin Spacey's performance as Jim Williams, the movie itself was widely panned.

Today the city is overrun with hustlers hawking *Midnight* items—everything from cookies to T-shirts. There's even a *Midnight* fan club (contact the Book Gift Shop and Museum, 127 E. Gordon St.; ☎ **912/233-3867**), and there are several *Midnight* Web sites (see "Internet Web Sites," above). This book even sketches out a walking tour that encompasses many of the famous sites from the book (see chapter 5).

Savannah's old-time aristocrats take a strong stance against the book; they feel Berendt invaded their privacy and published their dark secrets for the world to read. Jim Williams's sister, Dorothy Williams Kingery, occupies Mercer House today and isn't too happy over the hysteria surrounding the book, either. She hired an attorney to secure for her a trademark on the facade of Mercer House that would prevent artisans from depicting the mansion on souvenirs without first obtaining a licensing agreement.

The *Washington Post* has declared that *Midnight* is "well on its way to becoming an American classic." In the same vein, Random House has announced that *Midnight* has joined its Modern Library series, a rare distinction for a living author.

sailing regatta, the Tybrisa Ball, a sportfishing tournament, a 10K run, the Jet Ski Jamboree, the Beach Volleyball Classic, and a laser show with fireworks. For details, contact the Savannah Maritime Committee at ☎ **912/236-3959.** Early August.

September

- **Scottish Games and Highland Gathering,** Charleston. This gathering of Scottish clans features medieval games, bagpipe performances, Scottish dancing, and other traditional activities. For details, contact the Scottish Society of Charleston, P.O. Box 31951, Charleston, SC 29417 (☎ **803/884-4371**). Mid-September.

- **Savannah Jazz Festival,** Savannah. This festival features national and local jazz and blues legends. A jazz brunch and music are presented at different venues throughout the city. For details, contact Host South at ☎ **912/232-2222.** Mid-September.

October

- **MOJA Festival,** Charleston. The event celebrates the rich African-American heritage of the Charleston area with lectures, art exhibits, stage performances, historical tours, concerts, and much more. For details, contact the Charleston Office of Cultural Affairs, 133 Church St., Charleston, SC 29401 (☎ **803/724-7305**). Early October.

- **Corel Championships,** Hilton Head Island. In preparation for an end-of-the-year championship, world-class male tennis players compete in this $150,000 tournament. Call ☎ **803/842-1893** for details. Early October.

- **Tom Turpin Ragtime Festival,** Savannah. Tom Turpin, born in Savannah, was a major force in the development of ragtime. The festival honoring him includes concerts, seminars, parlor piano, and ragtime dance. For details, contact the Tom Turpin Ragtime Society at ☎ **912/233-9989.** Late October.

November

- ✪ **Georgia Bulldogs–Florida Gators Game,** Jacksonville, Florida, and Savannah. This football game may be held in Florida, but it's celebrated to the hilt in Savannah and throughout Georgia. It's not called the "World's Largest Outdoor Cocktail Party" for nothing. The Georgia–Florida game is mentioned in the book *Midnight in the Garden of Good and Evil* as "nothing less than a war between the gentlemen of Georgia and the Florida barbarians." Call ☎ **706/542-3000** for more information. First weekend in November or Halloween weekend if November 1 falls on a Monday.

Georgia

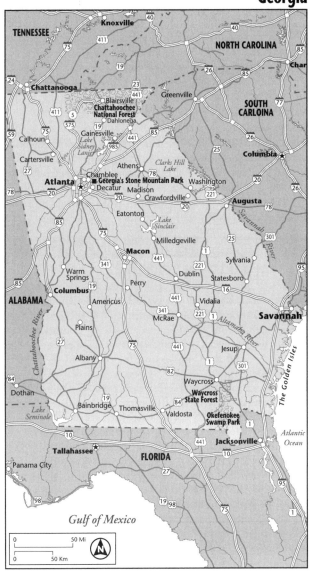

9

- **Festival of Trees,** Savannah. More than 75 uniquely decorated trees and wreaths festoon the area around the Marriott Riverfront Hotel, and a special gift shop is set up to accompany the event. For details, contact the Parent and Child Development Services at ☎ **912/238-2777.** Mid-November.

- **Crafts Festival and Cane Grinding,** Savannah. More than 75 crafts artists from four states sell and demonstrate their art. Music is provided by the Savannah Folk Music Society. For details, contact Oatland Island at ☎ **912/897-3773.** Mid-November.

December

- **Christmas 1864,** Savannah. Fort Jackson hosts the re-creation of its evacuation on December 20, 1864. More than 60 Civil War actors reenact the part of Fort Jackson's Confederate defenders, who were preparing to evacuate ahead of Union Gen. William T. Sherman. For details, contact the Coastal Heritage Society at ☎ **912/681-6895.** Early December.

3 Tips for Travelers with Special Needs

FOR TRAVELERS WITH DISABILITIES

The state of South Carolina provides numerous agencies to assist those with disabilities. For specifics, call the **South Carolina Handicapped Services Information System** at ☎ **803/777-5732.** Two other agencies that may prove helpful are the **South Carolina Protection & Advocacy System for the Handicapped** at ☎ **803/782-0639** and the **Commission for the Blind** at ☎ **803/734-7520.**

In Georgia, you can contact **Traveler's Aid** at ☎ **404/527-7400.** The **Georgia Department of Industry, Trade & Tourism** publishes *Georgia on My Mind,* a guide listing attractions and accommodations with access for persons with disabilities. To receive a copy, contact Tour Georgia, P.O. Box 1776, Atlanta, GA 30301 (☎ **800/VISIT-GA,** ext. 1903).

Mobility International USA, P.O. Box 10767, Eugene, OR 97440 (☎ **503/343-1284**), offers accessibility information and has many interesting programs for travelers with disabilities. It also publishes a quarterly newsletter called *Over the Rainbow* ($15 per year to subscribe). Help (accessibility information and more) is also available from the **Travel Information Service** (☎ **215/456-9600**) and the **Society for the Advancement of Travel for the Handicapped**

Getting Hitched in the Old South

With its historic homes, cobblestone streets, and age-old churches, Charleston is a beautiful spot for a wedding. And decadent Savannah is certainly a rival, for you can tie the knot aboard a sternwheeler or in a gorgeous house with Emma Kelly, "The Lady of 6,000 Songs," entertaining you.

The **Charleston Chapel for Weddings,** 22 Ashley Ave. (☎ 800/416-2779), is located in Charleston's downtown historic district and is intimate enough for two or large enough for a party of 60. Prices range from $150 for a simple service for two to $1,200 for a group up to 60, including amenities like horse-drawn carriages, limousines, flowers, and photography. They don't hold receptions, however. Reserve as far in advance as possible—some book 9 months ahead.

The **Absolutely Wonderful Wedding Service,** 25 Broad St. (☎ 803/723-9441), features a number of romantic wedding locations throughout Charleston and will pick up your marriage license at the Marriage License Bureau for you at no extra charge. The service has its own private Wedding Garden on historic Broad Street that will accommodate 15 to 20 people. Prices begin at $95 for a service at the location of your choice.

Other wedding-perfect locations in Charleston are the Thomas Bennett House (☎ 803/720-1203), Charleston Landing (☎ 803/852-4200), Dock Street Theatre (☎ 803/577-7400), Lowndes Grove Inn (☎ 803/723-3530), and Old Exchange Building (☎ 803/727-2165).

In Savannah, weddings can be held aboard the **Savannah River Queen,** a 325-passenger sternwheeler. Ceremonies are done on a BYOP ("bring your own preacher") basis and range from $27 to $70 per couple. Reservations are recommended far in advance: Contact the **River Street Riverboat Co.,** 9 E. River St. (☎ 912/232-6404).

Another possibility in Savannah is the **Gingerbread House,** 1921 Bull St. (☎ 912/234-7303), renowned as one of the country's finest examples of gingerbread carpentry. A basic ceremony can cost $300 (minister extra); more elaborate weddings start at $450. Emma Kelly has been known to play here and can be hired for your occasion. Reserve as far ahead as possible. If you're eloping, call to see if they can squeeze you in.

(SATH), 347 Fifth Ave., Suite 610, New York, NY 10016 (☎ **212/ 447-7284**).

A publisher called **Twin Peaks Press,** Box 129, Vancouver, WA 98666 (☎ **360/694-2462**), specializes in books for people with disabilities. Write for their *Disability Bookshop Catalog,* enclosing $4. One useful title is *Access to the World, a Travel Guide for the Handicapped,* by Louise Weiss, which can also be ordered from Henry Holt & Co. (☎ **800/247-3912**).

Accessible Journeys (☎ **800/TINGLES** or 610/521-0339) and **Flying Wheels Travel** (☎ **800/535-6790** or 507/451-5005) offer tours for people with physical disabilities. The **Guided Tour Inc.** (☎ **215/782-1370**) has tours for people with physical or mental disabilities, those with visual impairments, and seniors.

Amtrak (☎ **800/USA-RAIL**) provides redcap service, wheelchair assistance, and special seats at most major stations with 72 hours' notice. People with disabilities are also entitled to a 25% discount on one-way regular coach fares. Children ages 2 to 15 with disabilities can also get a 50% discount on already discounted one-way disabled adult fares. Documentation from a doctor or an ID card proving your disability is required. For an extra charge, Amtrak offers wheelchair-accessible sleeping accommodations on long-distance trains, and service dogs are permissible and travel free. Write for a free booklet called *Amtrak's America* from Amtrak Distribution Center, P.O. Box 7717, Itasca, IL 60143, which has a section detailing services for passengers with disabilities.

Greyhound (☎ **800/752-4841**) allows a person with disabilities to travel with a companion for a single fare and, if you call 48 hours in advance, they'll arrange help along the way.

FOR GAY & LESBIAN TRAVELERS

Gay hot lines in Charleston fall under the 24-hour crisis prevention network at ☎ **803/744-4357.** In addition, the **South Carolina Pride Center,** located in Columbia (☎ **803/771-7713**), functions as a conduit to other organizations, like the **Low Country Gay and Lesbian Alliance** (☎ **803/720-8088**).

The free *Etcetera* magazine is available in virtually every gay-owned or gay-friendly bar, bookstore, and restaurant in Georgia, the Carolinas, Tennessee, Alabama, and Florida. It boasts a bona fide circulation of 22,000 readers a week, a figure qualifying it as the largest gay and lesbian publication in the Southeast. If you'd like a copy in advance of your trip, send $2 for a current issue to P.O.

Box 8916, Atlanta, GA 30306. Or, when you arrive, call ☎ **404/ 888-0063** to find out where you can pick up an issue nearby. You can also call the same number for information on gay resources throughout the South.

Note that homophobia still reigns in the Bible Belt (especially among right-wing groups), but in general attitudes toward gays and lesbians are more tolerant and relaxed than they've been in years.

4 Getting There & Getting Around

BY PLANE

You can fly into Charleston on **Delta** (☎ 800/221-1212; www.delta-air.com), **Continental** (☎ 800/525-0280; www. flycontinental. com), **US Airways** (☎ 800/428-4322; www. usairways.com), and **United** and **United Express** (☎ 800/241-6522; www.ual.com).

You can fly directly into Savannah International Airport via **Delta** or **Continental.**

Another option is to fly into Atlanta's **Hartsfield International Airport.** From there you can get a connecting flight or rent a car and easily drive to either Charleston or Savannah in a few hours. **Delta** is the major carrier to Atlanta, connecting it to pretty much the entire country as well as 32 countries internationally. Other choices are **America West** (☎ 800/235-9292; www.americawest.com), **American** (☎ 800/433-7300; www.americanair.com), **British Airways** (☎ 800/247-9297; www.british-airways.com), **Continental Airlines** (☎ 800/525-3663; www.japanair.com), **KLM** (☎ 800/ 374-7747; www.klm.nl), **Lufthansa** (☎ 800/645-3880; www.lufthansa-USA.com), **Northwest** (☎ 800/225-2525; www.nwa.com), **Swissair** (☎ **800/221-4750**; www.swissair.com), **TWA** (☎ 800/221-2000; www.twa.com), **United,** and **US Airways.**

BY CAR

South Carolina has a network of exceptionally good roads. Even when you leave the highways for the state-maintained byways, driving is easy, and AAA services are available through the **Carolina Motor Club** in Charleston (☎ **803/766-2394**).

I-95 enters South Carolina from the north, near Dillon, and runs straight through the state to Hardeeville, on the Georgia border. If you're driving from the north, you can branch off onto I-26 to reach Charleston. The major coastal artery of South Carolina, U.S. 17, also runs through Charleston. The major east–west artery, I-26, runs from the northwest corner of the state through Columbia and then ends at Charleston.

South Carolina furnishes excellent travel information to motorists, and there are well-equipped, efficiently staffed visitor centers at the state border on most major highways (see "Visitor Information," above). If you have a cellular phone in your car and need help, dial ☎ #HP for Highway Patrol Assistance. In South Carolina, state law requires vehicles to have headlights on when windshield wipers are in use as a result of inclement weather.

If you're coming to Georgia from the north or south, I-95 will take you right to Savannah. If you're coming from the northwest, I-75 runs into Atlanta and south toward Macon; from there you can pick up I-16 to Savannah. State-run welcome centers at all major points of entry are staffed with knowledgeable, helpful Georgians who can often advise you as to time-saving routes. The seat belt laws are strictly enforced. In Georgia, you can call ☎ **404/656-5267** for 24-hour information on road conditions.

Before leaving home, it's a good idea to join the **American Automobile Association (AAA),** 12600 Fairlake Circle, Fairfax, VA 22033-4904 (☎ **703/222-6000**). For a very small fee, the association provides a wide variety of services, including trip planning, accommodation and restaurant directories, and a 24-hour toll-free phone number (☎ **800/222-4357**) set up exclusively to deal with members' road emergencies.

Leading car-rental firms are represented in both cities and at the airports. For reservations and rate information, call the following: **Avis** (☎ 800/331-1212), **Budget** (☎ 800/527-0700), **Hertz** (☎ 800/654-3131), or **Thrifty** (☎ 800/367-2277).

BY TRAIN

Amtrak (☎ **800/USA-RAIL**) services both Charleston and Savannah. Its tour packages include hotel, breakfasts, and historic tours of Charleston at bargain rates. Be sure to ask about the money-saving **All Aboard America** regional fares or any other current fare specials. Amtrak also offers attractively priced rail/drive packages in the Carolinas and Georgia.

BY PACKAGE TOUR

Collette Tours (☎ **401/728-3805**) offers the 6-day fly/drive Charleston/Myrtle Beach Show Tour, which guides you through a day of Charleston's most historic sites, visits a Civil War–era plantation in Georgetown, and ends up in Myrtle Beach with dinner and entertainment at Dixie Stampede, Broadway at the Beach, and Magic on Ice.

Mayflower Tours (☎ **800/365-5359**) runs a 7-day Myrtle Beach, Charleston, and Savannah tour that features an Atlanta city tour with Olympic sites and Stone Mountain, coastal touring on the Grand Strand in Myrtle Beach, Brookgreen Gardens, Pawley's Island, and Georgetown. It moves on to the historic city of Charleston, where you'll tour gracious homes, cobblestone streets, pre-Revolutionary buildings, the famous Battery, and the Old Market and Exchange. You'll stay the night after dinner and a Broadway-style variety show, *Serenade,* and travel to Savannah the next day, to board the Old Town Trolley and hear tales of the town's stately mansions and well-kept gardens.

FAST FACTS: South Carolina & Georgia

American Express   Services are available through Palmetto Travel Service, 4 Liberty St., Charleston (☎ **803/577-5053**), and at 5500 Abercorn St., Savannah, GA 31405 (☎ **800/528-4800** or 912/351-0770).

Area Codes   Charleston's area code is **803.** Savannah's area code is **912.**

Drugstores   The most popular chains in the Carolinas and Georgia are Eckerd, Revco, and Rite Aid. Though none of these offers 24-hour service, Eckerd does have stores in the larger cities that remain open until midnight.

Emergencies   Dial ☎ **911** for police, ambulance, paramedics, and fire department.

Liquor Laws   The minimum drinking age in both states is 21. Some restaurants in South Carolina are licensed to serve only beer and wine, those who do serve liquor serve it in minibottles, which can be added to cocktail mixers. Beer and wine are sold in grocery stores, but blue laws mandate that no alcohol can be bought or sold (in restaurants or in stores) on Sundays. All package liquor is sold through local government-controlled stores, commonly called ABC (Alcoholic Beverage Control Commission) stores.

In Georgia, you can buy alcoholic beverages in package stores between 8am and 11:45pm (except on Sunday, election days, Thanksgiving, and Christmas).

Newspapers & Magazines   The major papers in South Carolina are the *State* (Columbia), *Greenville News,* and *Charleston Post & Courier.* The *Sandlapper* is a local quarterly magazine. The *Atlanta Journal–Constitution* is Georgia's leading daily newspaper. *Southern Living* is a glossy publication concerned mainly with architecture, travel in the South, and gardening—profusely illustrated with color photography. Savannah's leading newspaper is the *Savannah Morning News,* with the *Savannah Tribune* and the *Herald of Savannah* geared to the African-American community.

Taxes   South Carolina has a 6% sales tax and Georgia a 5% to 6% sales tax.

Time Zone   South Carolina and Georgia are on eastern standard time, going on daylight saving time in summer.

Weather   In South Carolina, phone ☎ **803/822-8135** for an update; in Georgia, call ☎ **900/932-8437** (95¢ per minute).

2

Charleston: Haven of Grace & Charm

*I*n the closing pages of *Gone With the Wind,* Rhett tells Scarlett that he's going back home to Charleston, where he can find "the calm dignity life can have when it's lived by gentle folks, the genial grace of days that are gone. When I lived those days I didn't realize the slow charm of them." In spite of all the changes and upheavals over the years, Rhett's endorsement of Charleston still holds true.

If the Old South still lives throughout South Carolina's Low Country, it positively thrives in Charleston. All our romantic notions of antebellum days—stately homes, courtly manners, gracious hospitality, and, above all, gentle dignity—are facts of everyday life in this old city, even though there are a few scoundrels here and there, including an impressive roster of pirates, patriots, and presidents.

Its history may be dotted with earthquakes, hurricanes, fires, and Yankee bombardments, but Charleston remains one of the best-preserved cities in the Old South. It boasts 73 pre-Revolutionary buildings, 136 from the late 18th century, and more than 600 built before the 1840s. With its cobblestone streets and horse-drawn carriages, Charleston is a place of visual images and sensory pleasures. Tea, jasmine, and wisteria fragrances fill the air; the aroma of she-crab soup (the local favorite, a version of cream-of-crab soup) wafts from sidewalk cafes; and antebellum architecture graces the historic cityscape. "No wonder they're so full of themselves," said an envious visitor from Columbia; it may be the state capital, but it doesn't have Charleston's style and grace.

In its annual reader survey, *Condé Nast Traveler* consistently names Charleston as the fourth top city to visit in America, ahead of such perennial favorites as New York, Seattle, and San Antonio. Visitors are drawn here from all over the world—in fact, it's now quite common to hear German and French spoken along with English on the streets.

Charleston is and always has been a city of culture, exemplified by the paintings of Elizabeth O'Neill Verner, the decorative

*Charleston is ancient live oak trees, live jasmine, magnolias in
sequestered gardens, the sound of horses' hoofs over cobblestone streets
and the lyrical voices of flower ladies. It is the . . . cries of the colorful
street vendors calling SHEEEEEE-Crab and a hundred other delights.*
—Molly Heady Sillers, *Doin' the Charleston* (1976)

ironwork of Philip Simons, and even Ira Gershwin's *Porgy and
Bess*—and most definitely by the internationally renowned Spoleto
Festival USA.

Does this city have a modern side? Yes, but it's well hidden. Chic
shops abound, as do a few supermodern hotels. But you don't come
to Charleston for anything cutting edge. You come to glimpse an
almost-forgotten era.

A LOOK AT THE PAST

When Charles II of England magnanimously gave eight of his loyal
subjects the strip of land between the 29th and 35th parallels, these
"lord proprietors" sent out colonists to settle Albemarle Point and
the peninsula between the mouths of the Ashley and Cooper rivers.

By the mid-1770s, Charleston (originally named Charles Towne)
had become an important seaport. As desire for independence from
Britain grew, Charlestonians threw out the last royal governor and
built a fort of palmetto logs and sand (Fort Moultrie, which remained a working fort right on through World War II) on Sullivan's
Island. They repulsed a British fleet on June 28, 1776, and then sent
couriers to the Continental Congress in Philadelphia. The British
returned in 1780, however, and held the city until December 1782.
It took more than 300 ships to move them out—soldiers, Tory sup-
porters, slaves, and tons of loot.

In the 1800s, the economy of the South became ever more de-
pendent on slavery and the plantation system, and the region grew
ever more disaffected from the industrial North. Charleston gained
a reputation as a center of gentility and culture, where wealthy rice
and indigo planters pleasured themselves with imported luxuries and
built stately town houses (to which they regularly repaired for the
summer to escape backcountry mosquitoes and malaria). These aristocrats supported the first theater in the United States, held glittering
socials, and invented the planter's punch cocktail.

The election of Abraham Lincoln, who won the presidency without carrying a single Southern state, proved to be the straw that broke the camel's back. Tensions boiled over in 1860, as the first Ordinance of Secession, passed in Columbia, was signed in Charleston. Soon thereafter, South Carolinians opened fire from Fort Johnson against the Union-held Fort Sumter, and the Civil War was off and running. Though attacked again and again during the war, the city remained a Confederate stronghold until February 1865.

After the war, Charleston simply didn't have the money to rebuild as rapidly as Atlanta did. The demolition of old structures didn't begin until the 1900s, and by that time, fortunately, a preservation movement had developed. Many local families still own and live in the homes their planter ancestors built, and they still take pride in their well-manicured walled gardens. Charleston today remains a city without skyscrapers and modern architectural monstrosities.

Despite the ups and downs of family fortunes, Charlestonians manage to maintain a way of life that, in many respects, has little to do with wealth. The simplest encounter with Charleston natives seems invested with a social air, as though the visitor were a valued guest to be pleased. Yet there are those who detect a certain snobbishness in Charleston, and (truth be told) you'd have to stay a few hundred years to be considered an insider here.

1 Orientation

ARRIVING

Charleston International Airport is in North Charleston on I-26, about 12 miles west of the city. It's served by **Delta** (☎ 800/221-1212), **Continental** (☎ 800/525-0280), **US Airways** (☎ 800/428-4322), and **United** and **United Express** (☎ 800/241-6522).

Taxi fare into the city runs about $24; the **airport limousine** has a $9 fare (☎ 843/834-1998). All major car-rental facilities, including **Hertz** (☎ 800/654-3131) and **Avis** (☎ 800/331-1212), are available at the airport. Follow the airport access road to I-26 into the heart of Charleston.

If you're driving, the main north–south coastal route, U.S. 17, passes through Charleston; I-26 runs northwest to southeast and ends in Charleston. Charleston is 120 miles southeast of Columbia via I-26 and 98 miles south of Myrtle Beach via U.S. 17.

Amtrak trains arrive at 4565 Gaynor Ave., North Charleston (☎ 800/USA-RAIL). To reach the Historic District from here, you can catch a cab at the taxi stand or hop on an SCE&G bus, ride into Charleston, and transfer to the DASH (Downtown Area Shuttle) system.

VISITOR INFORMATION

The **Charleston Convention and Visitors Bureau,** 375 Meeting St., Charleston, SC 29402 (☎ **843/853-8000;** www. charlestoncvb.com), across from the Charleston Museum, provides maps, brochures, tour information, and access to South Carolina Automated Ticketing (SCAT), Charleston's events ticketing system. The helpful staff will assist you in finding accommodations and planning your stay. Numerous tours depart hourly from the Visitor Reception & Transportation Center (VRTC), also at 375 Meeting St.; rest-room facilities and parking are available. Be sure to allow time to view the 24-minute multi-image presentation "Forever Charleston" and pick up a copy of the visitor's guide. The center is open April to October, Monday to Friday from 8:30am to 5:30pm and Saturday and Sunday from 8am to 5pm; November to March, daily from 8:30am to 5:30pm.

CITY LAYOUT

Charleston's streets are laid out in an easy-to-follow grid pattern. Main north–south thoroughfares are **King, Meeting,** and **East Bay** streets; **Tradd, Broad, Queen,** and **Calhoun** streets bisect the city from east to west. South of Broad Street, East Bay becomes **East Battery.**

Unlike most cities, Charleston offers a most helpful map, and it's distributed free. Called The **Map Guide-Charleston,** it includes the streets of the Historic District as well as surrounding areas and offers tips on shopping, tours, and what to see and do. Maps are available at the Convention and Visitors Bureau (see above).

NEIGHBORHOODS IN BRIEF

Historic District   In 1860, according to one Charlestonian, "South Carolina seceded from the Union, Charleston seceded from South Carolina, and south of Broad Street seceded from Charleston." The city preserves its early years at its southernmost point, the conjunction of the Cooper and Ashley rivers. The White Point Gardens, right in the "elbow" of the two rivers, provide a sort of gateway into this area where virtually every home is of historic or architectural interest. Between Broad Street and Murray Boulevard (which runs along the south waterfront), you'll find such highlights as St. Michael's Episcopal Church, the Calhoun Mansion, the Edmonston–Alston House, the Old Exchange/Provost Dungeon, the Heyward–Washington House, Catfish Row, and the Nathaniel Russell House.

Downtown Extending north from Broad Street to Marion Square at the intersection of Calhoun and Meeting streets, this area encloses noteworthy points of interest, good shopping, and some historic churches. Just a few highlights are the Old City Market, the Dock Street Theatre, Market Hall, the Old Powder Magazine, the Thomas Elfe Workshop, Congregation Beth Elohim, the French Huguenot Church, St. John's Church, and the Unitarian Church.

Above Marion Square The visitor center is on Meeting Street north of Calhoun. The Charleston Museum is just across the street, and the Aiken–Rhett Mansion, Joseph Manigault Mansion, and Old Citadel are all within easy walking distance of one another in the area bounded by Calhoun Street to the south and Mary Street to the north.

North Charleston Charleston International Airport is in this area, where I-26 and I-526 intersect. This makes North Charleston a transportation hub of the Low Country. It's primarily a residential and industrial community, lacking the charms of the Historic District. It's also home to the North Charleston Coliseum, the largest indoor entertainment venue in South Carolina.

Mount Pleasant East of the Cooper River, minutes from the heart of the Historic District, this community is worth a detour. Filled with accommodations, restaurants, and some attractions, it encloses a Historic District known as the Old Village, on the National Register's list of buildings to preserve. Its major attraction is Patriots Point, the world's largest naval and maritime museum, and it's also home to the aircraft carrier *Yorktown*.

Outlying Areas Within easy reach of the city are Boone Hall Plantation, Fort Moultrie, and the public beaches at Sullivan's Island and Isle of Palms. Head west across the Ashley River Bridge to pay tribute to Charleston's birth at Charles Towne Landing and visit such highlights as Drayton Hall, Magnolia Gardens, and Middleton Place. One of the area's most popular beaches, Folly Beach County Park, is also west of the Ashley River.

2   Getting Around

BY CAR

If you're staying in the city proper, park the car and use it only for day trips to outlying areas. You'll find parking facilities scattered about the city, with some of the most convenient at Hutson Street and Calhoun Street, both near Marion Square; on King Street between Queen and Broad; and on George Street between King and Meeting. The two most centrally located garages are at Wentworth Street (☎ **843/724-7383**) and at Concord and Cumberland streets (☎ **843/724-7387**).

Leading car-rental companies in town and at the airport include **Avis** (☎ 800/331-1212 or 843/767-7038), **Budget** (☎ 800/527-0700 or 843/577-5195), and **Hertz** (☎ 800/654-3131 or 843/767-4552).

BY BUS

City bus fare is 75¢; service runs from 5:35am to 12:20am. Between 9:30am and 3:30pm, seniors and travelers with disabilities pay 25¢. Exact change is required. For route and schedule information, call ☎ **843/747-0922.**

BY TROLLEY

The Downtown Area Shuttle (DASH) is the quickest way to get around the main downtown area. The trolley runs daily from 6:35am to 10:30pm. The fare is 75¢, and you'll need exact change. You can buy a $2 pass good for the whole day at the **Convention and Visitors Bureau,** 375 Meeting Place (☎ **843/853-8000**). For routes, call ☎ **843/724-7420.**

BY TAXI

Leading taxi companies are **Yellow Cab** (☎ **843/577-6565**) and **Safety Cab** (☎ **843/722-4066**); each company has its own fare structure. Within the city, however, fares seldom exceed $4. You must call for a taxi; there are no pickups on the street.

FAST FACTS: Charleston

American Express   The local American Express office is located in downtown Charleston at 4 Liberty St., off of King Street (☎ **843/577-5053**); open Monday to Friday from 8:30am to 5:30pm, and Saturday from 9am to 1pm.

Dentist   Consult the **Orthodontic Associates of Charleston,** 86 Rutledge Ave. (☎ **843/723-7242**).

Doctor   For a physician referral or 24-hour emergency-room treatment, contact **Charleston Memorial Hospital,** 326 Calhoun St. (☎ **843/577-0600**). Another option is **Roper Hospital,** 316 Calhoun St. (☎ **843/724-2970**). Contact **Doctor's Care** (☎ **843/556-5585**) for names of walk-in clinics near you.

Emergencies   In a true emergency, dial ☎ **911.** If it's not a life-threatening situation, call ☎ **843/577-7077** for fire or police or ☎ **843/747-4000** for an ambulance.

Hospitals   Local hospitals operating 24-hour emergency rooms are **AMI East Cooper Community Hospital,** 1200 Johnnie Dodds Blvd., Mount Pleasant (☎ **843/881-0100**); **River Hospital North,** 2750 Spelssegger Dr., North Charleston (☎ **843/ 744-2110**); **Charleston Memorial Hospital,** 326 Calhoun St., Charleston (☎ **843/577-0600**); and the **Medical University of South Carolina,** 171 Ashley Ave., Charleston (☎ **843/ 792-2300**).

Liquor Laws   You must be 21 years of age to buy or consume alcohol.

Newspapers & Magazines   The *Charleston Post & Courier* is the daily newspaper in the metropolitan area.

Pharmacies   Try **CVS Drugs,** Wanda Crossing, Mount Pleasant (☎ **843/881-9435**), open Monday to Saturday from 8am to midnight and Sunday from 10am to 8pm.

Post Office   The **main post office** is at 83 Broad St. (☎ **843/ 577-0688**), open Monday to Friday from 8:30am to 5:30pm and Saturday from 9:30am to 2pm.

Rest Rooms   These are found throughout the downtown area, including Broad and Meeting streets, Queen and Church streets, and Market Street between Meeting and Church streets, and at other clearly marked strategic points in the historic and downtown districts.

Safety   The downtown area of Charleston is well lit and patrolled throughout the night to ensure public safety. People can generally walk about Charleston in the evening without fear of violence, though that's less true as the night wears on. The local trolley system, DASH, closes down at 10:30pm. After that, it's better to call a taxi than to walk through dark streets.

Taxes   The local sales tax is 6%.

Weather   Call ☎ **843/744-3207** for an update.

3 Accommodations

Charleston has many of the best and most historic inns in America, even topping Savannah. The opening and restoration of inns and hotels in the city has been phenomenal, though it's slowing down somewhat (after all, the market can absorb only so many hotel rooms). However, Charleston now ranks among America's top cities for hotels of charm and character.

Bed-and-breakfast options range from historic homes to carriage houses to simple cottages, and they're found in virtually every section of the city. We've reviewed our top choices below. One central reservation service is **Historic Charleston Bed and Breakfast,** 57 Broad St., Charleston, SC 29402 (☎ **800/743-3583** or 843/ 722-6606), which represents other choices as well.

The **Charleston Trident Convention and Visitors Bureau,** P.O. Box 975, Charleston, SC 29402 (☎ **843/853-8000**), offers a Courtesy Discount Card giving the holder from 10% to as much as 50% off certain hotels, restaurants, tours, and even purchases, from mid-November to mid-February. This is the ideal time to visit Charleston if saving money is important to you.

THE HISTORIC DISTRICT
VERY EXPENSIVE

Charleston Place Hotel. 130 Market St., Charleston, SC 29401. ☎ **800/611-5545** or 843/722-4900. Fax 843/724-7215. www. charlestonplacehotel.com. 487 units. A/C TV TEL. $189–$445 double; from $445 suite. Children under 17 stay free in parents' room. Seasonal packages available. AE, DC, MC, V. Parking $8.

Charleston's premier hotel, with far better amenities and facilities than its leading competitor (the Mills House Hotel), is a landmark that looks like a postmodern French chateau. It's big-time, uptown, glossy, and urban—or at least Prince Charles, a former visitor, thought so. Some hoteliers claim that this 1986 hotel represents the New South at its most confident, a stylish giant surrounded by a neighborhood of B&Bs and small converted inns. Acres of Italian marble grace the place, leading to plush, spacious, and well-furnished bedrooms inspired by colonial Carolina and containing all the amenities from luxury mattresses to deluxe toiletries.

Charleston Accommodations

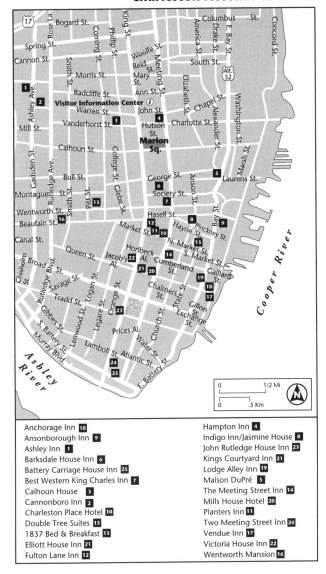

Anchorage Inn **18**
Ansonborough Inn **9**
Ashley Inn **1**
Barksdale House Inn **6**
Battery Carriage House Inn **25**
Best Western King Charles Inn **7**
Calhoun House **3**
Cannonboro Inn **2**
Charleston Place Hotel **10**
Double Tree Suites **15**
1837 Bed & Breakfast **13**
Elliott House Inn **21**
Fulton Lane Inn **12**

Hampton Inn **4**
Indigo Inn/Jasmine House **8**
John Rutledge House Inn **23**
Kings Courtyard Inn **21**
Lodge Alley Inn **19**
Maison DuPré **5**
The Meeting Street Inn **14**
Mills House Hotel **20**
Planters Inn **11**
Two Meeting Street Inn **24**
Vendue Inn **17**
Victoria House Inn **22**
Wentworth Mansion **16**

A Few Notes on Rates

Hotels and motels are priced in direct ratio to their proximity to the 789-acre Historic District; if prices in the center are too high for your budget, find a place west of the Ashley River and drive into town for sightseeing and dining.

During the Festival of Gardens and Houses and the Spoleto Festival, rates go way up, with owners charging pretty much what the market will bear. Advance reservations are essential.

When booking a hotel, ask about any package plans that might be available. It pays to ask because deals come and go; they're most often granted to those staying 3 to 4 days.

The hotel's premier restaurant, **Louis' Charleston Grill,** is reviewed under "Dining," below. There's also a more casual cafe. Services include 24-hour room service, baby-sitting, laundry, and a masseur. You'll also find a whirlpool, a men's steam bath, a health club, an aerobics studio, and a sundeck.

✪ **Wentworth Mansion.** 149 Wentworth St., Charleston, SC 29401. ☎ **843/853-1886.** Fax 843/720-5290. www.wentworthmansion.com. 21 units. A/C TV TEL. $275–$675 double. Rates include breakfast. AE, DC, DISC, MC, V. Free parking.

Commissioned in 1886 by wealthy cotton merchant Francis Silas Rodgers, this old Charlestonian home clings tightly to its past. Though the home has undergone renovations such as the addition of an elevator and air-conditioning, more than 80% of the original structure has been preserved, boasting 14-foot-high ceilings, stained-glass windows, and marble floors. All the spacious rooms are beautifully furnished with fireplaces, king rice beds (four-posters in which the posts are carved with rice sheathes; rice was a principal crop in colonial Charleston), and whirlpools. In addition, each unit has a private bathroom with glass-walled showers and dual showerheads. Units are tastefully furnished with 18th-century-style draperies and Asian rugs.

The Wentworth's rooftop cupola treats guests to a panoramic view of the city from the Ashley to the Cooper rivers. Breakfast includes fresh baked breads and cinnamon rolls. Evening dinner is served in the hotel's new restaurant, **Circa 1886.** Wine and sherry are offered in the library or on the sunporch. A sense of modern comfort embraces this old-fashioned abode in a tranquil residential area on the edge of the Historic District.

EXPENSIVE

✪ **Anchorage Inn.** 26 Vendue Range, Charleston, SC 29401. ☎ **800/ 421-2952** or 843/723-8300. Fax 843/723-9543. 19 units. A/C TV TEL. $105– $155 double; $155–$200 suite. Rates include continental breakfast and afternoon wine and cheese snack. AE, MC, V. Parking $8.

There's no garden, and other than a heraldic shield in front, there are few concessions to ornamentation on the inn's exterior (it was built in the 1840s as a warehouse to store cotton). It functioned as an office building until 1991, when investors radically renovated and upgraded the interior. The Anchorage boasts the only decorative theme of its type in Charleston: a mock Tudor interior with lots of dark paneling, references to "Olde" England, canopied beds with matching tapestries, pastoral or nautical engravings, leaded casement windows, and sometimes half-timbering. Because the inn is immediately adjacent to unremarkable buildings on either side, the architects designed all but a handful of rooms with views overlooking the lobby. Light is indirectly filtered through the lobby's skylights, which can be a plus during Charleston's hot summers. Each guest room is uniquely shaped, and the most expensive ones have bona fide windows overlooking the street outside.

Battery Carriage House Inn. 20 South Battery, Charleston, SC 29401. ☎ **800/775-5575** or 843/727-3100. Fax 843/727-3130. www. charlestoninns.com. 11 units. A/C TV. $149–$299 double. Rates include continental breakfast. AE, DISC, MC, V. Free parking. No children under 12.

In one of the city's largest antebellum neighborhoods, this inn offers midsize rooms in a carriage house behind the main building (constructed as a private home in 1843). In other words, the owners have saved the top living accommodation for themselves but have restored the carriage-house rooms according to a high standard, including whirlpools in some bathrooms. Look elsewhere if you demand an inn with lots of public space. That you don't get, but the location is idyllic, a short walk from the Battery, a seafront peninsula where you can easily imagine a flotilla of Yankee ships enforcing the Civil War blockades. Recent renovations have added four-poster beds and a colonial frill to the not overly large rooms. Alas, if you call, you're likely to get only a recorded message until the owners can call you back. In nice weather, breakfast is served in a landscaped brick courtyard.

Fulton Lane Inn. 202 King St. (at the corner of Market St.), Charleston, SC 29401. ☎ **800/552-2777** or 843/720-2600. Fax 843/720-2940. www.charminginns.com. 32 units. A/C TV TEL. $125–$240 double; $200–$285 suite. Rates include continental breakfast. MC, V. Parking $5.

ⅈ Family-Friendly Accommodations

Best Western King Charles Inn *(see p. 36)*   Children under 18 stay free here in their parents' room. The location is only a block from the Historic District's market area, and families gather for relaxation at the small pool. This is one of the best family values in Charleston.

Ansonborough Inn *(see p. 32)*   A good choice for families who'd like to stay in one of the historic inns as opposed to a cheap motel on the outskirts. A converted warehouse, it offers rooms with ceilings so high that many can accommodate sleeping lofts for the kids.

Double Tree Suites *(see p. 33)*   These suites contain full kitchens or wet bars with microwaves and refrigerators and offer the extra space that families need. Some units are bilevel, giving more privacy.

Knights Inn *(see p. 37)*   Families with cars may be tempted to anchor here in North Charleston, 11 miles from the Historic District. The suites are among the most reasonable in the area, and each has a kitchenette so that you can prepare some meals "at home."

Set amid the dense concentration of businesses in Charleston's commercial core, this hotel is composed of two contiguous houses, one built of brick in 1913, its neighbor of stucco in 1989. You'll find a hearty welcome for children, a summery decor with bright colors, and (in some suites) cathedral ceilings. Some rooms have whirlpool tubs and working gas fireplaces, and though most are larger than you'd expect, there's a conspicuous lack of antique furniture; however, it doesn't seem to bother the clientele at all. Breakfast, brought to the rooms on silver trays, is the only meal served. No smoking.

Indigo Inn/Jasmine House. 1 Maiden Lane, Charleston, SC 29401. ☎ **800/ 845-7639** or 843/577-5900. Fax 843/577-0378. 40 units (Indigo Inn), 10 units (Jasmine House). A/C TV TEL. $139–$225 double in Indigo Inn; $169–$275 double in Jasmine House. Rates include continental breakfast. AE, DISC, MC, V. Free parking.

These hotels, across the street from each other, share the same owners and the same reception area in the Indigo. Conceived as a warehouse for indigo in the mid–19th century and gutted and reconstructed in the 1980s, the Indigo offers midsize rooms with standardized 18th-century decor and comfortable furnishings. Rooms in the Jasmine House (an 1843 Greek Revival mansion whose exterior is painted buttercup yellow) are more individualized. Each has a ceiling of about 14 feet, a color scheme and theme markedly different from any of its neighbors, crown moldings, whirlpool tubs, and floral-patterned upholstery. Both inns serve breakfast; parking is available only in the lot at the Indigo.

✪ **John Rutledge House Inn.** 116 Broad St., Charleston, SC 29401. ☎ **800/ 476-9741** or 843/723-7999. Fax 843/720-2615. www.charminginns.com. 19 units. A/C MINIBAR TV TEL. Summer, $235–$335 double, $365 suite; off-season, $165–$280 double, $220–$290 suite. Rates include continental breakfast. AE, DC, DISC, MC, V. Free parking.

Many of the meetings that culminated in the formation of the United States were conducted in this fine 18th-century house, now one of Charleston's most prestigious inns. We think it towers over its major rivals, such as the Planters Inn and the Ansonborough. Its builder was one of the signers of the Declaration of Independence and later served as chief justice of the U.S. Supreme Court. Impeccably restored to its Federalist grandeur, it's enhanced with discreetly concealed electronic conveniences. Bedrooms come in a range of styles and shapes and often include antiques among the furnishings. Appointments are luxurious, ranging from deluxe mattresses to hair dryers and first-class toiletries. Tea and afternoon sherry are served in a spacious upstairs sitting room, where mementos of the building's history and antique firearms, elaborate moldings, and a marble fireplace help to enhance the distinguished aura.

Kings Courtyard Inn. 198 King St., Charleston, SC 29401. ☎ **800/ 845-6119** or 843/723-7000. Fax 843/720-2608. www.charminginns.com. 44 units. A/C TV TEL. $115–$185 double. Children under 12 free in parents' room. Off-season 3-day packages available. Rates include breakfast. AE, MC, V. Parking $5.

The tiny entry to this 1853 inn in the Historic District is deceiving because it opens into a brick courtyard with a fountain. A fireplace warms the small lobby. Besides the main courtyard, two others offer fine views from the breakfast room. The owners bought the building next door and appropriated 10 more rooms into the existing inn. Your midsize room might be fitted with a canopied bed, Oriental rugs over hardwood floors, armoires, and even a gas fireplace. All have refrigerators. Rates include evening chocolates and turndown service; there's also a whirlpool.

Lodge Alley Inn. 195 E. Bay St., Charleston, SC 29401. ☎ **800/845-1004** (outside SC), 800/821-2791 (in SC), or 843/722-1611. Fax 843/722-1611, ext. 7777. 93 units. A/C MINIBAR TV TEL. $139–$169 double; $199–$310 suite; $219–$310 duplex. Children under 12 stay free in parents' room. AE, MC, V. Free valet parking.

This sprawling historic property extends from its entrance on the Old Town's busiest commercial street toward a quiet brick courtyard in back. In the 19th century, this was a trio of warehouses; today, it evokes a mini-Louisiana village, with a central square, a fountain, landscaped shrubs in back, and easy access to the hotel's Cajun restaurant, the French Quarter. Accommodations include conventional hotel rooms, suites, and duplex units with sleeping lofts. Throughout, the decor is American country, with pine floors and lots of colonial accents. Some units have fireplaces, and most have retained the massive timbers and brick walls of the original warehouses. The staff is usually polite and helpful, but because the hotel hosts many small conventions, they might be preoccupied with the demands of whatever large group happens to be checking in or out.

Mills House Hotel. 115 Meeting St. (between Queen and Broad sts.), Charleston, SC 29401. ☎ **800/874-9600** or 843/577-2400. Fax 843/722-2112. www.millshouse.com. 214 units. A/C TV TEL. $149–$279 double; $229–$499 suite. Children under 19 stay free in parents' room. AE, CB, DC, DISC, MC, V. Parking $15 nearby.

Upscale and conservative, this hotel is a landmark. When it was built in 1853, it was hailed as the finest hotel in America south of New York City and hosted every big name of the antebellum era and the gilded age. Regrettably, it sank into disrepair by the 1930s, became an eyesore and a hazard, and was eventually bought for $135,000 in 1967—less than the price of its original construction.

Much to the dismay of the new owners, the core wasn't structurally sound enough for refurbishment. But they salvaged its architectural adornments, and after demolishing the core, a copy of the original, with lower ceilings and more rooms, was erected in its place. The hotel prides itself on its lack of razzle-dazzle and its well-mannered professionalism. The rooms are furnished with antique reproductions and, most often, half-tester beds. Accommodations come in a wide range of shapes and sizes, though most windows tend to be small. It may not be the most prestigious large hotel in Charleston anymore, but it nonetheless continues to attract loyal guests who appreciate its slightly faded charms.

The hotel's **Barbadoes Room** is one of the finest in town (see "Dining," below). No breakfast is served, however. Services include room service, laundry, and baby-sitting, and there's a small indoor pool.

Planters Inn. 112 N. Market St. (at Meeting St.), Charleston, SC 29401. ☎ **800/845-7082** or 843/722-2345. Fax 843/577-2125. www. plantersinn.com. 68 units. A/C TV TEL. $185–$250 double; $300–$500 suite. AE, MC, V. Parking $11.

For many years, this distinguished brick-sided inn next to the City Market languished. In 1994, it was acquired by a group of hoteliers who knew how to maintain an upper-crust historic inn, and a massive renovation was begun. Further expansion was carried out in 1997. The multimillion-dollar result has transformed the place into a cozy but tasteful and opulent enclave of colonial charm. You'll find a lobby filled with reproductions of 18th-century furniture and engravings, a staff clad in silk vests, and a parking area with exactly the right amount of spaces for the number of rooms. The guest rooms are spacious; with marble-sheathed baths, luxury mattresses, and a unique 18th-century decor. The suites are appealing, outfitted much as you'd expect from an upscale private home. Afternoon tea is served in the lobby, and the well-recommended **Peninsula Café** is described under "Dining, below."

✪ **Two Meeting Street Inn.** 2 Meeting St., Charleston, SC 29401. ☎ **843/723-7322.** www.innbook.com. 9 units. A/C TV. $155–$275 double. Rates include continental breakfast and afternoon tea. No credit cards. Free parking. No children under 12.

In an enviable position near the Battery, this Victorian house was built in 1892 as a wedding gift from a prosperous father to his daughter. Wraparound porches open onto panoramic views of the harbor. Inside, the proportions are as lavish and gracious as the gilded age could provide. You'll see stained-glass windows, mementos, and paintings that were either part of the original architecture or collected by the present owners, the Spell family. Most of the good-size rooms contain four-poster beds and ceiling fans; some offer access to a network of balconies.

Vendue Inn. 19 Vendue Range, Charleston, SC 29401. ☎ **800/845-7900** or 843/577-7970. Fax 843/577-2913. www.charlestonvendueinn.com. E-mail: vendueinn@navi-gator.com. 45 units. A/C TV TEL. $145–$275 double; $160–$290 suite. Rates include buffet breakfast and afternoon wine and cheese. AE, DC, DISC, MC, V. Parking $6.

On the site of what functioned in the 1800s as a warehouse for French-speaking dockworkers, this charming, small inn manages to convey some of the personalized touches of a B&B. Its public areas meander along a series of narrow labyrinthine spaces, and the collection of antiques and colonial decorative pieces evokes a slightly cramped inn in Europe. The rooms don't necessarily mimic the European model of the lobby, however, and in some cases they appear to have been the result of decorative experiments, with themes based on aspects of Florida, rococo Italy, or 18th-century Charleston. Marble floors and tabletops, wooden sleigh beds, and even wrought-iron canopy beds are featured in many.

The inn's restaurant, the **Library at Vendue Inn,** is recommended under "Dining, below." One of the best aspects of the place is the rooftop bar, whose view extends out over the waterfront of historic Charleston.

MODERATE

Ansonborough Inn. 21 Hassell St., Charleston, SC 29401. ☎ **800/522-2073** or 843/723-1655. Fax 843/577-6888. 34 units. A/C TV TEL. Summer $130–$200 double; off-season, $120–$130 double. Prices $20–$40 higher Sat–Sun and holidays. Children 7–12 $10, 13 and over $20 in parents' room. Rates include continental breakfast. AE, DISC, MC, V. Parking $5.

This is one of the oddest hotels in the Historic District. Once they get past the not-very-promising exterior, most visitors really like the unusual configuration of rooms. Set close to the waterfront, the Ansonborough occupies a massive building designed around 1900 as a warehouse for paper supplies. The lobby features exposed timbers and a soaring atrium filled with plants. Despite the building's height, it contains only three floors, allowing rooms with ceilings of between 14 and 16 feet and, in many cases, sleeping lofts. The rooms are outfitted with copies of 18th-century furniture and accessories, though the baths are reminiscent of a roadside motel's (molded fiberglass shower stalls and imitation marble countertops). A panoramic terrace with a hot tub has been added to the rooftop.

Ashley Inn. 201 Ashley Ave., Charleston, SC 29403. ☎ **800/581-6658** or 843/723-1848. Fax 843/579-9080. www.charleston-sc-inns.com. E-mail: ashley@cchat.com. 7 units, one 2-bedroom carriage house. A/C TV. $79–$155 double; $120–$165 suite; $140–$190 carriage house. Rates include full breakfast and afternoon tea. AE, DISC, MC, V. Free parking off-street.

Partly because of its pink clapboards and the steep staircases you climb to reach the public areas, this imposing B&B may remind you of a house in Bermuda. Built in 1832 on a plot of land that sold for a mere $419, it's even more appealing in its decor than the Cannonboro Inn, with which it shares the same Michigan-based owners. Breakfast and afternoon tea are served on a wide veranda overlooking a brick-floored carport whose centerpiece is a fountain/goldfish pond evocative of Old Charleston. The public rooms, with their high ceilings and deep colors, are attractive. The guest rooms are lavish, boasting antiques and reproductions as well as queen-size four-posters. The carriage house (shared with the Cannonboro) has a living room, a full kitchen, two bedrooms, and 1$^1/_2$ baths; it can accommodate up to six when the pullout sofa is used. If you have lots of luggage or difficulty climbing stairs, know in advance that negotiating this inn's steep and frequent stairs might pose a problem.

Double Tree Suites. 181 Church St., Charleston, SC 29401. ☎ **843/577-2644.** Fax 843/577-2697. 181 units. A/C TV TEL. $139–$229 1-bedroom suite; $229–$489 2-bedroom suite. AE, DC, DISC, MC, V. Parking $12 in underground garage.

Fairly anonymous, this inn contains many of the amenities of a conventional hotel, including a bar/lounge and a fitness center. A somber 1991 building adjacent to the City Market, it offers all suites, each with some type of cooking equipment. Kitchen facilities range from a wet bar, a refrigerator, and a microwave to more fully stocked kitchenettes with enough utensils to prepare a simple dinner. Regardless of their amenities, the accommodations tend to receive heavy use, since they appeal to families, tour groups, and business travelers. However, they were renovated in 1995. There's a coin-operated Laundromat on the premises.

1837 Bed & Breakfast. 126 Wentworth St., Charleston, SC 29401. ☎ **843/723-7166.** Fax 843/722-7179. 9 units. A/C TV. $79–$145 double. Rates include full breakfast. AE, MC, V. Free parking off-street.

Built in 1837 by cotton planter Nicholas Cobia, this place was restored and decorated by two artists. It's called a "single house" because it's only a single room wide, making for some interesting room arrangements. Our favorite is no. 2 in the Carriage House; it boasts authentic designs, exposed brick walls, a warm decor, a beamed ceiling, and three windows. All units have refrigerators and separate entrances, and one contains canopied poster rice beds (four-posters in which the posts are carved with rice sheaves; rice was a principal crop in colonial Charleston).

On one of the verandas you can sit under whirling ceiling fans and enjoy your breakfast or afternoon tea. Sausage pie, eggs

Benedict, and homemade breads are served at breakfast. The parlor room has cypress wainscoting and a black marble fireplace, while the breakfast room is really part of the kitchen.

Elliott House Inn. 78 Queen St. (between King and Meeting sts.), Charleston, SC 29401. ☎ **800/729-1855** or 843/723-1855. Fax 843/722-1567. www.elliotthouseinn.com. 25 units. A/C TV TEL. $94–$137 double. Rates include continental breakfast. AE, DISC, MC, V. Parking $11.

Historians have researched anecdotes about this place going back to the 1600s, but the core of this charming inn was built in 1861 as a private home, probably for slaves. The very hip staff offers a warm welcome, and you'll note lots of colonial inspiration in the decor of the comfortable and carefully maintained rooms. But despite all the grace notes and landscaping (the flower beds are touched up at 2-week intervals), the place has a raffish, indoor/outdoor motel–style quality that some guests find appealing. The units are arranged on tiers of balconies surrounding a verdant open courtyard. Conversation waxes free and easy beneath the city's largest wisteria arbor, near a bubbling whirlpool that can accommodate up to 12. Each room contains a four-poster bed (no. 36 is especially appealing). If possible, avoid the units with ground-level private outdoor terraces. The terraces are too cramped to really use, don't have attractive views, and tend to be plagued with mildew because of their location.

Hampton Inn. 345 Meeting St., Charleston, SC 29401. ☎ **800/426-7866** or 843/723-4000. www.hamptoninn.com. 172 units. A/C TV TEL. $89–$160 double; $149–$179 suite. Children under 18 stay free in parents' room. Rates include continental breakfast. AE, DC, DISC, MC, V. Parking $9.

A 10-minute walk from the City Market, near the Historic District, this Hampton Inn (a motor hotel) is preferred to the other Hampton Inn (a motel) at 11 Ashley Pointe Dr. Opposite the visitors' center (where many tours depart), it has some of the familiar Hampton Inn designs and features along with reproduction appointments. The colonial lobby is filled with natural woods and oriental rugs. The fireplace is a warm addition, and coffee and tea are always available. You won't find much in the way of views, but there's a fine outdoor pool with a deck. The boxy rooms, though pretty standard, are attractive, with pastel florals and modern baths. Housekeeping is of a good standard.

Maison DuPré. 317 E. Bay St., Charleston, SC 29401. ☎ **800/844-4667** or 843/723-8691. Fax 843/723-3722. 15 units. A/C TV TEL. $95–$215 double; $185–$215 suite. Rates include continental breakfast and afternoon tea. DISC, MC, V. Free parking.

This B&B evokes the aura of a country inn in France. Its central core dates from 1803, when it was built by a French-born tailor, but enlargements and improvements have incorporated three adjacent houses (two were hauled in from other neighborhoods) and two carriage houses into one well-organized whole. The components are unified by a brick-paved courtyard, with fountains, cast-iron furniture, and plantings.

Inside, you'll find bold 18th-century colors and a range of good-quality reproductions of antique sleigh beds, armoires, and four-posters. Rooms are individualized and come in a wide range of shapes and sizes; each is well appointed with firm mattresses and first-class plumbing. Many of the paintings were executed by the owner, Lucille Mulholland, who, with her husband, Robert, makes afternoon tea a pleasant event.

Meeting Street Inn. 173 Meeting St., Charleston, SC 29401. ☎ **800/ 842-8022** or 843/723-1882. Fax 843/577-0851. www.aesir.com/ meetingstreet. 56 units. A/C TV TEL. $185–$215 Fri–Sat; $125–$215 Thurs–Sun. Rates include continental breakfast. AE, DC, DISC, MC, V. Parking $8–$12.

The architectural design, from the 1870s, was influenced by the pink-sided buildings a Charleston merchant might've visited in Barbados a few decades earlier. Like the West Indian buildings it emulates, it might be in need of a coat of paint by the time you visit. That only helps to enhance a thoroughly romantic flair, especially at night, when moonlight filters down into the brick-paved courtyard. The midsize rooms are furnished with four-poster beds, armoires, and wood shutters, and the baths are pretty standard. There's no restaurant on the premises, but many lie within walking distance. We prefer some of the other inns in this price range, but this is a perfectly acceptable backup.

Victoria House Inn. 208 King St., Charleston, SC 29401. ☎ **800/933-5464** or 843/720-2944. Fax 843/720-2930. www.charminginns.com. E-mail: vhi@charminginns.com. 18 units. A/C MINIBAR TV TEL. $205 double; $255 suite. Rates include continental breakfast. AE, DISC, MC, V. Parking $5.

Constructed in 1889 as a branch of the YMCA, this brick-sided building retains some of its institutional flavor outside, despite a richly textured veneer of draperies and upholstery inside. Associated with the more upscale (and more expensive) John Rutledge House, it has a small but cheerful lobby with elaborate moldings, an elevator, and easy access to the shops and boutiques lining its street-level facade. Many rooms, ranging from small to midsize, have wallpaper in patterns of flowers and vines and reproductions of antique furnishings, and all have good beds and smoothly functioning plumbing. Breakfast is the only meal served.

INEXPENSIVE

Barksdale House Inn. 27 George St., Charleston, SC 29401. ☎ **843/ 577-4800.** Fax 843/853-0482. 14 units. A/C TV TEL. $90–$195 double. Rates include continental breakfast. MC, V. Free parking. No children under 7.

This is a tidy and well-proportioned Italianate building, constructed as an inn in 1778, near the City Market. It was massively altered and enlarged by the Victorians. Behind the inn, guests enjoy a flagstone-covered terrace, where a fountain splashes. The midsize rooms, most of which are reasonably priced, often contain four-poster beds and working fireplaces, and about six have whirlpool tubs. Throughout, the furnishings, wallpaper, and fabrics evoke the late 19th century. Sherry and tea are served on the back porch in the evening.

Best Western King Charles Inn. 237 Meeting St. (between Wentworth and Society sts.), Charleston, SC 29401. ☎ **800/528-1234** or 843/723-7451. Fax 843/723-2041. 91 units. A/C TV TEL. Summer $159 double; off-season $99 double. Children under 18 stay free in parents' room. AE, DC, DISC, MC, V. Free parking.

One block from the Historic District's market area, this hotel has a small pool, a helpful staff, and a colonial-inspired restaurant where breakfast is served. The midsize rooms are better than you might expect from a motel, and each comes with standardized but comfortable furnishings, including good beds. Some have balconies, but the views are limited. Though short on style, the King Charles is reliable, a good value, and convenient to most everything.

Calhoun House. 273 Calhoun St., Charleston, SC 29401. ☎ and fax **843/ 722-7341.** 4 units. A/C. $80–$135 double. Rates include continental breakfast. No credit cards. Free parking off-street.

It stands in isolated grandeur, a distinguished historic house hemmed in by more modern buildings. Fronted with double verandas supported with differing orders of neoclassical columns, it was built in 1855 by a Confederate colonel and judge and occupied after that by two of the city's elected officials. Today, it functions as a warm and hospitable guest house where owners Jim Wylie and Frank Lail welcome a mostly gay and lesbian crowd. The rooms are filled with 19th-century antiques and, to a greater degree, recent reproductions. Some of the units are in a circa 1840 carriage house, with 14-inch brick walls, and a few contain a TV. Continental breakfasts are served communally from a well-stocked buffet.

Cannonboro Inn. 184 Ashley Ave., Charleston, SC 29403. ☎ **800/235-8039** or 843/723-8572. Fax 843/723-8007. www.charleston-sc-inns.com. E-mail: cannon@cchat.com. 8 units. A/C TV. $69–$110 double; $140–$190 suite. Rates include full breakfast. AE, DISC, MC, V. Free parking. No children under 11.

Built in 1856 as a home for a rice planter, this buff- and beige-colored house opened as a B&B in 1990. The decor isn't as carefully coordinated or as relentlessly upscale as at many of its competitors in town; instead, there's a sense of folksy, comfortable informality. Though there's virtually no land around this building, a wide veranda on the side creates a "sit and talk for a while" mood. Each small to midsize room contains a canopy bed; old-fashioned bow-fronted furniture; and a cramped, somewhat old-fashioned bath. The carriage house is shared with the Ashley Inn (see above).

NORTH CHARLESTON
INEXPENSIVE

Knights Inn. 2355 Aviation Ave., North Charleston, SC 29418. ☎ **800/845-1927** or 843/744-4900. Fax 843/745-0668. www.knightsinn.com. 242 units. A/C TV TEL. $45–$55 double; $75–$85 suite. Rates include continental breakfast. AE, DC, DISC, MC, V. Free parking. 11 miles NW of Historic District off I-26.

There aren't many places in the Charleston area where families can rent suites, complete with kitchenettes, costing from $75 a night. But this is one of them. The double rooms starting at $45 a night also attract the serious budgeteer. And there's more good news: Seventeen of the standard doubles contain kitchenettes (the suites have them too, but inconveniently, none come with dishes). The rooms, as you'd expect, are in the standard motel format, and the suites are little more than a small living room plus a bedroom. A coin laundry and two pools make this place especially popular with families traveling in the hot, humid months.

Ramada Inn. 2934 W. Montague Ave., North Charleston, SC 29418. ☎ **800/272-6232** or 843/744-8281. Fax 843/744-6230. 155 units. A/C TV TEL. Mar–Oct $59–$79 double; off-season $39–$49 double. Extra person $10. AE, DC, DISC, MC, V. Free parking. 8 miles NW of Charleston off I-26.

The Ramada is hardly in the same class as the historic inns already previewed, but it's kind to the frugal vacationer. Mainly an outpost for the weary interstate driver, the inn is convenient to the airport and the major traffic arteries, and it provides free transportation to and from the airport. However, Charleston's downtown mass-transit system doesn't service this area, so be warned. Your buck gets more than you might expect at this well-maintained chain member, where a refrigerator and microwave are available on request. You don't get charm—but then, at prices beginning at $39 a night off-season, you can't really go wrong. You do get proper service and decent maintenance, however. The restaurant serves three meals a day and within walking distance is a Red Lobster and other choices. The hotel also offers a Ramada Live Lounge with entertainment nightly, ranging from country music to karaoke and comedy.

MOUNT PLEASANT
INEXPENSIVE

Masters Economy Inn. 300 Wingo Way, Mount Pleasant, SC 29464. ☎ **800/633-3434** or 843/884-2814. Fax 843/884-2598. 120 units, 26 with kitchenette. A/C TV TEL. $60–$65 double; $65–$70 double with kitchenette, $51–$56 double with king-size bed. Children under 18 stay free in parents' room. Rates include continental breakfast. AE, DC, DISC, MC, V. Free parking. 3 miles E of Charleston on U.S. 17.

As the name suggests, this Savannah-based chain lures the budget-conscious traveler with its trademark green sign. Many families favor this place over the high-priced inns of historic Charleston. The standard rooms with kitchenettes also help keep food costs down. Don't expect luxury at any of these chain members—still, what you get isn't bad. The rooms are well maintained and furnished in a typical motel style with twin beds. They're more than adequate, and no one has ever been known to complain about the rates. For the business traveler, there's a meeting room and fax service. Nearby dining options are plentiful, including a branch of Shoney's, several steak houses, and more than a dozen fresh seafood restaurants.

NEAR THE AIRPORT
MODERATE

Charleston Hilton Hotel. 4770 Gore Dr., Charleston, SC 29406. ☎ **800/445-8667** or 843/747-1900. Fax 843/744-2530. www.charleston.net/com/hilton. E-mail: hilton@charleston.net. 296 units. A/C TV TEL. $104–$169 double; $200–$315 suite. Rates include continental breakfast. AE, DC, MC, V. Free parking.

This place, a 15-minute drive north of the old town's center, is close to the junction of Montague Avenue and I-26, a 5-minute drive from the airport. Its moderate rates make it an appealing choice for leisure travelers who don't mind the long haul from the Historic District. Its amenities are clean, modern, comfortable, and suitable for business travelers or visitors who don't have their hearts set on quaint charm. It offers 24-hour room service, convention space and meeting facilities, a bar, an indoor/outdoor restaurant, and both indoor and outdoor pools. The midsize rooms, in the standard Hilton "motel" format, are comfortable and what you'd expect, though views open onto the highway.

INEXPENSIVE

La Quinta Motor Inn. 2499 La Quinta Lane, North Charleston, SC 29405. ☎ **843/797-8181.** Fax 843/569-1608. 122 units. A/C TV TEL. $69 double; $89 suite. Children under 18 stay free in parents' room; cribs free. AE, DC, DISC, MC, V. Free parking. Take I-26 north to Ashley-Phosphate Rd. (exit 209).

As the inn is conveniently located near the airport, you can call it directly from the airport baggage-claim area for free shuttle service. The boxy rooms in this clean, comfortable, well-run chain motel are standard but comfortable, and the beds are extra long. No-smoking rooms are available, and pets are welcome. There's also a pool. Shoney's restaurant next door provides room service from 6am to 11pm.

4 Dining

Foodies from all over the Carolinas flock to Charleston for some of the finest dining in the South. You get not only the most refined cookery of the Low Country but also an array of French and international specialties. Space doesn't permit us to preview all the outstanding restaurants, much less the merely good ones, but we've rounded up our very top choices.

A culinary experience unique to Charleston is the **Market Street Food Court,** between South Market and Church streets. Daily from 8am to 5pm, you can patronize a dozen or so little places contained in the food court area of the City Market. Some begin their day by serving breakfast, but most make their money at lunch, offering their menus to both the business community and visitors. The decor is inexpensive—mostly brick with canvas flags and cheap multicolored chairs. You can buy Chinese, Japanese, Italian, pizza, Greek, or American fare, in addition to subs, sandwiches, and cookies. Swensen's Ice Cream and A. W. Shuck's Oyster Bar are also here.

THE HISTORIC DISTRICT
EXPENSIVE

✪ **Anson.** 12 Anson St. ☎ **843/577-0551.** Reservations recommended. Main courses $17–$20. AE, DC, DISC, MC, V. Sun–Thurs 5:30–10pm, Fri–Sat 5:30–11pm. LOW COUNTRY/MODERN AMERICAN.

We simply love this place. Locals know they're likely to spot Charleston's society types here; newcomers recognize it as a hip

big-city venue with all the softly upholstered grace notes you'd expect in New York or Chicago, but with added touches of Low
Country charm. The setting is a brick-sided warehouse built a century ago to store ice. The present owners have added ornaments of
superb taste, including New Orleans–style iron balconies,
Corinthian pilasters salvaged from demolished colonial houses, and
lots of Victorian rococo.

The well-trained staff in long white aprons will describe to you
dishes inspired by traditions of the coastal Southeast. But this isn't
exactly down-home cooking, as you'll soon see after sampling the
get-*Gourmet* magazine-on-the-phone fried cornmeal oysters with
potato cakes; the lobster, corn, and black-bean quesadillas; the
cashew-crusted grouper with champagne sauce; or the rack of lamb
in a crispy Dijon-flavored crust with mint sauce. Our favorite is the
crispy flounder, which rival chefs have tried to duplicate but just
can't match.

Barbadoes Room. 115 Meeting St. (in the Mills House Hotel). ☎ **843/
577-2400.** Reservations recommended for dinner. Main courses $16–$21.
AE, DC, DISC, MC, V. Daily 11am–2pm; Mon–Sat 6:30–10pm, Sun 5:30–10pm.
SOUTHERN/SEAFOOD.

This is the showcase dining area in one of the city's most reputable
hotels. It was selected as the site of a dinner held in honor of Prince
Charles and Princess Diana when they were in Charleston. The
decorative theme evokes the planter's life of the 18th century, when
many local traders grew rich from trade with Europe, the West
Indies, and Africa. Plantation fans whirl air gently in a room accented with high ceilings and arches. Scarlett could have gotten
Rhett back had she prepared such menu items as Charleston she-
crab soup, pan-fried Low Country crab cakes, grilled salmon glazed
with honey jalapeño sauce, pork tenderloin with curried fruit
compote, blackened shrimp and scallops with grit cakes, and ginger-
encrusted tuna with apple relish. Dessert might be a mud pie as
dense and dark as the swamplands that flank the nearby coastline
(but infinitely more appetizing). The chef shows precision and sen-
sitivity in most dishes, and that's why the locals keep coming back.

✪ **Louis' Charleston Grill.** 224 King St. (in the Charleston Place Hotel).
☎ **843/577-4522.** Reservations recommended. Main courses $16–$22.
AE, DC, MC, V. Sun–Thurs 6–10pm, Fri–Sat 6–11pm. MODERN LOW
COUNTRY/AMERICAN.

When the Omni Hotel (now the Charleston Place) was built
in the mid-1980s, its architects included a marble-floored,

Charleston Dining

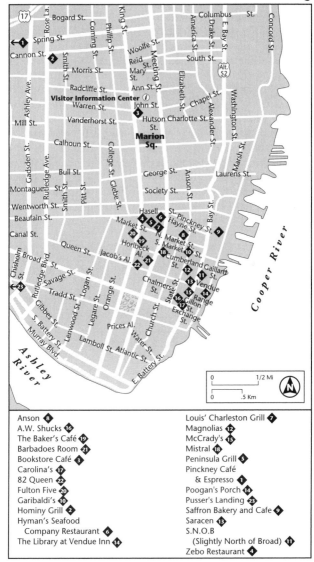

Anson **8**
A.W. Shucks **16**
The Baker's Café **19**
Barbadoes Room **21**
Bookstore Café **3**
Carolina's **17**
82 Queen **22**
Fulton Five **20**
Garibaldi's **10**
Hominy Grill **2**
Hyman's Seafood
   Company Restaurant **6**
The Library at Vendue Inn **14**

Louis' Charleston Grill **7**
Magnolias **12**
McCrady's **15**
Mistral **18**
Peninsula Grill **5**
Pinckney Café
   & Espresso **1**
Poogan's Porch **14**
Pusser's Landing **23**
Saffron Bakery and Cafe **9**
Saracen **13**
S.N.O.B
   (Slightly North of Broad) **11**
Zebo Restaurant **4**

mahogany-sheathed dining room whose opulence surpassed that of many of Europe's grand and formal dining salons. After fits and stops, the space was eventually leased to Louis Osteen, a South Carolinian who turned it into one of the top 25 restaurants in America, according to the editors of *Esquire*. He has since moved on and been replaced by Bab Wagner, who comes from Wild Boar in Nashville. However, the decor and menu remain unchanged—in the words of one of the staff, "If it ain't broke, don't fix it."

Unlike the decor, the good-tasting food does pay homage to local traditions. Putting a fresh twist on classic dishes is the rule. Menu items change with the season and the chef's inspiration but may include grilled lamb ribs with shallot-flavored pepper butter, McClellanville lump crabmeat with lobster cakes and mustard sauce, pan-fried baby flounder with Vidalia onion marmalade, or veal chops with bourbon-flavored blue cheese.

McCrady's. 2 Unity Alley. ☎ **843/577-0025.** Reservations recommended. Main courses $15–$23; fixed-price dinners $35. AE, DC, MC, V. Mon–Fri 11:30am–2:30pm; Mon–Thurs 5:30–10pm, Fri–Sat 5:30pm–1am. AMERICAN/ CONTINENTAL.

George Washington tipped a few at this old tavern and is said to have lost a set of false teeth during a drunken banquet here. All vestiges of colonial rowdiness are now gone, although the setting in one of the most historic buildings in Charleston remains. For years, this was the location of the Restaurant Million upstairs. The appropriately named Million was the most expensive restaurant in South Carolina, and many former patrons still arrive from around the world looking for it. It's gone and McCrady's is a worthy substitute for the departed. It's also an ideal spot for drinks, either before or after dinner. Join the locals in the sitting area around the fireplace. The cookery aims to please and succeeds. Witness such starters as pecan-crusted prawns or potato gnocchi in a savory tomato sauce. The oven-roasted sea bass with chile peppers is a pleasant revelation, as is the perfectly grilled salmon or the sautéed grouper. Other main courses are uniformly appealing to the palate, including herb-marinated rack of lamb. McCrady's also offers one of the best wine lists in Charleston.

✪ **Peninsula Café.** 112 N. Market St. (in the Planters Inn, at Meeting St.). ☎ **843/723-0700.** Reservations recommended for dinner. Main courses $17–$28. AE, DC, DISC, MC, V. Sun–Thurs 5:30–10pm, Fri–Sat 5:30–11pm. Bar open 4:30pm until the last customer leaves. SOUTHERN AMERICAN.

👥 Family-Friendly Restaurants

Hyman's Seafood Company Restaurant *(see p. 49)*   When given a choice, the children of Charleston like to be taken here, where the menu does a virtual song and dance to please them. The children's menu caters to their every desire. Choices range from a shrimp dinner to hot dogs to grilled cheese to an array of sandwiches and hamburgers. Kids have a hard time deciding between apple pie, cheesecake, and the melt-in-your-mouth fudge brownies.

Magnolias *(see p. 45)*   Southern hospitality and charm keep this place buzzing day and night. Lunch is the best time for families and children, with an array of soups, appetizers, salads, sandwiches, and pastas. But in-the-know local kids go easy on these, saving room for the daily array of homemade Southern desserts, perhaps a warm cream-cheese brownie with white-chocolate ice cream and chocolate sauce.

Pinckney Café & Espresso *(see p. 50)*   Near the City Market, this warm and casual spot is coffeehouse in decor, but with a surprising array of food to please families with small children. Try one of the Pinckney pasta dishes. At lunch, a wide array of sandwiches and omelets is featured.

Stylish and amusing, this is one of the Historic District's most likable and best-managed restaurants, a fit rival to the nearby Anson. Outfitted with postmodern wood-grained flair and tucked away behind the kind of cocktail lounge where you might be tempted to linger a bit longer than you should, it's known for its ultrahip staff, superb food, and an ambience reminiscent of an upscale European bistro.

The food is imaginative and "worth the detour," as Michelin might say. There's also a choice of dishes for low-cholesterol, low-calorie dining. Tantalizing menu items include bronzed mahimahi, lightly spiced tuna steak with curried salsa, herb-grilled tenderloin of pork, grilled ostrich steak with port-and-leek sauce, and mint-pesto loin of lamb.

MODERATE

Carolina's. 10 Exchange St. ☎ **843/724-3800.** Reservations required. Main courses $9–$23. AE, DC, DISC, MC, V. Daily 5:30–11pm. AMERICAN.

Perhaps because of its name and because of the skill of its designers in adapting an antique warehouse into a stylish minimalist restaurant, this place is usually included on any local's short list of noteworthy bistros. Despite its nod to yesteryear, it sports a black, pink, and white decor. The result is a skillful and aggressively marketed compendium of old-time dishes with uptown flair. Examples are shrimp and crabmeat wontons, salmon with coriander sauce, loin of lamb with jalapeño chutney, the best crab cakes in town, and an elaborate version of local grouper cooked in a crust of almonds and black sesame seeds and topped with crabmeat and lemon-butter sauce. As you dine, admire the antique French movie posters on the walls.

82 Queen. 82 Queen St. ☎ **843/723-7591.** Reservations recommended for dinner. Main courses $16–$22. AE, MC, V. Daily 11:30am–3pm and 6–10:30pm. LOW COUNTRY.

This is Charleston's most unusual compendium of real estate—three 18th- and 19th-century houses clustered around an ancient magnolia tree, with tables placed in its shade. If you ask, someone will list an even older set of dates connected with the property (it was part of a land grant issued in 1688), but most diners prefer to concentrate on the Low Country cuisine. The menu is filled with flavor and flair, with dishes that include an award-winning she-crab soup laced with sherry, charcoal-grilled spicy oysters with sesame and soy sauce, a surprisingly zesty Carolina bouillabaisse, a New Orleans–style shrimp-and-chicken gumbo with andouille sausage and okra, and crab cakes with sweet pepper and basil rémoulade sauce. For dessert, the bourbon pecan pie is wicked.

Fulton Five. 5 Fulton St. ☎ **843/853-5555.** Reservations recommended. Main courses $13–$26. AE, CB, DC, MC, V. Mon–Thurs 5:30–11pm, Fri–Sat 5:30pm–midnight. NORTHERN ITALIAN.

When you've grown tired of the she-crab soup and Low Country grits, retreat to the Fulton Five, with its cozy Mediterranean charm and decor of muted brown shutters and handsome green walls. This is the setting for great Northern Italian cuisine that attracts local families seeking value. The menu changes frequently but is always imbued with an authentic Italian flavor. Try, if featured, scallops pancetta with balsamic glaze, followed by braised veal shank perfectly flavored or one of the varieties of pasta (our favorite is tagliatelle with shrimp and green olives). Top the meal with a selection from the ever-changing dessert menu. The kitchen staff promises you good food at a reasonable price and delivers.

Library at Vendue Inn. 19 Vendue Range. ☎ **843/577-7970.** Lunch salads, sandwiches, and platters $5–$9; dinner main courses $17–$20. AE, DC, DISC, MC, V. Mon–Sat 11:30am–2:30pm; Mon–Thurs 6–10pm, Fri–Sat 5:30–10pm. SOUTHERN/INTERNATIONAL.

This place lies at the end of a labyrinth of narrow corridors that interconnect with the reception area of the Vendue Inn. Its most unusual aspects are its diminutive size and its seemingly awkward division into a network of small dining rooms, each in a decorative theme unrelated to its neighbors. The most visible of the dining areas looks like a library (with an admittedly tiny collection of reading material), whose scholarly atmosphere is softened with candlelight and napery.

The cuisine is innovative, even progressive, as you'll soon discover when faced with such appetizers as ravioli and shrimp with roasted herb garlic dressing or barbecue shrimp and grits. One delectable pasta, a first for most diners, is made with blackened oysters and saffron Alfredo sauce. Other palate-tempting specialties include half a crispy duck, pan-seared grouper, Greek-style stuffed flounder, and fried lobster tail. Dessert highlights are pecan pie and chocolate torte.

Magnolias. 185 E. Bay St. ☎ **843/577-7771.** Reservations recommended. Main courses $15–$25. AE, DC, MC, V. Sun–Thurs 11:30am–10pm, Fri–Sat 11:30am–11pm. SOUTHERN.

This place manages to elevate the vernacular cuisine of the Deep South into a postmodern art form suitable for big-city foodies. After the Savings and Loan debacle of the Reagan years, its owners acquired the city's venerable but decrepit Customs house, constructed in the 1820s and rebuilt in the 1890s. After awesome expenditures on renovations, the space now resembles a sprawling network of connected loft apartments in New York City, with heart-pine floors, faux-marble columns, and massive beams. Everybody's favorite lunch is an open-faced veal meat loaf sandwich, though we find it rather dull. The soups and salads tend to be excellent, however, especially one made with field greens with lemon-lingonberry vinaigrette and crumbled blue cheese. Down South dinners include everything from Carolina carpetbaggers filet with Parmesan-fried oysters, green beans, and Madeira-and-béarnaise sauce to chicken and dumplings with shiitake mushrooms.

Mistral. 99 S. Market St. ☎ **843/722-5708.** Reservations recommended. Main courses $12–$18; children's menu $5. AE, DC, DISC, MC, V. Sun–Thurs 11am–11pm, Fri–Sat 11am–midnight. FRENCH.

Across a narrow street from the crowded kiosks of what was 19th-century Charleston's food and vegetable markets, this is the kind of bistro you'd find in a working-class district of New Orleans. There's a comfortably outfitted bar at one end of the room, a diffident and sometimes skeptical reception, and accessories that include posters of Paris movie halls and old-time French movie stars. Daily specials are posted on chalkboards. Menu items include crab cakes with fried shrimp; noisette of mahimahi dredged in pecan flour; bouillabaisse; chicken with rosemary-cream sauce; and a succulent vegetarian penne pasta prepared with eggplant, peppers, goat cheese, and gorgonzola. Most of these are right on the mark, though the cookery is inconsistent. Live music is presented Tuesday to Saturday nights.

Pusser's Landing. 17 Lockwood Dr. ☎ **843/853-1000.** Reservations recommended for dinner. Main courses $12–$24. AE, DC, DISC, MC, V. Sun–Wed 11am–10pm, Thurs–Sat 11am–11pm. CARIBBEAN/SEAFOOD.

Located downtown at the City Marina, Pusser's offers some of the finest seafood in Charleston, many dishes with Caribbean zest and flair. Lunch or dinner is served at the water's edge, overlooking the Ashley River. Choice cuisine is offered with views of the marina and its sailboats. The large, vibrant dining room is decorated with ship models and antiques, making it a comfortable family setting. Menu items include Low Country shrimp and grits; classic sandwiches; and Caribbean dishes, such as chicken rôti, conch fritters, and a large and delectable steam pot of seafood to share. There is also a separate menu for their vast selection of beers and rum drinks. Finish with a classic key-lime pie.

Saracen. 141 E. Bay St. ☎ **843/723-6242.** Reservations recommended. Main courses $11–$20. AE, CB, DC, MC, V. Dining room Tues–Sat 6–10pm; bar Tues–Fri 5pm–2am, Sat 6pm–midnight. MODERN AMERICAN/INTERNATIONAL.

Its name derives from the style of architecture of the 19th-century building that contains it: Saracen Revival. Constructed in 1853 as the headquarters of the Farmers and Exchange Bank, this building is said to be the only authentic example of the style in the United States. Restaurateur Charlie Farrell, who learned her culinary techniques in Louisiana and Paris, ripped out the interior's second floor in the 1980s, painted the soaring ceiling blue with white stars, and created a hushed and often solemn setting that (except for the good food) has been likened to a church interior. Menu items are eclectic and occasionally experimental. Sauces are light, and there's a deft touch of seasonings. Examples are duck breast with honey-thyme sauce and cider vinegar, and delectable orange-flavored crème brûlée.

The building's upper balcony is home to **Charlie's Little Bar,** a cozy watering hole that features live jazz and blues every Friday and Saturday after 9:30pm.

S.N.O.B. (slightly North of Broad). 192 E. Bay St. ☎ **843/723-3424.** Reservations accepted for 6 or more. Main courses $14–$28. AE, MC, V. Mon–Fri 11:30am–3pm; daily 5:30–11pm. SOUTHERN.

In this snazzily rehabbed warehouse you'll find an exposed kitchen, a high ceiling crisscrossed with ventilation ducts, and vague references to the South of long ago, including a scattering of wrought iron. The place promotes itself as Charleston's culinary maverick, priding itself on updated versions of the vittles that kept the South alive for the first 300 years of its history; however, the menu seems tame compared with the innovations being offered at many of its upscale Southern-ethnic competitors. Once you get past the hype, you might actually enjoy the place. Former diners have included Timothy Dalton, Sly Stallone, and superlawyer Alan Dershowitz. You can order main courses in a medium or large size, a fact appreciated by dieters. Grilled dolphin glazed with pesto on a bed of tomatoes; grilled beef tenderloin with green-peppercorn sauce, topped with a deviled crab cake; honey-and-sesame–crusted sea bass with roasted beets; and sautéed jumbo sea scallops with Asian spices and wilted greens are examples of the well-prepared but not particularly Southern menu. For dessert, it's the sour cream apple pie for us.

INEXPENSIVE

A. W. Shucks. 70 State St. ☎ **843/723-1151.** Reservations not necessary. Main courses $9–$17. AE, DC, DISC, MC, V. Sun–Thurs 11:30am–10pm, Fri–Sat 11am–11pm. SEAFOOD.

This is a true oyster bar, a sprawling, salty tribute to the pleasures of shellfish and the memorabilia of the fishers who gather them. A short walk from the Public Market stands this solid building that's been heavily restored (it was once a warehouse for Nabisco). The setting is filled with rough timbers, a long bar where thousands of crustaceans have already been cracked open and consumed, and a dining room. The best and most satisfying choices on the menu include oysters and clams on the half shell, seafood chowder, deviled crab, shrimp Creole, and oysters prepared in at least half a dozen ways. Chicken and beef dishes are listed, but they're nothing special. A wide selection of international beer is sold. Absolutely no one cares how you dress—it's hard to maintain an elegant wardrobe anywhere near the premises of an oyster roast.

Baker's Café. 214 King St. ☎ **843/577-2694.** Main courses $6–$10. DC, MC, V. Mon–Fri 8am–2:30pm, Sat–Sun 9am–2:30pm. INTERNATIONAL.

The menu selection here is more complete than you'll find in a coffee shop. The rose-colored walls, ceiling fans, track lighting, local art, wood-slatted chairs, and plum/brown tables create a cozy ambience. Egg dishes are a specialty, including eggs Florentine, eggs Copenhagen, and the local favorite: two poached eggs on a bed of Canadian snow crab, Hollandaise, and rusks. Simple but good-tasting selections include croissants, muffins, Danish pastries, and scones. Well-stuffed sandwiches are also served. Brunch is popular on weekends.

Bookstore Café. 412 King St. (at Hutson St.). ☎ **843/720-8843.** Main courses $4–$8. MC, V. Mon–Fri 9am–2:30pm, Sat–Sun 8am–2pm. AMERICAN.

There isn't a big selection of books, but that doesn't keep Charleston's Greenwich Village set away. The wallpaper looks like bookshelves, and the baskets, ceiling fans, and wood tables and chairs make the artsy decor work. Specials are written on a chalkboard. Breakfast begins with classic shrimp and grits with eggs, accompanied by Madeira sauce, though you can order three-egg omelets as well (even one made for vegetarians, another with poached salmon). Potato casseroles are a feature at lunch; folly is made with country ham, fresh tomato, broccoli, onions, pomme (potato) sauce, mushrooms, and peppers. Fresh-tasting soups, crisp salads, and stir-fries round out the bill of fare. The beer bread is homemade.

California Dreaming. 1 Ashley Pointe Dr. ☎ **843/766-1644.** Reservations recommended. Main courses $7–$17. AE, MC, V. Sun–Thurs 11am–10pm, Fri–Sat 11am–11pm. AMERICAN.

The building is a replica of a Civil War fort on the Ashley River. The casual dining restaurant offers house specialties such as prime rib, broiled steaks, signature salads, baby-back ribs, broiled seafood, sandwiches, burgers, and low-fat items. The restaurant also has a full-service bar. The cookery here is diversified enough to keep patrons returning again and again. It is reasonably priced and professional, although no one has accused the kitchen of having an overactive imagination. This is familiar fare, almost '50s in its offerings, but that is exactly why many of the locals come here.

Garibaldi's. 49 S. Market St. ☎ **843/723-7153.** Reservations recommended. Main courses $8–$16. AE, MC, V. Sun–Thurs 5:30–10:30pm, Fri–Sat 5:30–11pm. ITALIAN/SEAFOOD.

In the center of the historic Charleston Market, Garibaldi's is a successful place that also has branches in Columbia and Savannah. The interior, with its bistro atmosphere, is decorated with wicker pieces, ladderback chairs, track lights, ceiling fans, and Italian memorabilia. You might start with a salmon appetizer and continue with a pasta selection. The seafood specials are good, too, including the dolphin, stuffed grouper, and blackened tuna. The chef makes his own desserts and offers outdoor dining in fair weather.

Henry's on the Market. 54 N. Market St. ☎ **843/723-4363.** Reservations recommended. Main courses $14–$19. AE, DC, MC, V. Mon–Fri 4–10pm, Sat–Sun 2–11pm. LOW COUNTRY.

This is the oldest established restaurant and bar offering casual fine dining in Charleston. The second-floor setting has an extraordinary view of the surrounding market and downtown area. Henry's utilizes Charleston's local produce and seafood to create menu items, such as crab soup, baked oysters, poached mussels, grilled portobello mushrooms, Southern fried catfish, or the very Southern barbecued shrimp with hominy grits. The restaurant's unique and diversified cuisine is enhanced with live blues and jazz performances Thursday through Sunday.

✪ **Hominy Grill.** 207 Rutledge Ave. ☎ **843/937-0931.** Brunch $5–$8; lunch main courses $5–$7; dinner main courses $9–$15. AE, MC, V. Mon–Fri 7:30am–2:30pm, Sat–Sun brunch 9am–2:30pm; Mon–Sat 7–9:30pm. LOW COUNTRY.

Owned and operated by chef Robert Stehling, Hominy Grill features beautifully prepared dishes inspired by the Low Country. It has gained a devoted local following that comes here to feast on such specialties as a barbecued chicken sandwich, avocado-and-wehani rice salad and grilled vegetables, okra-and-shrimp beignets, and (a brunch favorite) smothered eggs or poached eggs on homemade biscuits with mushroom gravy. At night, try the oven-fried chicken with spicy peach gravy (yes, that's right) or the grilled duck breast with eggplant and sautéed greens. Stehling claims that he likes to introduce people to new stuff away from pasta or potatoes. Many of his dishes, including salads, are prepared with grains like barley and cracked wheat. At breakfast, go for the buttermilk biscuits, the meaty bacon, and the home-style fried apples. The catfish stew with cornbread at lunch is a temptation on a cold and rainy day, and the banana bread is worth writing home about.

Hyman's Seafood Company Restaurant. 215 Meeting St. ☎ **843/723-6000.** Reservations not necessary. Seafood dinners and platters $8–$15. AE, DISC, MC, V. Daily 7am–11pm. SEAFOOD.

It was opened a century ago by a family of Russian immigrants and has remained true to the old-fashioned traditions that thousands of diners find appealing. The building containing Hyman's sprawls over most of a city block, near Charleston Place, in the commercial heart of Charleston's business district. Inside is a take-out deli loaded with salmon, lox, and smoked herring, all displayed in the style of New York's great kosher delis. Technically, the restaurant contains two sit-down sections: one devoted to deli-style sandwiches, chicken soup like mama made, and fresh salads; the other to a delectably messy choice of fish, shellfish, lobsters, and oysters. We ignore the endorsement of eternal Sen. Strom Thurmond but take more seriously the praise of such luminaries as Barbra, Oprah, and Misha.

Pinckney Café & Espresso. 18 Pinckney St. (at Motley Lane). ☎ **843/ 577-0961.** Reservations required for parties of 6 or more. Main courses $10– $17. No credit cards. Tues–Sat 11:30am–3pm and 6–9pm. AMERICAN.

Two blocks north of the City Market, this spot is casual, warm, and inviting. Picture a yellow-frame 19th-century home turned coffee-house and restaurant. You'll find wide hardwood floors, comfortable slatted chairs, a fireplace, and a porch with ceiling fans for outdoor dining. The crowd is rather yuppie-ish. On the menu (written on a chalkboard brought to your table) will be creamy lemon broccoli soup with rosemary and thyme, sandwiches, omelets, and main courses. Specials may include a spinach quesadilla with seasoned spinach and Jack and feta cheese, all stuffed in a crisp flour tortilla and served with sour cream and salsa; turkey marsala; salmon cakes with shallot-and-dill cream sauce and stone-ground grits; or Pinckney's homemade cheese tortellini with shrimp and scallops in tomato-and-scallion cream sauce. On the lighter side are specialty coffees, including the Café Market Street (espresso with cocoa, sugar, cinnamon, nutmeg cream, and whipped cream) and the cappuccino float (with ice cream). Wine and beer are available.

Poogan's Porch. 72 Queen St. ☎ **843/577-2337.** Reservations recom- mended. Main courses $13–$15. AE, MC, V. Mon–Sat 11:30am–9:30pm, Sun 10:30am–9:30pm. LOW COUNTRY.

Poogan's Porch is a local gem, located in the heart of Old Charles- ton. This award-winning restaurant has been serving its authentic Southern cooking since 1976. Known as the "Home of Southern Hospitality," celebrities, politicians, visitors, and locals alike equally enjoy the relaxed setting. Dinner is served indoors or outside on the porches and patio. The building is believed to be haunted by the ghost of Zoe St. Anad. Don't worry, though—she hasn't made any house calls in some time.

Dishes include such satisfying Low Country specialties as jambalaya, gumbo, she-crab soup, seasonal seafood, Cajun duck, Southern fried catfish, quail, alligator, and for dessert peanut butter pie.

Saffron Bakery and Cafe. 333 By St. ☎ **843/722-5588.** Reservations not necessary. Main courses $5–$9. Daily 7am–10pm. AE, MC, V. MEDITERRANEAN.

This artisan-style bakery, cafe, and gourmet shop was voted "Charleston's Best Bakery." For Southern breakfast favorites, start with shrimp and grits, and for lunch or dinner try any of the enormous Mediterranean salads, fresh pastas, deli sandwiches, or Middle Eastern selections such as roasted lamb stewed with cilantro and parsley and served with saffron rice. In the gourmet shop you can get custom breads, pastries, croissants, muffins, cookies, chocolates, teas and coffees, and imported delicacies from around the globe.

Zebo Restaurant. 275 King St. ☎ **837/577-7600.** Main courses $10–$16. AE, DC, DISC, MC, V. Mon–Fri 11:30am–10pm, Sat–Sun 11:30–11pm. CONTINENTAL.

Zebo has something to offer everyone with its high-energy nightlife, microbrewery, and great meals. Modern light fixtures and patterned fabric contrast nicely with mustard-colored, marbelized walls. Some of the best contemporary dining in Charleston is offered in this relaxed atmospheric setting. Flavor-filled menu items include beef tenderloin, fresh fish, pasta, salads, corn-fried oysters, ice creams, and sorbets. There is also a wood-burning pizza oven and microbrewery for local beer. Specials change daily. Zebo's also features live music after dinner, and the second floor provides an additional bar and billiards room.

THE MUNICIPAL MARINA
INEXPENSIVE

Marina Variety Store. 17 Lockwood Blvd. ☎ **843/723-6325.** Lunch main courses $5–$10; dinner main courses $10–$15. AE, MC, V. Daily 6:30am–9:30pm. SEAFOOD/LOW COUNTRY.

For more than a quarter of a century, this spot has been serving locals and boat owners who put into the adjacent dock along the Ashley River next to the municipal marina. You can feed the entire family here without doing serious injury to your pocketbook. The restaurant occupies one side of a store that sells fishing supplies and souvenirs and overlooks the yacht basin. You can enjoy down-home Low Country specialties like okra soup or chili, well-stuffed sandwiches, or fried-fish dinners, all at budget prices. Breakfast is served until 11am. Picture windows frame the comings and goings of all sorts of boats; maybe you'll even see a Chinese junk sail past. You place your order at the counter, and waitresses bring the food to comfortable booths.

MOUNT PLEASANT
MODERATE

Supper at Stack's. 101 Pitt St. (in the Captain Guild's Inn). ☎ 843/884-7009. Reservations required. Fixed-price 4-course dinner $29. AE, MC, V. Tues–Sat 6–10pm. LOW COUNTRY.

Housed in a historic B&B (though it's not associated in any managerial way) in the 19th-century suburb of Mount Pleasant, 7 miles from the heart of historic Charleston, this is the culinary equivalent of a folksy, family-oriented inn. The menus are without a shred of European pretense and are listed on a chalkboard at one end of the old-fashioned dining room. In the shadow of a 19th-century icebox, which the owners have converted into a modern refrigerator, you can order such downhome specialties as catfish, salmon, duck, and leg of lamb, as well as wholesome desserts like you wished your grandmother used to make. Beer and wine are served.

The Wreck. Mt. Pleasant Docks, 106 Hadrell Point. ☎ 843/884-0052. Reservations not accepted. Main courses $11.50–$21. Sun–Thurs 5:30–9pm, Fri–Sat 5:30–10pm. SOUTHERN/SEAFOOD.

Southern fried seafood "in the rough" is the house specialty here, attracting "bubba guys and gals." The Wreck offers a casual setting in a comfortable atmosphere. Meals are served in a screened porch. Deviled crab, fish, or fried oysters are fresh and served daily. Meals are served with such downhome favorites as hushpuppies, red rice, and coleslaw. At night there are also stone crab claws, fish stew, steak, and bread pudding for dessert—ideal Bill Clinton food.

5 Seeing the Sights

We always head for the **Battery** (if you want to be official about it, the White Point Gardens) to get into the feel of this city. It's right on the end of the peninsula, facing the Cooper River and the harbor. There's a landscaped park, shaded by palmettos and live oaks and filled with walkways lined with old monuments and other war relics. The view toward the harbor looks out to **Fort Sumter.** We like to walk along the sea wall on East Battery and Murray Boulevard and sink slowly into the history of Charleston. You might then venture into the neighborhood to see the architecture.

WALKING TOUR—
Old Charleston

This is really a two-in-one tour, since we've made a distinction (as do Charlestonians) between "south of Broad Street" and "north of Broad Street." If you have the luxury of 2 days to devote to this charming city, we strongly recommend that you explore each area in depth on successive days.

Start: White Point Gardens at the Battery.

Finish: Aiken–Rhett Mansion, Elizabeth Street between Mary and Judith streets.

Time: 6 hours without touring historic attractions; add from a half an hour to an hour for each tour.

Best Times: Any time except midday, when the heat can be steamy, especially in summer. Early evening is pleasant if you don't plan to tour attractions.

Worst Times: Rush hours Monday to Friday, when there's too much traffic.

We start south of Broad Street. Turning your back to the water, you'll face a row of graceful large houses that line South Battery. When you walk away from the park, it's as if you're going through a sort of gateway into the rest of town.

Once off South Battery, note that almost every home is of historic or architectural interest. For most of the stops below you'll find detailed information elsewhere in this chapter. After a stroll through White Point Gardens, walk up Meeting Street to the:

1. **Calhoun Mansion,** 16 Meeting St., then return to South Battery Street and walk east 2 blocks alongside one gracious mansion after another. Loiter a moment or two at East Battery Street to savor the harbor view, then turn north to the:

2. **Edmondston–Alston House,** 21 E. Battery. Cross the street and spend a few minutes in the waterfront park. Continue north to the next intersection and turn left on Water Street for 1 block, then turn right on Church Street and continue north to the:

3. **Heyward–Washington House,** 87 Church St. Continuing north, you'll pass:

4. **Catfish Row,** a row of connected buildings from 89 to 91 Church St. Its real name is Cabbage Row (after the vegetables that used to be sold on the sidewalk). Duboise Heyward changed its name in his novel *Porgy,* and when he and George Gershwin collaborated on the opera *Porgy and Bess,* its fame spread all over the world.

   At Church and Elliott streets, turn left to reach:

5. **St. Michael's Episcopal Church,** at Meeting and Broad streets. Look inside, then stroll through the adjoining graveyard, with centuries-old headstones.

   🌑 **TAKE A BREAK** If it's lunchtime or you just want a sandwich, burger, or drink, head for **Sticky Fingers,** 235 Meeting St. (☎ 843/853-RIBS), which has a full bar. With a telephone number like that, you know the chef specializes in ribs, and they're succulent here and will definitely leave you with sticky fingers as the name of the joint promises. It's real family dining.

   Now we'll head north of Broad Street. While you're in the vicinity, you may want to stop in at:

6. **City Hall,** at Broad and Meeting streets, to have a look at the portrait gallery in the Council Chamber. The famous John Trumbull portrait of George Washington is here, along with Samuel F. B. Morse's painting of James Monroe.

   The adjacent park at:

7. **Washington Square** holds monuments to a whole slew of prominent South Carolinians, as well as the Fireproof Building, this country's first.

   Walk 2 blocks north to Queen Street and turn right to reach the:

8. **Dock Street Theatre,** on the corner of Queen and Church streets. Continue east toward the waterfront and turn south at Church Street to visit the:

9. **French Huguenot Church,** Church Street between Queen and Chalmers.

   Now turn north on Church Street and walk the few blocks to the:

10. **Old City Market,** at East Bay and Market streets. It's a fascinating collection of open stalls under brick sheds with tile roofs stretching for roughly 3 blocks. On either side of the open sheds, old market buildings have been leased to small boutiques filled with craft items, linens, cookware, clothing, gifts, and such.

Walking Tour—Old Charleston

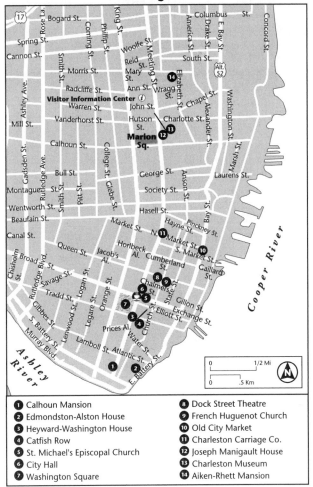

1 Calhoun Mansion
2 Edmondston-Alston House
3 Heyward-Washington House
4 Catfish Row
5 St. Michael's Episcopal Church
6 City Hall
7 Washington Square
8 Dock Street Theatre
9 French Huguenot Church
10 Old City Market
11 Charleston Carriage Co.
12 Joseph Manigault House
13 Charleston Museum
14 Aiken-Rhett Mansion

Back at the corner of Meeting and North Market, you'll find a stand for the:

11. **Charleston Carriage Co.** This may be an ideal time to treat yourself to a horse-drawn carriage ride through many of the streets that you've just been walking, as well as a few more (see "Organized Tours," below).

Our course is now along Meeting Street several blocks north to the:

12. **Joseph Manigault House,** Meeting Street between John and Hutson. At this intersection, plan a leisurely interval at the:

13. **Charleston Museum,** this country's oldest, with several fine collections of 18th-century silver and other interesting exhibits.

When you can tear yourself away, walk north on Meeting to Wragg Street and turn right for the:

14. **Aiken–Rhett Mansion,** 48 Elizabeth St., which was Civil War headquarters for Gen. P. G. T. Beauregard and his Confederate troops. It's now closed to the public. A brick facade and white Greek columns are the trademark features of this circa 1817 home. Former slave quarters still stand at the back.

A NATIONAL MONUMENT

Fort Sumter National Monument. In Charleston Harbor. ☎ **843/ 883-3123.** Fort, free; boat trip, $10.50 adults, $5.50 children 6–11, free for children 5 and under.

It was here that the first shot of the Civil War was fired on April 12, 1861. Confederate forces launched a 34-hour bombardment of the fort. Union forces eventually surrendered, and the "Rebels" occupied federal ground that became a symbol of Southern resistance. However, their action led to a declaration of war in Washington. Stubbornly, the Confederate troops held onto Sumter for nearly 4 years, which is an amazing feat since it was almost continually bombarded by the Yankees. When evacuation finally came, the fort was nothing but a heap of rubble.

Park rangers today are on hand to answer your questions about this rare attraction, which played such a large role in the nation's history. You can explore gun emplacements and visit a small museum filled with artifacts related to the siege. A complete tour of the fort takes about 2 hours.

Though you can travel to the fort via your own boat, most people seek out **Fort Sumter Tours,** 205 King St., Suite 204 (☎ **843/ 722-1691**), offering the only tour to Fort Sumter, the "Harbor and Fort Sumter Tour" (see "Organized Tours," later in this chapter, for more on this company). You can board at either of two locations: Charleston's City Marina on Lockwood Boulevard or Mount Pleasant's Patriots Point, site of the world's largest naval and maritime museum. Sailing times change every month or so, but generally from March to Labor Day there are three sailings per day from each location, beginning at 9:30 or 10:45am. Winter sailings are more curtailed. Call for details. Each departure point offers ample parking, and the boats carrying you to Fort Sumter are sightseeing yachts built for the purpose; they're clean, safe, and equipped with modern conveniences.

HISTORIC HOMES

Calhoun Mansion. 16 Meeting St. (between Battery and Lamboll sts.). ☎ 843/772-8205. Admission $15 adults, $7 children 5–10, free for children under 5. Wed–Sun 10am–4pm. Tours every 15 minutes; last tour 4pm. Closed holidays and in Jan.

This 1876 Victorian showplace is complete with period furnishings (including a few original pieces), porcelain and etched-glass gas chandeliers, ornate plastering, and woodwork of cherry, oak, and walnut. The ballroom's 45-foot-high ceiling has a skylight.

✪ **Edmondston–Alston House.** 21 E. Battery. ☎ **843/722-7171.** Admission $8. Guided tours Tues–Sat 10am–4:30pm, Sun–Mon 1:30–4:30pm.

In High Battery, an elegant section of Charleston, this house (built in 1825 by Charles Edmondston, a merchant and wharf owner) was one of the earliest constructed in the city in the late Federalist style. After economic reverses, he sold it to Charles Alston, a Low Country rice planter, who modified the style, changing it to the more popular Greek Revival. The house has remained in the Alston family, who now open the first two floors to visitors. You can see their heirloom furnishings, silver, and painting collection. It was here in 1861 that General Beauregard joined the Alston family to watch the bombardment of Fort Sumter. Robert E. Lee once found refuge here when his hotel uptown caught fire.

Heyward–Washington House. 87 Church St. (between Tradd and Elliott sts.). ☎ **843/722-0354.** Admission $7 adults, $4 children 3–12, free for children 2 and under. Combination ticket including Charleston Museum and Joseph Manigault House $12. Mon–Sat 10am–5pm, Sun 1–5pm. Tours every half hour; last tour 4:30pm.

In a district of Charleston called Cabbage Row stands this 1772 house. It was built by Daniel Heyward, the Rice King, and was the setting for Dubose Heyward's *Porgy.* President Washington bedded down here in 1791. It was also the home of Thomas Heyward Jr., a signer of the Declaration of Independence. Many of the fine period pieces in the house were the work of Thomas Elfe, one of America's most famous cabinetmakers. The restored kitchen from the 1700s is the only historic kitchen in the city open to the public. It stands behind the main house, as do the servants' quarters and a garden.

Joseph Manigault House. 350 Meeting St. (diagonally across from the visitors' center on the corner of John St.). ☎ **843/723-2926.** Admission $7 adults, $4 children 3–12, free for children 2 and under. Combination ticket including Heyward–Washington House and Charleston Museum $18. Mon–Sat 10am–4:30pm, Sun 1–5pm.

This 1803 Adams-style residence on the register of National Historic Landmarks was the home of a wealthy rice planter. The house features a curving central staircase and an outstanding collection of Charleston, American, English, and French period furnishings.

Nathaniel Russell House. 51 Meeting St. ☎ **843/724-8481.** Admission $7, free for children under 5. Guided tours Mon–Sat 10am–5pm, Sun and holidays 2–5pm.

One of America's finest examples of Federal architecture, this 1808 house was completed by Nathaniel Russell, one of Charleston's rich merchants. Over the years it has been put to many uses, including stints as a girls' school and a convent. The house has been celebrated architecturally for its "free-flying" staircase, spiraling unsupported for three floors. The staircase's elliptical shape is repeated throughout. The interiors are ornate and still decorated with period furnishings; check out the elegant music room with its golden harp and neo-classical sofa.

AN AQUARIUM

South Carolina Aquarium. 350 Concord St. ☎ **843/720-1900.** Call for exact admissions. Discounts for children, students, and seniors. Mar–Oct daily 9am–5pm; Nov–Feb daily 10am–5pm.

Charleston's latest major attraction makes its debut in the spring of 2000. Located at the edge of the historic Charleston Harbor, this prominent 93,000-square-foot structure not only overlooks the water but provides views of the dolphins, the ships, and the landscape of the Cooper River from its decks. There are 60 exhibits on display and more than 10,000 living organisms, representing 500 species. Among these are otters, birds, turtles, fish, venomous snakes, other reptiles and amphibians, aquatic invertebrates, and insects. The aquarium has set up an exhibit that guides visitors through different habitats of the five major regions of the Southeast Appalachian Watershed in South Carolina. In addition, the museum has set up

Charleston Attractions

Aiken-Rhett Mansion ❷
American Military Museum ❺
Calhoun Mansion ⓫
Charleston Museum ❸
The Citadel ❶
Dock Street Theatre ❼
Edmondston-Alston House ❿

Gibbes Museum of Art ❻
Heyward-Washington House ❽
Joseph Manigault House ❸
Nathaniel Russell House ❾
Old Exchange & Provost
  Dungeon ⓭
South Carolina Aquarium ❹
White Point Gardens ⓬

Impressions

Just as one generation of Charlestonians had recovered from the Revolution, the next generation was indiscreet enough to start the Civil War—the "War of Northern Aggression" you can still hear it called here—and the Yankees and carpetbaggers plundered the city all over again. For decades, the old Charlestonians were left huddled in their crumbling mansions "too poor to paint and too proud to whitewash." I can remember visiting Charleston with my parents in the Depression years, and looking upon its Georgian houses and Greek temples as a vast classical ruin.

—Charles Kuralt, *Charles Kuralt's America* (1995)

interactive displays, an education center, a Discovery Lab, and special toddler exhibits.

NEARBY PLANTATIONS

✪ **Boone Hall Plantation.** 1235 Long Point Rd., Mount Pleasant. ☎ **843/ 884-4371.** Admission $12 adults, $10 seniors 55 and over, $6 children 6–12, free for children 5 and under. Apr–Labor Day Mon–Sat 8:30am–6:30pm, Sun 1–5pm; day after Labor Day–Mar Mon–Sat 9am–5pm, Sun 1–4pm. 9 miles N of Charleston on U.S. 17.

You approach this unique 783-acre cotton plantation via a famous avenue of oaks, huge moss-draped trees planted in 1743 by Capt. Thomas Boone. The plantation was settled by Maj. John Boone in 1681. The first floor of the main house is elegantly furnished and open to the public. Outbuildings include the circular smokehouse and slave cabins constructed of bricks made on the plantation. The place was used for background shots in *Gone With the Wind* and the miniseries *North and South*.

✪ **Charleston Tea Plantation.** 6617 Maybank Hwy. ☎ **800/222-8327** or 843/559-0383. Free admission. April–Dec Mon–Fri 10am–4pm; Jan–Mar Mon–Fri 10am–3pm. 15 miles S of Charleston on Wadmalaw Island.

This plantation is the only one in America that grows tea, sold as American Classic tea. The plantation has been growing tea since 1799, when a French botanist brought the first tea plants to Charleston. Today, they use a state-of-the-art harvesting machine (designed on the site) that you can see during free tours offered during the harvest season. Private tours, costing $5 per person, are available for groups of 20 or more; you must make an appointment. Note that inclement weather cancels any tour. Be sure to buy some tea while you're there—you won't find anything fresher in the stores.

Drayton Hall. 3380 Old Ashley River Rd. ☎ **843/766-0188.** Admission $8 adults, $6 children 12–18, $4 children 6-11, free for children 5 and under. Mar–Oct daily 9am–4pm; Nov–Feb daily 10am–3pm, with tours commencing on the hour. Closed Jan 1, Thanksgiving, and Dec 25. 9 miles NW of Charleston on Hwy. 61.

This is one of the oldest surviving plantations, built in 1738 and owned by the Drayton family until 1974. Framed by majestic live oaks, the Georgian Palladian house is a property of the National Trust for Historic Preservation. Its hand-carved woodwork and plasterwork represent New World craftsmanship at its finest. Since such modern elements as electricity, plumbing, and central heating have never put in an appearance, the house is much as it was in its early years.

✪ **Magnolia Plantation.** 3550 Ashley River Rd. ☎ **843/571-1266.** Garden, $10 adults, $9 seniors, $8 children 13–19, $5 children 6–12, free for children under 6; plantation house tour $6 extra. Audubon Swamp Garden, $5 adults, $3 children 6–12. Nature train, $5 adults, $4 students, $3 children 6–12. Plantation and gardens, daily 8am–5pm. Children under 6 are not allowed on the plantation house tour. 9 miles N of Charleston.

Ten generations of the Drayton family have lived here continuously since the 1670s. They haven't had much luck keeping a roof over their heads: The first mansion burned just after the Revolution, and the second was set afire by General Sherman. But you can't call its replacement modern. A simple pre-Revolutionary house was barged down from Summerville and set on the basement foundations of its unfortunate predecessors.

The flowery gardens of camellias and azaleas—among the most beautiful in America—reach their peak bloom in March and April but are colorful year-round. You can tour the house, the gardens (including an herb garden, a horticultural maze, a topiary garden, and a biblical garden), and a petting zoo; visit a waterfowl refuge; and walk or bike through wildlife trails. Other sights are an antebellum cabin that was restored and furnished, a plantation rice barge on display beside the Ashley River, and a Nature Train that carries you on a 45-minute ride around the plantation's perimeter.

Low Country wildlife is visible in marsh, woodland, and swamp settings. The Audubon Swamp Garden, also on the grounds, is an independently operated 60-acre cypress swamp offering a close look at egrets, alligators, wood ducks, otters, turtles, and herons.

✪ **Middleton Place.** 4300 Ashley River Rd. ☎ **843/556-6020.** Admission Mar–Oct, $15 adults, $7 children 6–12; off-season, free for children 5 and under to tour gardens and stable yard. Gardens and stable yard daily 9am–5pm; house Tues–Sun 10am–4:30pm, Mon 1:30–4:30pm. 14 miles NW of Charleston on Hwy. 61.

This was the home of Henry Middleton, president of the First Continental Congress, whose son Arthur was a signer of the Declaration of Independence. Today the National Historic Landmark includes this country's oldest landscaped gardens, the Middleton Place House, and the Plantation Stableyards. The gardens, begun in 1741, reflect the elegant symmetry of European gardens of that period. Ornamental lakes, terraces, and plantings of camellias, azaleas, magnolias, and crape myrtle accent the grand design.

Middleton Place House was built in 1755, and in 1865 all but the south flank was ransacked and burned by Union troops. It was restored in the 1870s as a family residence and today houses collections of fine silver, furniture, rare first editions by Catesby and Audubon, and portraits by Benjamin West and Thomas Sully. In the stable yards, craftspeople demonstrate life on a plantation of yesteryear. There are also horses, mules, hogs, cows, sheep, and goats.

A plantation lunch is served at the Middleton Place Restaurant, a replica of a rice mill. *American Way* magazine cited this restaurant as one of the top 10 representing American cuisine at its best. Specialties include she-crab soup, hoppin' John (a traditional Southern dish of rice and black-eyed peas, flavored with salt pork), and ham biscuits, along with okra gumbo, Sea Island shrimp, and corn pudding. Lunch is served daily from 11am to 3pm. Dinner is served only on Friday and Saturday from 5 to 9pm and is likely to include panned-fried quail with ham, sea scallops, or broiled oysters. For dinner reservations, call the number above (reservations aren't usually needed at lunch).

A SLICE OF COLONIAL LIFE

✪ **Charles Towne Landing.** 1500 Old Towne Rd. ☎ **843/852-4200.** Admission $5 adults, $2.50 seniors and children 6–14, free for children 5 and under and travelers with disabilities. Daily 9am–6pm. 10 miles W of Charleston on S.C. 171, between U.S. 17 and I-26.

This 663-acre park is on the site of the first 1670 settlement. Underground exhibits show the colony's history, and there's a re-creation of a small village, a full-scale replica of a 17th-century trading ship, and a tram tour for $1 (or you can rent a bike). Because trade was such an important part of colonial life, a full-scale reproduction of the 17th-century trading vessel *Adventure* is an excellent addition. After touring the ship, you can step into the Settler's Life Area and view a 17th-century crop garden where rice, indigo, and cotton were grown. There's no flashy theme-park atmosphere: What you see as you walk under huge old oaks, past freshwater lagoons, and through the Animal Forest (with animals of the same species that lived here in 1670) is what those early settlers saw.

SPECTACULAR GARDENS

See also **Magnolia Plantation** under "Nearby Plantations," above.

✪ **Cypress Gardens.** 3030 Cypress Garden's Rd. (U.S. 52), Moncks Corner. ☎ **843/553-0515.** Admission mid-Feb–Apr (not including boat rides), $7 adults, $6 seniors, $2 children 6–12, free for children 5 and under; off-season, $7 adults, $6 seniors, $2 children 6–12, free for children 5 and under. Daily 9am–5pm. Closed Jan. 24 miles N of Charleston.

This 163-acre swamp garden was used as a freshwater reserve for Dean Hall, a huge Cooper River rice plantation, and was given to the city in 1963. Today, its giant cypresses, draped with Spanish moss, provide an unforgettable setting for flat-bottom boats that glide among their knobby roots. Footpaths in the garden wind through a profusion of azaleas, camellias, daffodils, and other blooms. You share the swamp with alligators, pileated woodpeckers, wood ducks, otter, barred owls, and other abundant species. The gardens are worth a visit at any time of year, but they're at their most colorful from March to April.

MUSEUMS

American Military Museum. 40 Pinckney St. (near Church and Market sts.). ☎ **843/723-9620.** Admission $5 adults, $1 children 12 and under, free for military personnel in uniform. Mon–Sat 9:30am–6pm, Sun 1–6pm.

Dedicated to the men and women who've served in the U.S. Armed Forces, this museum displays uniforms and artifacts from all branches of the military. There are relics of virtually every armed conflict in which this country has been involved. Civil War buffs come here to look at that collection, but there are exhibits from the War of 1812, the Indian Wars, the Spanish–American War, World Wars I and II, and even the Korean and Vietnam wars.

✪ **Charleston Museum.** 360 Meeting St. ☎ **843/722-2996.** Admission $7 adults, $4 children 3–12, free for children 2 and under. Combination ticket including Joseph Manigault House and Heyward–Washington House $18. Mon–Sat 9am–5pm, Sun 1–5pm.

Charleston Museum, founded in 1773, was the first museum in America. Its collections preserve and interpret the social and natural history of Charleston and the South Carolina coastal region. The full-scale replica of the famed Confederate submarine *Hunley* standing outside is one of the most photographed subjects in the city. The museum also exhibits the largest Charleston silver collection, early crafts, historic relics, and the state's only children's Discover Me room, with hands-on exhibits.

Gibbes Museum of Art. 135 Meeting St. ☎ **843/722-2706.** Admission $6 adults, $5 seniors, $3 children 6–18, free for children 5 and under. Tues–Sat 10am–5pm, Sun–Mon 1–5pm. Closed holidays.

Opened in 1905 by the Carolina Art Association, the Gibbes Museum contains an intriguing collection of prints and drawings from the 18th century to the present. Landscapes, genre scenes, panoramic views of Charleston harbor, and portraits of South Carolinians are displayed. See especially *Thomas Middleton* by Benjamin West, *Charles Izard Manigault* by Thomas Sully, and *John C. Calhoun* by Rembrandt Peale. The collection of some 400 miniature portraits ranks as one of the more comprehensive in the country. The Wallace Exhibit includes 10 rooms, 8 replicated from historic American buildings and 2 from classic French styles. They range from a plain dining room in the house of a Martha's Vineyard sea captain to the elegant drawing room of Charleston's historic Nathaniel Russell House (see above).

CHURCHES & SYNAGOGUES

Congregation Beth Elohim. 90 Hasell St. (between King and Meeting sts.). ☎ **843/723-1090.** Free admission. Mon–Fri 10am–noon.

Dating from 1840, this is the oldest synagogue in continuous use in the United States and the second oldest in the country. The original, built in 1794, burned in 1838; its Greek Revival replacement is one of America's finest examples of that style. The synagogue was the birthplace of Reform Judaism in 1824. Attracted by the civil and religious freedom of South Carolina, Jews first arrived after 1670. By 1749, there were enough members to organize a congregation and to consecrate a small house of worship.

French Huguenot Church. 136 Church St. (at the corner of Church and Queen sts.). ☎ **843/722-4385.** Free admission. Services Sun at 10:30am.

This church (built 1844–45) is the fourth on this site; the first was constructed in 1687. In the early days, because much of the congregation came downriver by boat, services were planned so that the people could arrive on the ebb tide and go home on the flood. This is the only French Huguenot church in the United States that still uses the French liturgy.

St. Mary's Roman Catholic Church. 89 Hasell St. (between Meeting and King sts.). ☎ **843/722-7696.** Free admission. Daily 8am–4pm.

Built in 1839, this is the mother church of the Roman Catholic dioceses of South Carolina, North Carolina, and Georgia. An earlier church (1789) burned on this site in 1838.

✪ **St. Michael's Episcopal Church.** 14 St. Michael's Alley (at Meeting and Broad sts.). ☎ **843/723-0603.** Free admission. Mon–Fri 9am–4:45pm.

This is the city's oldest church, dating from 1761. Its eight bells (imported in 1764) are well traveled: They were seized back by the British in retaliation for the 1765 Stamp Act; after unexpectedly being returned to the United States, they were burned during the Civil War and had to cross the Atlantic again to be recast and returned in late 1867. Fittingly, the first song they played was "Home Again." In 1992, the bells were sent to England yet again (for returning this time) and were returned without incident in 1993. The church's chandelier, installed in 1803, has been lighted over time by candles, gas, and then electricity. Washington worshipped here during his 1791 Southern tour.

MORE ATTRACTIONS

The Citadel. Moultrie St. and Elmwood Ave. ☎ **843/953-5006.** Free admission. Daily 24 hours for drive-through visits; museum Sun–Fri 2–5pm, Sat noon–5pm. Closed religious and school holidays.

The all-male Citadel military academy was established at Marion Square in 1842 as an arsenal and to serve as a refuge for whites in case of a slave uprising. In 1922, it was moved to its present location, where it received worldwide notoriety in 1995, during the failed attempt of Shannon Faulkner to join the ranks as the Citadel's first female cadet.

After winning a legal battle to be admitted, Faulkner dropped out, citing continual harassment as the cause (however, she did show up for basic training about 30 pounds overweight and in poor physical shape). Her ordeal at the Citadel drew fiercely divided opinions. News of her resignation was greeted with whooping and dancing at the female-free campus. However, best-selling author Pat Conroy, a Faulkner supporter, said, "They made sure that everyone in America saw that that college hates women. They've made a blood sport of hating in South Carolina." Conroy's novel *The Lords of Discipline* is based on his 4 years at the school.

The Citadel adopted a more positive view of female cadets in the summer of 1996. Four women marched at the Citadel at the invitation of the college, which was forced into compliance by a near-unanimous Supreme Court decision in a similar case. The Citadel agreed to admit women in late June. School officials tried to put a happy spin on events, claiming that female cadets will increase the pool of candidates, reenergize the institution, and help to prepare all Citadel students "to meet the challenges of the 21st century." In fact, the young women who have followed Faulkner have proven to be a success in the eyes of the school and the state. This long struggle came full circle when Citadel cadet Nancy Mace became the first woman to graduate from the institution on May 8, 1998.

The campus of this military college, with its buildings of Moorish design, featuring crenellated battlements and sentry towers, is especially interesting on Friday, when the college is in session and the public is invited to a precision drill parade on the quadrangle at 3:45pm. For a history of the Citadel, stop at the **Citadel Memorial Archives Museum** (☎ **843/953-6846**), just inside the main gate at 171 Moultie St.

Fort Moultrie. Sullivan's Island, W. Middle St. ☎ **843/883-3123.** Admission $2 adults 16 and over, $1 seniors and children 15 and under. Apr–Sept daily 9am–5pm; winter daily 9am–5pm. Closed Dec 25. 10 miles E of Charleston; watch for signs.

Only a palmetto-log fortification at the time of the American Revolution, the fort was half completed when it was attacked by a British fleet in 1776, the year on which construction was launched. Col. William Moultrie's troops repelled the invasion in one of the Revolution's first decisive American victories. The fort was subsequently enlarged into a five-sided structure with earth-and-timber walls 17 feet high. The British didn't do it in, but an 1804 hurricane ripped it apart. By the War of 1812, it was back and ready for action.

Osceola, the fabled leader of the Seminoles in Florida, was incarcerated and eventually died here. In the 1830s, Edgar Allan Poe served as a soldier at the fort; he set his short story "The Gold Bug" on Sullivan's Island. The fort also played roles in the Civil War, the

Mexican War, and the Spanish–American War—even World Wars I and II. By 1947, it had retired from action.

Old Exchange & Provost Dungeon. 122 E. Bay St. ☎ **843/727-2165.** Admission $6 adults, $5.50 seniors, $3.50 children 7–12, free for children 6 and under. Daily 9am–5pm. Closed Jan 1, Thanksgiving, Dec 24–25 and 31.

This is a stop many people overlook; most local sightseeing companies stop here only if requested. However, it's one of the three most important colonial buildings in the United States because of the role it played as a prison during the American Revolution. In 1873, the building became City Hall. You'll also find here one of the nation's largest collections of antique chairs—in 1921, each of the Daughters of the American Revolution brought a chair here from home.

PARKS

Old Santee Canal State Park (☎ 843/899-5200) is one of the city's newest and finest parks. It was landscaped along the banks of the old Santee Canal, reached by taking I-26 west from the city center, exiting at Hwy. 52. Drive through Goose Creek to Moncks Corner to reach it. Admission is $2.50 for adults; free for children under 6. Miles of boardwalks and trails await you, and you can explore the natural beauty of the region at your leisure daily from 9am to 6pm. An Interpretive Center provides information about the area dating from 4000 B.C., and here you can rent canoes for rides along Biggin Swamp (yes, there are alligators). Less frightening are the ospreys and blue herons who also inhabit this wild and untamed area.

Family fun is promised at the **Palmetto Islands County Park** (☎ 843/884-0832) in Mount Pleasant, near Boone Hall. Instead of the wild nature of Old Santee, it offers more organized fun in the form of a big toy playground, mile-long canoe trails, picnic sites, an observation tower, a water playground, toddler slides, marsh boardwalks, and plenty of jogging trails and bicycle paths. Bordering Boone Hall Creek are public fishing and boating docks. The park is open daily: November to February from 10am to 5pm; May to August from 9am to 7pm; and March, April, September, and October from 9am to 6pm. Admission is $1.

Folly Beach County Park (☎ 843/588-2426) is a beach park with some 4,000 feet of ocean frontage along the Atlantic, plus some 2,000 feet of river frontage. Lifeguards protect swimmers along a 600-foot beachfront. Group picnics and Low Country oyster roasts seem a perennial feature around here at the **Pelican Watch Shelter** (☎ **843/795-7275**). There's a 300-vehicle parking lot, along with such amenities as dressing rooms, toilets, and outdoor showers. Equipment to rent includes beach umbrellas, beach chairs, and rafts. Cost is $4 per vehicle. It's open daily: April, September, and October from 10am to 6pm; May to August from 9am to 7pm; and November to March from 10am to 5pm.

If you don't have a car and still want to enjoy a park, make it the **Charleston Waterfront Park,** along 1,280 feet of waterfront property bordering Concord Street in the center of the city. City officials, by landscaping and cleaning up this area, revitalized a section of Charleston. Numerous benches for Forrest Gump types and picnic tables are available, as are a grassy public green and a pier. Admission is free. The park is open daily from 6am to midnight (but we don't advise hanging out here too late at night because of the danger of muggings).

ESPECIALLY FOR KIDS

For more than 300 years, Charleston has been the home of pirates, patriots, and presidents. Your child can see firsthand the **Great Hall at the Old Exchange,** where President Washington danced, and the **Provost Dungeons,** where South Carolina patriots spent their last days; and touch the last remaining structural evidence of the **Charleston sea wall.** Among the attractions listed above, children will take special delight in **Charles Towne Landing** and **Middleton Place.**

Kids and Navy vets will love the aircraft carrier **U.S.S. Yorktown** at Patriots Point, 2 miles east of the Cooper River Bridge. Its World War II, Korea, and Vietnam exploits are documented in exhibits, and general naval history is illustrated through models of ships, planes, and weapons. You can wander through the bridge wheelhouse, flight and hangar decks, chapel, sick bay, and several other areas, then view the film *The Fighting Lady,* depicting life aboard the carrier. The *Yorktown* is the nucleus of the world's largest naval and maritime museum. Also at Patriots Point, and welcoming visitors aboard, are the nuclear ship *Savannah,* the world's first nuclear-powered merchant ship; the World War II destroyer *Laffey;* the World War II submarine *Clamagore;* and the cutter *Ingham.* Patriots Point is open daily: April to September from 9am to 7:30pm and October to March from 9am to 5pm. Admission is $10 for adults, $9 for seniors over 62 and military personnel in uniform, $5 for children 6 to 11, and free for children 5 and under. Adjoining is the fine 18-hole public Patriots Point golf course for moms and dads. For further information, call ☎ **843/884-2727.**

Another kid pleaser, **Best Friend,** adjacent to the visitors' center on Ann Street (☎ **843/973-7269**), combines a museum and an antique train with a full-size replica of the 1830 locomotive that was the first steam engine in America to establish regularly scheduled passenger service. The present train was constructed from the original plans in 1928 and donated to Charleston in 1993. Hours are Monday to Saturday from 9am to 5pm and Sunday from 1 to 5pm; admission is free.

6 Organized Tours

The **Charleston Carriage Co.,** 96 N. Market St. (☎ 843/577-0042), offers narrated horse-drawn carriage tours through the Historic District daily from 9am to dusk. The cost is $17 for adults, $15 for seniors, and $8 for children.

Palmetto Carriage Tours, 40 N. Market St., at Guignard (☎ **843/723-8145**), uses mule teams instead of the usual horse and carriage for its guided tours of Old Charleston. Tours originate at the Rainbow Market. The cost is $16 for adults, $14 for seniors, $5 for children 4 to 11, and free for children 3 and under.

The Civil War era comes alive again on a unique walking tour conducted by **Jack Thomson** (☎ **843/722-7033**), a guide well versed in the lore of the "War of Northern Aggression." You can stroll down cobblestone streets and listen to firsthand accounts and anecdotes recounting the embattled city of Charleston during its years of siege by Union troops. Tours depart at 9am Monday to Sunday (March to Dec) from the Mills House Hotel Courtyard at 115 Meeting St. Adults pay $15 and children under 12 go free; reservations are appreciated.

One of the best offbeat walking tours is the **Charleston Tea Party Walking Tour** (☎ **843/577-5896**), lasting 2 hours and costing $13 for adults and $6 for children up to 12. Departing year-round Monday to Saturday from 9:30am to 2pm, tours originate at Kings Courtyard Inn, 198 Kings St. The tour goes into a lot of nooks and crannies of Charleston, including secret courtyards and gardens. And, of course, there's tea at the end.

Architectural tours of Charleston's 18th-century structures within the original "walled city" begin at 10am, and tours of 19th-century architecture along Meeting Street and the Battery start at 2pm. Departures are in front of the Meeting Street Inn, 173 Meeting St. Tours last 2 hours and are given Monday and Wednesday to Saturday. The cost is $13 and is free for children 12 and under. For reservations, call ☎ **843/893-2327.**

Fort Sumter Tours, 205 King St., Suite 204 (☎ **843/722-1691**), offers a "Harbor and Fort Sumter Tour" by boat (see the entry for Fort Sumter under "Seeing the Sights"). It also has an interesting "Charleston Harbor Tour," with daily departures from Patriots Point. The 1¹/₂-hour cruise passes the Battery, Charleston Port, Castle Pinckney, Drum Island, Fort Sumter, and the aircraft carrier *Yorktown,* then sails under the Cooper River Bridge and on to other sights. The cost is $10 for adults, $5 for children 6 to 11, and free for children 5 and under.

7 Beaches & Outdoor Pursuits

BEACHES   Three great beaches are within a 25-minute drive of the center of Charleston. If you're lucky enough to stumble onto a traditional Carolina beach party, you might be introduced to the Shag, South Carolina's state dance, as well as beach music sounds made famous in the state's beach communities by such bands as the Tams and the Drifters.

In the West Islands, **Folly Beach,** which had degenerated into a tawdry Coney Island–type amusement park, is making a comeback following a multimillion-dollar cleanup (though even after the effort, it remains the least pristine of the area's beaches). The best bathroom and changing facilities west of the Holiday Inn are here. At the western end of the island is the **Folly Beach County Park,** including bathrooms, parking, and shelter from the rain.

In the East Cooper area, both **Isle of Palms** (see chapter 3) and **Sullivan's Island** offer miles of beaches, most bordered by beachfront homes. Windsurfing and jet skiing are popular here, but you shouldn't engage in these activities in front of the islands' commercial districts.

✪ **Kiawah Island** has the area's most pristine beach, far preferable than Folly (see chapter 3).

BIKING   Charleston is basically flat and relatively free of traffic except on its main arteries at rush hour, so biking is a popular local pastime and is relatively safe. Many of the city parks also have trails set aside for bikers.

Your best bet for rentals is the **Bicycle Shoppe,** 280 Meeting St. (☎ 843/722-8168), which rents bikes for $4 per hour or $15 for a full day. A credit-card imprint is required as a deposit.

BOATING & SAILING   A true Charlestonian is at home on the sea as much as on land. Many local families spend their Sunday afternoons sailing. One of the best places for rentals is **Wild Dunes Yacht Harbor,** Isle of Palms (☎ 843/886-5100), where 16-foot boats big enough for four rent for $250 for 4 hours, plus fuel. The Harbor also rents jet skis for $75 for 1 hour, second person $15, and third free (☎ 843/886-8456). A larger pontoon boat, big enough for 10, goes for $500 for 4 hours, plus fuel.

DIVING   Several outfitters are available in the Charleston area, providing rentals and ocean charters but also instruction for neophytes. Local divers favor **Aqua Ventures,** 426 W. Coleman Blvd., Mount Pleasant (☎ 843/884-1500), which offers diving trips off the local shoreline costing $60 to $80 per person. You can rent diving equipment; costs are $6 for a tank and $10 for a regulator. Hours are Monday to Saturday from 10am to 6pm.

Another possibility is the **Wet Shop,** 5121 Rivers Ave. (☎ 843/744-5641), which rents scuba equipment for $45 a day, including two tanks, a regulator, a wet suit, a diving knife, and a weight belt. Hours are Monday to Saturday from 10am to 6pm.

FISHING   The Low Country's numerous creeks and inlets are filled with flounder, trout, and spot-tail or channel bass, among other freshwater catches. Offshore fishing charters are also available, and reef fishing is an option (you'll find a variety of fish like cobia, black sea bass, or king mackerel). Anglers also venture to the Gulf Stream for sailfish, marlin, wahoo, dolphin, and tuna. Some of the best striped bass fishing available in America is at nearby Lake Moultrie. For those who'd like a true Low Country experience, a crabbing excursion can be arranged.

The **Folly Beach Fishing Pier** at Folly Beach opened in 1995. The wooden pier, 25 feet wide, extends 1,045 feet into the Atlantic Ocean. Facilities include rest rooms, a tackle shop, and a restaurant. It's accessible for travelers with disabilities.

Deep-sea fishing or inshore fishing is best arranged at the previously recommended **Wild Dunes Yacht Harbor,** Isle of Palms (☎ 843/886-5100). A fishing craft holding up to six rents for $650 for 6 hours, including everything but food and drink. Reservations must be made 3 days in advance.

GOLF　Charleston is said to be the home of golf in America, and Charlestonians have been playing the game since the 1700s, when the first golf clubs arrived from Scotland. (Back then, golfers wore red jackets for greater visibility.) With 17 public and private courses, there's a golf game waiting for every buff.

The **Wild Dunes Resort,** Isle of Palms (☎ **843/886-6000**), offers two championship courses designed by Tom Fazio. The Links is a 6,722-yard, par-72 layout taking you through marshlands, over or into huge sand dunes, through a wooded alley, and finally to a pair of oceanfront finishing holes once called "the greatest east of Pebble Beach, California." The course opened in 1980 and has been ranked in the top 100 greatest courses in the United States by *Golf Digest* and the top 100 in the world by *Golf. Golf Digest* also ranks the Links as the 13th greatest resort course in America. The Harbor Course offers 6,402 yards of Low Country marsh and Intracoastal Waterway views. This par-70 layout is considered target golf, challenging players with two holes that play from one island to another across Morgan Creek. Greens fees at these courses range from $35 to $100, depending on the season. You can rent clubs at either course for $25 for 18 holes, and professional instruction costs $45 for a 45-minute session. Both courses are open daily from 7am to 6pm year-round.

Your best deal if you'd like to play at any of the other Charleston area golf courses is to contact **Charleston Golf Partners** at ☎ **800/247-5786** or 847/549-9770. It represents 15 courses, with packages starting at $99 per person from May to June and September to December 1. In off-season, packages start at $79 per person. Prices include greens fees on one course, a hotel room based on double occupancy, and taxes. Call Monday to Friday from 10am to 6pm. Travel professionals will customize your vacation with golf course selections and tee times. They can also arrange rental cars and airfares.

HIKING & CAMPING　There are several possibilities in the Charleston area. The most interesting hiking trails begin around **Buck Hall** in the Francis Marion National Forest, McClellanville (☎ **843/887-3257**). The area also has 14 camping sites costing $15 per night, plus a boat ramp and fishing. The park lies some 40 miles north of the center of Charleston via U.S. 52. The site consists of some 250,000 acres of swamps, with towering oaks and pines.

Other hiking trails are at the **Edisto Beach State Park,** State Cabin Road, on Edisto Island (☎ **843/869-2156**).

HORSEBACK RIDING   Our pick is the **Seabrook Island Resort,** 1002 Landfall Way, Seabrook Island (☎ **843/768-1000**), though reservations for these guided rides are needed 3 to 4 days in advance. It not only has an equestrian center but also offers trail rides and beach rides. The beach ride for advanced riders only leaves at 9am daily, costing $65 per person; and the trail ride also for advanced riders leaves at 9am daily, going for $55 per person. Rides for beginners are also offered, lasting 1 hour and costing $45.

PARASAILING   **Island Water Sports,** South Beach Marina (☎ **843/671-7007**), allows you to soar up to 800 feet over the waves. The cost ranges from $39 to $49, depending on the number of feet of line used. It's open April to October, daily from 9am to 7:30pm.

TENNIS   As with golf, Charlestonians have been playing tennis since the early 1800s. The **Charleston Tennis Center,** Farmfield Avenue (west of Charleston on Hwy. 17), is your best bet, with 15 well-maintained outdoor courts, lit for night play. The cost is only $3 to reserve court time. Hours are Monday to Thursday from 8:30am to 10pm, Friday from 8:30am to 7pm, Saturday from 9am to 6pm, and Sunday from 10am to 6pm.

Another possibility is the **Shadowmoss Plantation Golf & Country Club,** 20 Dunvegan Dr. (☎ **843/724-7402**), where you can play tennis free daily from 7am to 8pm.

WINDSURFING   Long a favorite of windsurfers, the Low Country coast is known for its temperate waters and wide-open spaces. You can arrange windsurfing through **McKevlin's Surf Shop,** 1101 Ocean Blvd., Isle of Palms (☎ **843/886-8912**). Boards rent for $15 per 24 hours. It's open Friday to Sunday from 10am to 6pm.

8 Shopping

King Street is lined with many special shops and boutiques. The **Shops at Charleston Place,** 130 Market St., is an upscale complex of top designer clothing shops (Gucci, Jaeger, Ralph Lauren, and more), and the **State Street Market,** just down from the City Market, is another cluster of shops and restaurants.

ANTIQUES
George C. Birlant and Co. 191 King St. ☎ **843/722-3842.**

If you're in the market for 18th- and 19th-century English antique furnishings, this is the right place. This Charleston staple prides itself on its Charleston Battery Bench, which is seen (and sat upon) throughout the Battery. The heavy iron sides are cast from the original 1880 mold, and the slats are authentic South Carolina cypress. It's as close to the original as you can get.

Livingston Antiques. 163 King St. ☎ **843/556-6162.**

For nearly a quarter of a century, discriminating antiques hounds have patronized this dealer's showroom. Both authentic antiques and reproductions good enough to fool most eyes are sold. If you're interested, the staff will direct you to their 30,000-square-foot warehouse on West Ashley.

ART
African-American Art Gallery. 43 John St. ☎ **843/722-8224.**

With some 2,900 square feet of exhibition space, this is the largest African-American art gallery in the South. The original artwork is changed every 2 months. On permanent display are the works of name African artists, including Dr. Leo Twiggs and historical artist Joe Pinckney.

Audubon Wildlife Shop & Gallery. 245 King St. ☎ **800/453-BIRD** or 843/723-6171.

The finest gallery of its kind in South Carolina, this outlet attracts birders and others to view its collection of not only Audubon prints but also botanical and wildlife prints, both original and reproduction. Wildlife posters are also sold. There's a collection of telescopes and binoculars for Low Country bird-watching. A framing service is available.

Lowcountry Artists. 184 East Bay St. ☎ **843/577-9295.**

In a former bookbindery, this gallery is operated by eight local artists who work in oil, watercolor, drawings, collage, woodcuts, and other media.

Waterfront Gallery. 167 E. Bay St. (at Queen St.). ☎ **843/722-1155.**

Facing Waterfront Park, this gallery is the premier choice for viewing the work of South Carolina artists, with the largest assemblage of such art in town. Some 21 local artists are presented, with original works beginning at $95. For sale are pieces ranging from sculpture to oils.

Wells Gallery. 103 Broad St. ☎ **843/853-3233.**

Artists from the Low Country and all over the Southeast are on display at this Charleston gallery. Specializing in Low Country landscapes, the gallery offers works by two of South Carolina's most respected artists: Betty Anglain Smith and Mickey Williams. Prices range from $300 to $12,000.

BOOKS

Atlantic Books. 310 King St. ☎ **843/723-4751.**

Amelia and Gene Woolf offer thousands of good used books at moderate prices, along with a collection of rare books. Their specialties are books on South Carolina and the Civil War. They also have a good collection of the works of Southern authors, along with modern first editions and books on Americana, children's literature, and nautical subjects.

Hoppin' John's. 30 Pinckney St. ☎ **843/763-5252.**

Foodies will love this bookstore, which features only books devoted to food. You can learn about cuisine from the world over, from Africa to Wales and, of course, the Low Country. Southern cookbooks are also featured prominently; the owner has even written a cookbook himself.

CIVIL WAR ARTIFACTS

Sumter Military Antiques & Museum. 54 Broad St. ☎ **843/577-7766.**

Relics from that "War of Northern Aggression" are sold here. You'll find a collection of authentic artifacts that range from firearms and bullets to Confederate uniforms and artillery shells and bullets. There are some interesting prints, along with a collection of books on the Civil War.

CRAFTS & NEEDLEWORK

Charleston Crafts. 87 Hasell St. ☎ **843/723-2938.**

This is a permanent showcase for Low Country craft artists who work in basically all known materials, including metal, glass, paper, clay, wood, and fiber. Handmade jewelry is also sold, along with basketry, leather works, traditional crafts, and even homemade soaps. Gifts range from traditional to modern.

Claire Murray. 295 King St. ☎ **843/722-0900.**

Claire Murray, a well-known artist, specializes in beautifully crafted hooked-rug designs. Locally, she's credited with having revived this almost disappearing craft. Designs are available in not only hooked rugs but counted-cross stitch and needlepoint. Her kits are complete with all the materials needed to create such work yourself.

Clown's Bazaar. 9 Broad St. ☎ **843/723-9769.**

Store owner Deanna Wagoner's heart is as big as her smile. Her store is indeed one of a kind—the city's only tax-exempt, self-help crafts organization. Originally, it was in Katmandu, Nepal, founded to help Third World families help themselves. Economic and political circumstances forced the store's relocation to Charleston, but the objective of helping Third World families hasn't changed. The store features handmade carvings, silks, brasses, and pewter from exotic locales such as Africa, Nepal, India, Bangladesh, and the Phillipines, as well as wooden toys and books, including some in Gullah, a lost language that is still spoken in some areas of the city. Oh, and if you are looking for clown dolls, Deanna has those, too.

FASHION

Ben Silver. 149 King St. ☎ **843/577-4556.**

One of the finer men's clothiers in Charleston, this is the best place to get yourself dressed like a member of the city's finest society. It specializes in blazers and buttons: It has a collection of more than 600 blazer button designs, which are unique in the city. Ben Silver's features house names and designs only, so don't go looking for Ralph Lauren here.

Carol J's of Charleston. 40 N. Market St. (in the Rainbow Market). ☎ **843/853-8889.**

Embroidered and appliquéd women's apparel, along with accessories and gifts, are sold here at this outlet in Charleston's center. Leisure wear with matching accessories is a special feature. Various collectibles are also sold, and the staff will custom design for you.

Nancy's. 342 King St. ☎ **843/722-1272.**

On the main street, Nancy's specializes in clothing for the woman who wants to be both active and stylish. Complete outfits in linen, silk, and cotton are sold, along with accessories like belts and jewelry. Nancy's aims for a "total look."

FURNISHINGS

✪ **Historic Charleston Reproductions.** 105 Broad St. ☎ **843/723-8292.**

It's rare that a store with so much to offer could be nonprofit, but that's the case here. All items are "approved" by the Historic

Charleston Foundation, and all proceeds benefit the restoration of various historic projects in Charleston.

The name couldn't be more apt, as the place specializes in a number of licensed replica products ranging from furniture to jewelry. The pride of the store is its home furnishings collection by Baker Furniture, an esteemed company based in Michigan. What makes this collection unique is that the mahogany pieces are adaptations of Historic Charleston antiques: rich dark wood with an authentic feel that you can find only here.

Charleston is a city that prides itself on the iron works around town, and if one of the iron designs catches your eye, you might find a replica of that in the form of jewelry. Also featured is a collection of china from Mottahedeh.

The store operates shops in several historic houses, and for slightly more than basic souvenirs, see the **Francis Edmunds Center Museum Shop** at 108 Meeting St. (☎ **843/724-8484**).

GIFTS & PERFUME

Hamilton House. 102 Broad St. ☎ **800/688-9690** or 843/853-0290.

In this 1844 antebellum home, two floors of merchandise will appeal to the traditionalist and the Victorian in you. Antiques and accessories for the home are sold, including teapot lamps, dried and silk florals, paintings, toiletries, lace, and cut crystal.

Scents Unlimited. 92 N. Market St. ☎ **843/853-8837.**

You'll find favorite fragrances here, and the prices for the most part are relatively reasonable. The shop evokes a perfumery in Europe. Scents creates its own exclusive brands and also features classic and popular fragrances.

JEWELRY

Dazzles. 226 King St. (in Charleston Place). ☎ **843/722-5951.**

One-of-a-kind jewelry is sold, along with the finest collection of handmade 14-karat-gold slide bracelets in town. Some of the jewelry is of heirloom quality. The staff will help you create jewelry of your own personal design, including a choice of stones.

Geiss & Sons Jewelers. 116 E. Bay St. ☎ **843/577-4497.**

Jewelry here is custom designed by Old World–trained craftspeople. This is a direct offshoot of a store opened by the Geiss family in Brazil in 1919. It's an official watch dealer for names like Rolex, Bertolucci, and Raymond Weil. Repair jobs are given special attention here.

Muller Jewelers. 129B Market St. ☎ **843/853-1938.**

In business for more than a quarter of a century, Muller is one of Charleston's leading jewelers. Some of its timepieces are unique, and it also sells fine crystal and china, along with silver and other items for the home. The store designs custom-made pieces.

JOGGLING BOARDS

Old Charleston Joggling Board Co. 652 King St. ☎ **843/723-4331.**

Since the early 1830s, joggling boards have been a Charleston tradition, the creation of Mrs. Benjamin Kinloch Huger, who sought a mild form of exercise for her rheumatism. Mrs. Huger's Scottish cousins sent her a model of a joggling board, suggesting that she sit and gently bounce on it for exercise. (A joggling board is a 16-foot wooden plank placed on the seats of two separate "ends," each resembling a rocking chair.) Its fame spread, and the board soon turned up in gardens and on patios and porches throughout the Charleston area. After World War II, joggling boards became rare because of the scarcity of timber and the high cost of labor. However, the tradition was revived in 1970. The company also produces a joggle bench, a duplicate of the joggling board but only 10 feet long and 20 inches from the ground.

9 Charleston After Dark

THE PERFORMING ARTS

Charleston's major cultural venue is the 463-seat **Dock Street Theatre,** 133 Church St. (☎ **843/965-4032**), built in 1736. It burned down in the early 19th century, and the Planters Hotel (not related to the Planters Inn) was constructed around its ruins. In 1936, the theater was rebuilt on its original site, around the ruins of the Planters Hotel. Since then it has been home to the **Charleston State Company,** a nonprofit theater group offering classes and education in the technical and dramatic aspects of theater. The season is from mid-September to May. Dock Street hosts various companies throughout the year, with performances ranging from Shakespeare to *My Fair Lady.* It's most active at the annual Spoleto Festival in May and June. Admission prices are generally $16 for adults, $14 for seniors, and $10.50 for students with ID. The box office is open Monday to Thursday from noon to 5pm, Friday and Saturday from 10am to 8pm, and Sunday from 10am to 3pm.

The Robert Ivey Ballet, 1910 Savannah Hwy. (☎ **843/ 556-1343**), offers both classical and contemporary as well as

Late-Night Bites

If you want a place to hang out and people-watch or perhaps meet someone, head for the casual **Café Rainbow,** 282 King St. (☎ 843/853-9777). Patrons are always playing chess on the large board in the front window, while others sit on sacks of coffee beans and watch. The menu is light, with items priced from $2 to $4.50. Try a quiche, croissants with jam, home-made Belgian waffles with berries and nuts, muffins, or cookies; or you can visit just for coffee, cafe mocha, hot cocoa, or iced mochaccino.

Step back to the 1950s at **Mickey's Diner,** 137 Market St. (☎ 843/723-7121), where even at 3am you can order the kind of food that Elvis used to fill up on. Breakfast is served around the clock. The decor is right out of the old diner days—red, white, and black, with chrome-trimmed red booths, pink and blue neon, 1950s photos, and a jukebox playing period favorites. On the menu is French toast, blueberry pancakes, sausage and gravy with biscuits, and a number of sandwich standards. The brownie with ice cream is the perennial Girl Scout dessert choice; wine and beer are also served.

Following a night of jazz or blues, **Kaminsky's Most Excellent Café,** 78 N. Market St. (☎ 843/853-8270), is a good spot for resting your feet and ordering just the power boost you need to make it through the rest of the evening. The handsome bar offers a wide selection of wines and, out of the traffic flow, is ideal for people-watching. The desserts are sinful, especially the Italian cream cake and the mountain chocolate cake.

children's ballet programs. This 40-member troupe performs four to six major shows annually, with two geared toward children. The group performs at various venues throughout the Charleston area, with general admission prices costing $15 for adults and $10 for children, students, and seniors.

The **Charleston Symphony Orchestra,** 14 George St. (☎ 843/723-7528), performs throughout the state, but its main venue is the Gaillard Auditorium at Charleston Southern University. This troupe of 40 permanent members, which can reach out to embrace another 80 local musicians if needed, has a season from September to May. Small chamber concerts to full orchestral programs are performed.

A local distributor of tickets is **SCAT** (call ☎ **843/577-4500** for tickets or information about performances).

The **Footlight Players,** 20 Queen St. (☎ **843/722-7521**), is a small players group that's the best-known local community theater, with a season extending from October to May. Call for tickets or information Monday to Friday from noon to 5pm or from noon to curtain time on days of actual performances.

The **Charleston Ballet Theater,** 477 King St. (☎ **843/ 723-7334**), is one of South Carolina's finest professional ballet companies. The season begins in late October, with productions such as *Dracula* continuing into the early spring. Ticket prices vary with shows.

MUSIC & DANCE CLUBS

Club Habana. 177 Meeting St. ☎ **843/853-5900.** No cover.

This eclectic cigar and martini bar serves an array of appetizers, fruit plates, and cheeses. Patrons can enjoy exotic drinks or fine coffees, while listening to jazz, salsa, and rock-and-roll. It's open Monday to Friday from 5pm to 2am and Saturday and Sunday from 3pm to 3am.

Cumberland's. 26 Cumberland St. ☎ **843/577-9469.** Cover $2–$15.

If your musical tastes run from Delta blues to rock to reggae, this is the place for you. The dominant age group at this bar depends on the act playing. You will find that the generation gap isn't strong here, with college students toasting glasses with midlifers. Music is the common bond, and the cover charge depends on which group is booked for the night.

Harold's Country Club. 97 Hwy. 17A, Yemassee. ☎ **843/589-4360.** No cover.

A Dinner Cruise

Your most memorable evening in Charleston might be aboard the luxury yacht ✪ **Spirit of Charleston,** enjoying a 3-hour cruise that features a four-course dinner and live entertainment and dancing, as the vessel glides through Charleston harbor. The cost is $34.95 ($37.95 on weekends), not including drinks or service. Departures are from City Marina on Lockwood Boulevard. For schedules and bookings, contact Fort Sumter Tours, 205 King St. (☎ **843/ 722-1691**).

If you want to venture out of Charleston to see how the other half lives, put on your best good ol'boy bubba attitude and head for Harold's Country Club. Forget the stereotypes in Southern Gothic novels of the first half of the century, and chances are that you'll have a really good time. This so-called country club is a former gas station that's been converted to a bar and grill. You can play pool or pinball and learn that there is only one kind of beer: col'beer.

Henry's. 54 N. Market St. ☎ **843/723-4363.** No cover.

One of the best places for jazz in Charleston, this club features a live band on Friday and Saturday. Otherwise, you get taped Top 40 music for listening and dancing. Happy hour, with drink discounts and free appetizers, is Monday to Friday from 4 to 7pm. Open Monday to Friday from 4pm to 2am, Saturday and Sunday from 11:30am to 2am.

Indigo Lounge. 5 Faber St. ☎ **843/577-7383.** No cover.

Acme proved to be such a popular bar in Mount Pleasant that it has moved its operation to this more convenient site. In spite of its name, no food is served. This is strictly a dance club with a deejay playing alternative rock, and the occasional live band appears. It's open daily from 8pm to 4am.

Jukebox. 4 Vendue Range (across from the Waterfront Park). ☎ **843/ 723-3431.** Cover $3 men, $2 women Fri–Sat 9pm–1am.

One of the most popular clubs in town, Jukebox offers a deejay playing not only Top 40 music but hits from the 1950s and 1960s. At various times throughout the evening, bartenders and staffers will perform skits, dance, or lip sync to their favorite songs. There's a buffet for grazing from 5 to 8pm Wednesday to Saturday. The club is open Monday to Friday from 5pm to 2am and Saturday from 7:30pm to 2am.

Music Farm. 32 Ann St. ☎ **843/722-8904.** Cover free–$15.

This club is self-described as being "Charleston's premier music venue." The club covers nearly every taste of music, from country to rock. You're as likely to hear funkster George Clinton as you are country legend George Jones. The club hosts local and regional bands, as well as national acts. Past performers include rock bands Cracker and Morphine and country act David Allen Coe. Note the cover will depend on the performer.

BARS & PUBS

Charleston Sports Pub & Grill. 41 S. Market St. ☎ **843/853-2900.** No cover.

This popular sports bar is smack in the center of activity at South Market Street. Inside, you'll find two dozen TV monitors so that you won't miss a split second of any sports action, and the decor consists of lots of sports memorabilia. There are also tables outside, with some under cover.

First Shot Lounge. 115 Meeting St. (in the Mills House Hotel). ☎ **843/577-2400.** No cover.

Our preferred watering hole is this old standby where we've seen such visiting celebrities as Gerald Ford and Elizabeth Taylor (not together) over the years. The bar is one of the most elegant in Charleston—a comfortable place to sit back and enjoy a relaxed cocktail. If you get hungry, the kitchen will whip you up some shrimp and grits.

The Griffon. 18 Vendue Range. ☎ **843/723-1700.** No cover.

A lot of Scotch and beer is consumed at this ever-popular Irish pub. A full array of home-cooked specials from the old country are served as well, including such pub grub favorites as steak pies, bangers and mash, and the inevitable fish-and-chips. On Friday and Saturday nights, seafood is available.

Mike Calder's Pub. 288 King St. ☎ **843/577-0123.** No cover.

Mike Calder's is a local favorite, with 15 imported beers on tap from England, Scotland, and Ireland. The bartender's special is a Bloody Mary. A menu offers soups, salads, sandwiches, and steaks, and on Friday and Saturday seafood is featured. All the food is homemade.

Tommy Condon's Irish Pub. 160 Church St. ☎ **843/577-3818.** No cover.

In a restored warehouse in the City Market area, this Irish pub (also a family restaurant) is filled with memorabilia of Old Ireland. The bartender turns out such drinks as a Leprechaun punch, real Irish ale, and Irish coffee. The menu offers not only Irish food but Low Country specials like shrimp and grits or jambalaya. The pub hosts a full bar with happy hours featuring reduced drink prices Monday to Friday from 5 to 7pm. Live Irish entertainment is on tap Wednesday to Sunday from 8:30pm to closing. Regular hours are daily from 11:30am to midnight, with no food served after 10pm.

Southend Brewery & Smoke House. 161 E. Bay St. ☎ **843/853-4677.** No cover.

Charleston's largest brew pub offers their own ice cold, hand-crafted beers, succulent baby-back ribs with their own special barbecue sauce, and spicy hot pizzas. The pub also features nightly performances or a simple game of pool. You can relax in the cigar lounge. It's open daily from 11:30am to 1am.

Vendue Inn Bar. 23 Vendue Range (in the Vendue Inn). ☎ **843/723-0485.** No cover.

Although mostly intended for and patronized by hotel guests, the Vendue Inn's rooftop bar has stunning views for everyone. It's a good place to mix and mingle with Charleston's young workforce; you will definitely get a chance to see and meet some of the young minds of the New South.

Vicery's Bar & Grill. 15 Beaufain. ☎ **843/577-5300.** No cover.

This is one of the most popular gathering places in Charleston for young people, especially students. It's also a good dining choice, with an international menu, including jerk chicken and gazpacho. What makes it popular is the 16-ounce frosted mug of beer for $1 and the convivial atmosphere.

Wild Wing Café. 36 N. Market St. ☎ **843/722-WING.** No cover.

This is the hot spot in the market district. The bar is busy, really busy, most nights. The atmosphere is casual, as is the dress of the mostly young crowd, and the food is your typical chicken-wings-and-quesadillas type. After all those hot-spiced wings, the cold beer keeps flowing. Napkins—big terry-cloth numbers—help you wipe up the grease on those sticky fingers.

GAY & LESBIAN BARS

The Arcade. 5 Liberty St. ☎ **843/722-5656.** Cover $2–$5.

Set in the heart of historic Charleston, on the premises of what was a 1930s movie theater, this is the largest and most high-energy dance bar in Charleston. Catering with equal ease to gays and lesbians, it features between two and four bars (depending on the night). The atmosphere ranges from conversational to manic.

Déja Vu II. 445 Savannah Hwy., West Ashley. ☎ **843/554-5959.** Cover $3–$5.

Opened in 1995, this is the warmest lesbian bar in the Southeast. Rita Taylor, your host, transformed what was a supper club into a cozy enclave with two bars and live entertainment on weekends (usually from all-girl bands). The crowd is almost exclusively gay and 75% female. Gay men are welcome—the ambience is unpretentious and charming, definitely not exclusionary to sympathetic patrons of any ilk. Platters of simple country food are offered if you're hungry.

Dudley's. 346 King St. ☎ **843/723-2784.** Cover $1.

This is the clubbiest and (in its low-key way) the most welcoming gay bar in Charleston. Some regulars compare it to a gay man's version of TV's *Cheers* because of its wood paneling and brick interior and its amused and bemused sense of permissiveness. Most of the dialogue occurs on the street level, where an advance call from nonmembers is considered necessary to guarantee admittance. Upstairs is a "game room" with pool tables and very few places to sit. The bar is open daily from 4pm to 2am.

3

Side Trips from Charleston

*F*rom historic small towns to the intriguing landscapes of South Carolina's barrier islands, Charleston is surrounded by intriguing places to explore. You can see the following destinations as quick day trips, but we've recommended a few lodging and restaurant choices in case you decide to linger.

For specifics on many of the outdoor activities, see "Beaches & Outdoor Pursuits" in chapter 2.

1 Isle of Palms

A residential community bordered by the Atlantic Ocean 10 miles north of Charleston, this island, with its salt marshes and wildlife, is a major vacation retreat along the coastline of the Carolinas. Charlestonians have been flocking to the island for holidays since 1898; the first hotel opened here in 1911.

The attractions of Charleston are close at hand, but the Isle of Palms is a self-contained destination, with **shops, dining,** an array of **accommodations,** two **championship golf courses,** and 7 miles of **white-sand beach.** Sailing and windsurfing are popular, and you can even go crabbing and shrimping in the creeks.

GETTING THERE I-26 intersects with I-526 heading directly to the island via the Isle of Palms Connector (S.C. 517).

ACCOMMODATIONS

Boardwalk Inn. In the Dunes Resort, Isle of Palms, Charleston, SC 29415. ☎ **800/845-8880** or 843/886-600. Fax 843/886-2916. www.wildunes.com. E-mail:reservations@wildunes.com. 93 units. A/C MINIBAR TV TEL. Winter $139–$199 double; autumn $159–$239 double; spring $169–$279 double; summer $179–$289 double. Golf packages available. AE, DC, DISC, MC, V. Free parking.

This newest addition to the Wild Dunes Resort (see below) offers four-star service on the resort premises, with full room service and a concierge. Furnished in the spirit of Historic Charleston, the inn features modern amenities such as firm mattresses but still gives you a feeling of tradition and Low Country charm. Data ports are available in each good-size room in case your getaway requires some business attention. The service is top-notch and the hospitality so inviting that the place has already established much repeat business. On-site is a pool, but guests usually use the facilities and enjoy all the privileges of the Wild Dunes Resort.

✪ **Wild Dunes Resort.** Isle of Palms (P.O. Box 20575), Charleston, SC 29413. ☎ **800/845-8880** or 843/886-6000. Fax 843/886-2916. www.wilddunes.com. E-mail: reservations@wilddunes.com. 280 villas, 32 cottages. A/C TV TEL. $195–$416 villa or cottage. Golf packages available. AE, DC, DISC, MC, V. Free parking.

A bit livelier than Kiawah Island, its major competitor, this 1,600-acre resort boasts not only two widely acclaimed golf courses but also an array of other outdoor activities. The resort's own private beach stretches over 2^1/$_2$ miles. Set on landscaped grounds, this complex of villas and cottages lies on the north shore. Many families settle in for a long stay, almost never venturing into Charleston. Each accommodation is individually decorated; many have only one bedroom but others as many as six. The furnishings are done in a tasteful resort style, and the units have kitchens, washers/dryers, and spacious baths with dressing areas. Some of the best ones have screened-in balconies.

Dining: Edgard's Restaurant specializes in both standard American fare and regional dishes. Its lounge remains open nightly to 2am.

Amenities: Racquet club, yacht harbor on the Intracoastal Waterway, nature trails, bicycling, children's programs, 17 clay tennis courts and 10 hard-surface courts, 20 pools, activities like surf casting and an array of water sports.

2 Kiawah Island

This private residential and resort community, sprawling across 10,000 acres, lies 21 miles south of Charleston. Named for the Kiawah Indians who inhabited the islands in the 17th century, today it consists of two resort villages, **East Beach** and **West Beach.**

The community fronts a 10-mile stretch of **Atlantic beach;** magnolias, live oaks, pine forests, and acres of marsh blanket the island. The best beach is at **Beachwalker County Park** on the southern end of the island. Go before noon on Saturday and Sunday, however, as the limited parking is usually gone by then. Canoe rentals are available for use on the Kiawah River, and the park offers a boardwalk, bathrooms, showers, and a changing area.

Kiawah boasts many challenging **golf courses,** including one designed by Jack Nicklaus at Turtle Point (*Golf Digest* rates this one among the top 10 courses in South Carolina). Golf architect Pete Dye designed a 2^1/$_2$-mile oceanfront course to host the 1991 PGA Ryder Cup Match. *Tennis* magazine rates Kiawah as one of the nation's top **tennis resorts,** with its 28 hard-surface or Har-Tru clay courts. Anglers are also attracted to the island, especially in spring and fall.

GETTING THERE To get here from Charleston, take S.C. 17 South to S.C. 700 West (Maybank Hwy.) to Bohicket Road. From there, follow the signs into Kiawah.

ACCOMMODATIONS

Kiawah Island Resort. 12 Kiawah Beach Dr., Kiawah Island (P.O. Box 12357), Charleston, SC 29412. ☎ **800/654-2924** or 843/768-2122. Fax 843/768-6099. 150 inn units, 500 villas and town houses. A/C TV TEL. $129–$179 double; $135–$230 villa; $325–$900 town house. AE, DC, DISC, MC, V. Free parking.

The resort offers a wide range of accommodations—from rooms at the inn to villas and town houses with as many as four bedrooms. A self-contained community, the complex opened in 1976 at West Beach village. Since then, East Beach village has joined the community, though West Beach is the only one with shops. Regular hotel-like rooms are available in four buildings, opening onto the lagoon or the Atlantic. King-size or two double beds are available, along with private balconies and combination baths. The villas and town houses, which you can rent in various configurations, are casually furnished, with complete kitchens and amenities like washers and dryers.

Dining: Several dining options await you, at such rooms as the Jasmine Porch and Veranda and the Indigo House. Tables face the lagoon at the Park Café. Low Country and international dishes are featured.

3 Edisto Island

Isolated and enveloped with a kind of melancholy beauty, Edisto is some 45 miles south of Charleston. Named after its early Native American inhabitants, the island saw the arrival of the first Europeans (the Spanish) in the 1500s. In the century that followed, the English appeared, forming permanent settlements and cultivating indigo and rice. But by the late 18th century, sea island cotton was the crop that brought wealth to the islanders. Some plantations from that era are still standing.

Edisto Island today attracts families from Charleston and the Low Country intent on a beach holiday, as the island is known for its profusion of **white-sand beaches.** The **water sports** you can enjoy include surf casting, deep-sea fishing, shrimping, and sailing.

GETTING THERE   To get here, take U.S. 17 west from Charleston for 21 miles, then head south along Hwy. 174 the rest of the way.

HITTING THE BEACH   Edisto Beach State Park, State Cabin Road, Edisto, SC 19438 (☎ **843/869-2156**), sprawls across 1,255 acres, opening onto 2 miles of beach. There's also a well-signposted nature trail. You can bring a picnic lunch to enjoy under one of the shelters. In addition, the park has 103 **camping sites** with full hookups (only 5 sites have no hookups). Camp sites cost $20 per night or $17 off-season (the same price for RV hookups). Five cabins are available for rent, ranging from $64 daily. There are two restaurants within walking distance of the camp, plus a general store nearby.

ACCOMMODATIONS

Rooms are extremely limited on the island. You may want to stay nearby and visit just for 1 day.

Fairfield Ocean Ridge. 1 King Cotton Rd., Edisto Island, SC 29438. ☎ **843/869-2561.** www.fairfieldvacation.com. 40 units. A/C MINIBAR TV TEL. $220 1-bedroom villa; $295 2-bedroom villa; $360 2-bedroom deluxe villa. MC, V.

Located at the south end of Edisto Beach, this 300-acre time-share resort is a favorite summer rendezvous for Charleston families who come to fish, bird-watch, and beachcomb. Golf, jet skiing, parasailing, and tennis are among the other recreational activities. Accommodations include villas and condos, and range from a one-bedroom villa to a two-bedroom duplex villa with sleeping lofts. Each is complete with a kitchen and is individually furnished according to the owner's taste. Most rooms have VCRs; fax service is available at the rental office. A restaurant on the premises serves a free continental breakfast only on Monday.

DINING

Old Post Office. Hwy. 174 at Store Creek. ☎ **843/869-2339.** Main courses $17–$21. MC, V. Mon–Sat 6–10pm. SOUTHERN.

This is the most prominent building you're likely to see as you drive across Edisto Island, about 5 miles from the beach. As the weathered clapboards and old-time appearance imply, this structure was built as a post office/general store. Partners David Gressette and Philip Bardin, who transformed the premises in 1988, prepare a worthwhile array of Low Country Southern cuisine and serve it in copious portions. Try Island corn-and-crabmeat chowder, Orangeburg onion sausage with black-bean sauce, fried quail with duck-stock gravy, or "fussed-over" pork chops with hickory-smoked tomato sauce and mousseline. All main courses are accompanied by salads, vegetables, and bread.

4 Summerville

This historic town, listed on the National Register of Historic Places, is where Charlestonians used to go to escape summer heat and malaria. It's a treasure trove of **19th-century buildings** (mainly 1850 to the early 1900s), many built by Low Country rice planters. **Gardens** of azaleas, wisteria, and camellias bloom in town.

Today, Summerville is known for its old **country stores** and **antiques shops,** most on East Richardson Avenue, Main Street, and Old Trolley Road. Names of stores range from Antiques 'n Stuff to Granny's Attic—corny but appropriate. For **outdoor pursuits,** the town maintains two lighted recreational fields, three parks, and four playgrounds with six tennis courts. Picnics are possible at **Givhans Ferry State Park** nearby and at **Francis Beidler Forest.**

GETTING THERE   Summerville is 25 miles north of Charleston on I-26 (exit 199).

ACCOMMODATIONS

Woodlands Resort & Inn. 125 Parson Rd., Summerville, SC 29483. ☎ **800/ 774-9999** or 843/875-2600. Fax 843/875-2603. www.woodlandsinn.com. E-mail: reservations@woodlands.com. 27 units. A/C TV TEL. Mon–Fri $225 double, $275 suite; Sat–Sun $275 double, $350 suite. AE, DC, DISC, MC, V.

A 30-minute drive from Charleston, Woodlands is one of the finest places to stay in the Low Country. This white-pillared Classical Revival building, originally constructed in 1906, stands on 42 landscaped acres. The standard rooms are furnished in traditional style with king- or queen-size beds, sitting areas, VCRs, and large baths. The inn also offers eight luxurious suites with large whirlpool tubs.

Dining: A full Southern breakfast (including grits, of course) arrives every morning, and later in the day you can sample Low Country cooking in the full-service 85-seat restaurant, the **Dining Room** at the Woodlands. The only five-star restaurant in the state, it attracts many locals.

Amenities: Room service, laundry, massage, croquet, tennis, swimming, and biking; golf available nearby.

DINING

McNeill's. 105 S. Cedar St. ☎ **843/832-0912.** Reservations recommended. Main courses $6–$18; sandwiches $7. AE, DISC, MC, V. Tues–Fri 11am–2:30pm; Tues–Sat 5:30–9pm. AMERICAN/LOW COUNTRY.

Since 1994, this place has been packing them in, with locals and visitors alike sampling the superb cookery of Chef Herman McNeill. Among the dishes on this distinctive and ever-evolving menu are shrimp and bacon ravioli with an oregano cream sauce and crab cakes served with Granny Smith apple slices. Veal McNeil is veal cutlets tossed in a roasted garlic and honey cream sauce. Our favorite is the pan-roasted chicken with an orange-scented barbecue sauce and bacon. You'll welcome the seafood risotto with lots of crabmeat, shrimp, and scallops, and especially the shrimp and grits, a local favorite. Well-stuffed sandwiches make a good luncheon choice.

5 Beaufort

Below Charleston and 30 miles north of Hilton Head, Beaufort (*bew*-fort) is an old seaport with narrow streets shaded by huge live oaks and lined with **18th-century homes** (the oldest was built in 1717 and is at Port Republic and New streets). This was the second area in North America discovered by the Spanish (1520), the site of the first fort (1525) on the continent, and of the first attempted settlement (1562).

And if you find that Beaufort looks familiar, that's probably because this town has been used as a setting for several films, including *The Big Chill, Forrest Gump,* and *The Prince of Tides.*

GETTING THERE   If you're traveling from the north, take I-95 to exit 33, then follow the signs to the center of Beaufort. From the south, including Hilton Head, take I-95 to exit 8 and follow the signs.

VISITOR INFORMATION   The **Beaufort Chamber of Commerce,** 1006 Bay St. (P.O. Box 910), Beaufort, SC 29901 (☎ **843/ 524-3163**), offers self-guided tours and lots of other information about this historic town. It's open daily from 9am to 5:30pm. If you plan to come in early to mid-October, write the **Historic Beaufort Foundation** (P.O. Box 11, Beaufort, SC 29901), for specific dates and details on their 3 days of antebellum house-and-garden tours.

Beaufort, June 6, 1863

Dear Mother,

*This is an odd sort of place. All the original inhabitants are gone—
and the houses are occupied by Northerners.*

Your loving son,

Robert Gould Shaw

EXPLORING THE TOWN

The **Spirit of Old Beaufort,** 210 Scott's St. (☎ 843/525-0459),
takes you on a journey through the old town, exploring local history,
architecture, horticulture, and Low Country life. You'll see houses
not accessible on other tours. Your host, clad in period costume, will
guide you for 2 hours on Tuesday to Saturday at 10 and 11:30am
and 1:15 and 3:30pm. The cost is $10 for adults, $7.50 for teens,
free for children 12 and under. Tours depart from just behind the
John Market Verdier House Museum (below).

The **John Market Verdier House Museum,** 801 Bay St.
(☎ 843/524-6334), is a restored 1790 house that has been partially
furnished to depict the life of a merchant planter from 1790 to
1825. It's one of the best examples of the Federal period and was
once known as the Lafayette building, since the Marquis de
Lafayette is said to have spoken here in 1825. It's open Monday to
Friday from 11am to 4pm, charging $4 for adults and $2 for children and students.

St. Helen's Episcopal Church, 501 Church St. (☎ 843/
522-1722), traces its origin from 1712. On Monday to Saturday
from 10am to 4pm, you can see its classic interior and visit its graveyard, where tombstones served as operating tables during the Civil
War. Free admission.

In the surrounding area, the most interesting excursion is to
Parris Island (☎ 843/525-3650), 10 miles south of the center of
Beaufort, site of the famous U.S. Marine Corps Recruit Depot.
Opened in 1891, the depot grew to become the main recruit training center in the United States. The visitor center, in Building 283,
is open daily from 10am to 4:30pm. There you can learn about driving and bus tours (free) around the grounds. Among the things to
see are an Iwo Jima monument, a monument to the Spanish

settlement of Santa Elena (1521), and a memorial to Jean Ribaut, the French Huguenot and founder of Charlesfort in 1562. Sword drills and parade marches are interesting to watch, and even better is the music of the Marine Corps Band. The **Parris Island Museum,** Building 111 (☎ **843/525-2951**), tells the history of the island from 1521. Free admission, and it's open Saturday to Wednesday 10am to 4:30pm, Thursday 10am to 7pm, and Friday 8am to 4:30pm.

ACCOMMODATIONS

✪ **Beaufort Inn.** 809 Port Republic St., Beaufort, SC 29902. ☎ **843/ 521-9000.** Fax 843/521-9500. www.beaufortinn.com. 13 units. A/C MINIBAR TV TEL. $125–$225 double. Rates include full breakfast and afternoon tea. AE, DISC, MC, V. Free off-street parking.

This is Beaufort's most appealing hotel, the preferred lodging for whatever movie star happens to be shooting a film in town. Built in 1907 by a prosperous lawyer, it became the town's most respectable inn just after the 1929 stock market crash. Today, the woodwork and moldings inside are among the finest in Beaufort, and its four-story circular staircase is the subject of numerous photos and architectural awards. The good-size rooms, each decorated in a brightly colored style different from the others, are conversation pieces. All are equipped with data ports, and the staff supplies white robes; some units also contain a fireplace. The inn's wonderful restaurant is reason enough to stay here (see the entry in "Dining," below).

Best Western Sea Island Inn. 1015 Bay St., Beaufort, SC 29902. ☎ **800/ 528-1234** or 843/522-2090. Fax 843/521-4858. 43 units. A/C TV TEL. $79–$105 double. Rates include continental breakfast. AE, DC, DISC, MC, V.

This place was built in 1959 on the site of one of Beaufort's most historic hotels (nary a shred of the original building remains). What you'll find is a basic two-story motel, fairly unremarkable except for the touches of cast iron on the facade facing the street and elegant brown bricks that despite their newness manage to look antique. Very few of the rooms have sea views; most overlook a small pool separated from the rest of the motel in a brick-sided courtyard. Though the rooms are nothing special, they're comfortable and clean, with firm beds.

✪ **Cuthbert House Inn.** 1203 Bay St., Beaufort, SC 29901. ☎ **800/ 327-9275** or 843/521-1315. www.curthberthouseinn.com. E-mail: curtbert@ hangray.com. 8 units. A/C MINIBAR TV TEL. Jan–Feb $145–$165 double; Mar– Dec $155–$225 double. Rates include full breakfast and afternoon tea or refreshments. AE, DISC, MC, V. Free off-street parking.

This is one of South Carolina's grand old B&Bs; built in a classic Southern colonial style, it extends a type of hospitality that might've pleased Rhett Butler. One of Beaufort's showcase homes, the Cuthbert was built in 1790, and its current owner, Sharon Groves, has worked to modernize it without sacrificing its grace elements. (On the Eastlake room's fireplace mantel you can still see the graffiti carved by Union soldiers.) The midsize to spacious rooms are elegantly furnished in the plantation style, some with four-poster beds and cast-iron soaking tubs in the baths. The inn is filled with large parlors and sitting rooms furnished in antiques and has the spacious halls and 12-foot ceilings characteristic of classical homes. At breakfast in the conservatory, you can order delights like Georgia ice cream (cheese grits) and freshly made breads.

Rent House Inn. 601 Bay St., Beaufort, SC 29902. ☎ **834/524-9030.** 9 units. TV. Mar–Nov $125–$225 double; Dec–Feb $100–$195 double. Rates include full breakfast. AE, DISC, MC, V.

One of the most elegant historic homes in town, the inn looks across a quiet road toward a view of a saltwater estuary. Built in 1852 by owners of a plantation on nearby Dataw Island and used by Union troops during the Civil War as an officers' club, it was sold for back taxes, fell into disrepair, and hobbled along as a private home until someone transformed it into a B&B in the 1980s. Our favorite room is no. 7, a cellar accommodation outfitted incongruously (but charmingly) in a Southwestern theme. Eight of the rooms have working fireplaces, and each is well furnished and comfortable, with traditional styling, including firm beds.

Rhett House Inn. 1009 Craven St., Beaufort, SC 29902. ☎ **843/524-9030.** Fax 843/524-1310. www.rhetthouseinn.com. E-mail: rhetthse@hargray.com. 17 units. A/C TV TEL. $125–$225 double. Rates include full breakfast and afternoon tea. AE, DISC, MC, V. Free parking.

Spacious and graceful, this circa 1820 inn places an emphasis on nostalgia and glamour, with more style and better furnishings than many other B&Bs in this part of the state. None of this occurred effortlessly, as a dialogue with owners Steve and Marianne Harrison will quickly reveal. Each spacious room boasts a private entrance, a whirlpool tub, a fireplace, and a private porch. The inn's largest rooms are behind the main house in a circa 1850 building that has the distinction of having been the first Free Man (former slaves) school in South Carolina.

Two Suns Inn. 1705 Bay St., Beaufort, SC 29902. ☎ **800/532-4244** or 843/522-1122. Fax 843/522-1122. www.twosunsinn.com. E-mail: twosuns@islc.net.

6 units. A/C TV TEL. $104–$155 double. Rates include full breakfast and after-noon tea. AE, DC, DISC, MC, V. Free parking.

It was built in 1917 as one of the grandest homes in its prosperous neighborhood, with views over the coastal road and the tidal flatlands beyond. Every imaginable modern convenience was added, including a baseboard vacuum-cleaning system, an electric call box, and steam heat. However, it conspicuously lacked an entrance vestibule. In 1943, the Colonial Revival building was sold to the Beaufort Board of Education as housing for unmarried female teachers and allowed to run down. In 1990, a retired music teacher/bandleader, Ron Kay, with his wife, Carroll, bought the place as part of "an accidental stop along the way to North Carolina" and transformed it into a warmly decorated B&B. Part of its appeal stems from its lack of pretension, as a quick glance at the homey rooms and uncomplicated furnishings will show.

A NEARBY RESORT

Flat and marshy, with raised outcroppings of ancient trees and sand dunes, the 3,000 acres comprising **Fripp Island,** 19 miles south of Beaufort on U.S. 21, were never inhabited by European settlers, partly because of waterlogged soil, mangrove swamps, and bugs. It's the sea island most distant from the South Carolina mainland, reached via U.S. 21, which meanders through the marshes and creeks of three other islands. A refuge of waterfowl and reptiles, Fripp Island slumbered throughout the era when Hilton Head and its neighbors nearby were burgeoning.

But in 1990, an earlier (failed) attempt at development was renewed when a new group of investors bought the entire island for $8 million, poured another $10 million into its development, and began the long and difficult task of pulling the complex into the 20th century.

Fripp Island Resort. 1 Tarpon Blvd., Fripp Island, SC 29920. ☎ **800/845-4100** or 843/838-3535. Fax 843/838-9079. 310 units. A/C TV TEL. $95 suite with kitchenette; villas and cottages with kitchen: $165–$300 1 bedroom, $145–$310 2 and 3 bedrooms, $245–$350 4 bedrooms. Discounts for stays of 1 week; 15% reductions for Nov–Apr. AE, DC, DISC, MC, V.

This sprawling resort takes up the whole island, and access is limited to guests. Getting away from it all in a rugged Low Country setting is Fripp's greatest appeal. After you check into a Cape Cod–inspired main building (also site of a restaurant), you're shown to your villa. The style of the one- to four-bedroom villas ranges from Key West–style clapboard to California marina modern. The decor depends on the taste of the individual owner and may not agree with yours. The resort doesn't achieve the level of such major Hilton Head competitors as Palmetto Dunes or the Westin. But natural beauty abounds on the island, and there are extensive bicycle paths, 10 tennis courts, sandy beaches and dunes, scattered pools, and two 18-hole golf courses. Six restaurants are scattered about (though only four are open in winter).

DINING

✪ **Beaufort Inn Restaurant.** In the Beaufort Inn, 809 Port Republic St. ☎ **843/521-9000.** Reservations recommended. Main courses $15–$27. AE, DISC, MC, V. Mon–Sat 8–10am and 6–10pm; Sun 10am–2pm. INTERNATIONAL.

Stylish and urbane and awash with colonial lowland references, this is a carefully decorated restaurant where many locals like to come for special celebrations or important business dinners. The dining room has been featured on the Discovery Channel and on the Food Network's review show *Dining Around. Country Inns* magazine has rated this as one of the Southeast's top 10 dining experiences, and Ulbrich has been nominated as the Southeastern Chef of the Year. Stellar examples from the menu are Low Country shrimp Creole and roast duck breast with shallot-berry sauce.

Bistro DeJong. 205 West St. ☎ **843/524-4994.** Reservations required. Main courses $12–$21. AE, DC, DISC, MC, V. Mon–Sat 5:30–11pm. EUROPEAN/ FUSION.

Award-winning Chef Peter DeJong serves an interesting mix of Western and Eastern cuisine. The chef prepares a wonderful array of appetizers, including satays and Southern-style sushi. For the main course there's tender rack of lamb, pan-sautéed salmon in rosemary with vodka sauce over rice; butterfly shrimp; pecan-crusted grouper with lemon-caper-butter sauce over spinach, pesto, and fettuccine; and a variety of excellent steaks. One of the highlights featured in this restaurant is its exclusive wine list.

✪ **Emily's.** 906 Port Republic St. ☎ **843/522-1866.** Reservations recommended. Tapas $7; main courses $20–$23. AE, DISC, MC, V. Drinks and tapas Mon–Sat 4:30–10pm; main courses Mon–Sat 6:30–10pm. INTERNATIONAL.

This is our favorite restaurant in Beaufort, a warm spot where the ambience and attitude remind us of a restaurant in Scandinavia. That's hardly surprising, since its bearded owner is an émigré from Sweden who happened to feel comfortable in the South Carolina lowlands after years of life at sea. Some folks just go to the bar for sampling the tapas, which include miniature portions of tempura shrimp, fried scallops, alligator ribs, and at least 50 others. At the table, the menu items might include a cream of mussel-and-shrimp soup rich enough for a main course, filet "black and white" (beef and pork filets with béarnaise sauce), duck with orange sauce, Weiner schnitzel, and a changing assortment of the catch of the day—all served in stomach-stretching portions.

Ollie's by the Bay. 822 Bay St. ☎ **843/524-2500.** Reservations recommended. Lunch main courses $4–$16; dinner main courses $11–$21. AE, DC, DISC, MC, V. Mon–Sat 11:30am–3pm and 5–10pm. ITALIAN/SEAFOOD.

Ollie's by the Bay replaces the long-popular New Gadsby Tavern. The building is still the same, but with a decor evocative more of the Mediterranean. Whitewashed floors and Italian portraits on the walls, also whitewashed, make up the simple decor. Chefs Bob Maher and Jon Breda have designed an entirely new menu, featuring hot and cold antipasti, freshly made salads, and pastas ranging from spaghetti with shrimp, mussels, and calamari to creamy ravioli filled with spinach and cheese. From the grill emerges a 16-ounce T-bone steak or a delightful mahimahi with olive-orange tapenade. Other specialties are skillet-seared tuna; tender herb-flavored veal; and slow-roasted pork braised in a sauce of balsamic vinegar, red onions, and rosemary.

4

Hilton Head: One of the Southeast's Premier Resorts

*O*ne of America's great resort meccas, Hilton Head is the largest sea island between New Jersey and Florida. It's surrounded by the Low Country, where all the romance, beauty, and graciousness of the Old South survive. The coastline is among the most scenic in the Southeast: Graceful sea oats wave in the wind, anchoring broad white-sand beaches. Towering pines and wind-sculpted live oaks and palmettos, all draped in Spanish moss, line the rolling dunes.

The subtropical climate makes all this beauty the ideal setting for golf and fishing. Spring arrives early and summer lingers until late October. Far more sophisticated and upscale than Myrtle Beach and the Grand Strand, Hilton Head depends on 12 miles of beautiful uncrowded beach to draw visitors. Some of the finest saltwater fishing on the East Coast is in the surrounding waters and in the Gulf Stream some 60 miles offshore. Today the island's "plantations" (as most resort areas here call themselves) still preserve something of the leisurely lifestyle that's always held sway.

Though it covers only 42 square miles (it's 12 miles long and 5 miles wide at its widest point), Hilton Head feels spacious, thanks to judicious planning from the outset of development, in 1952. And that's a blessing, since about half a million resort guests visit annually (the permanent population is about 25,000). The broad beaches on its ocean side; sea marshes on the sound; and natural wooded areas of live oak, pine, bay, and palmetto trees in between have all been carefully preserved amid the commercial explosion. This lovely setting attracts artists, writers, musicians, theater groups, and craftspeople. The only "city" is Harbour Town, at Sea Pines Plantation, a Mediterranean-style cluster of shops and restaurants.

1 Orientation

GETTING THERE

It's easy to fly into Charleston and drive to Hilton Head. See chapter 1 for details on airlines and chapter 2 for details on car

Special Events

Springfest is a March festival featuring seafood, live music, stage shows, and tennis and golf tournaments. In early or mid-April, top tennis players congregate for the **Family Circle Magazine Cup Tennis Tournament,** held at the Sea Pines Racquet Club. Outstanding PGA golfers also descend on the island in mid-April for the **MCI Heritage Classic** at Harbour Town Golf Links. To welcome in fall, the **Hilton Head Celebrity Golf Tournament** is held on Labor Day weekend at Palmetto Dunes and Sea Pines Plantation.

rentals at the airport. (Hilton Head is about 65 miles south of Charleston.) If you're driving from other points south or north, take the Hilton Head exit off I-95 to reach the island. The island is 52 miles northeast of Savannah, located directly on the Intracoastal Waterway.

VISITOR INFORMATION

The **Hilton Head Visitors' and Convention Bureau** (Chamber of Commerce), 1 Chamber Dr., Hilton Head, SC 29928 (☎ 843/785-3673), offers free maps of the area and will assist you in finding places of interest and outdoor activities. It won't, however, make hotel reservations. It's open Monday to Friday from 8:30am to 5pm, Saturday from 9am to 6pm, and Sunday from noon to 4pm.

GETTING AROUND

U.S. 278 (the William Hilton Pkwy.) is the divided highway that runs the length of the island. Hilton Head has seen the problems of popularity, and to relieve traffic congestion it now boasts the **Cross Island Expressway,** which serves as an extension of U.S. 278.

If you'd like to leave the driving to someone else, **Yellow Cab** (☎ 843/686-6666) has flat two-passenger rates determined by zone; an extra person is charged $2.

Note that many of our recommendations below are located on the grounds of the **Sea Pines Plantation.** To enter the plantation if you're not a registered guest at the resort, you must pass through a gate, where you're charged $3.

2 Accommodations

Hilton Head has some of the finest properties in the Deep South, with more than 3,000 hotel and motel rooms on the island, plus

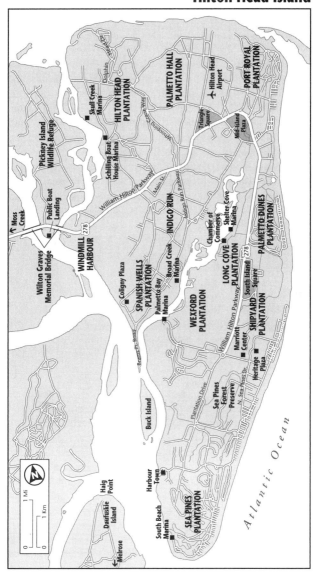

6,000 villas. Prices are high, unless you book into one of the motels run by national chains. Most places will discount rates from November to March, and golf and tennis packages are offered almost everywhere. Instead of paying typical rack rates, always ask about special discounts or get your travel agent to search for a deal.

The oldest and most comprehensive service on the island, the **Hilton Head Central Reservation Service,** P.O. Box 5312, Hilton Head Island, SC 29938 (☎ **800/845-7018** in the U.S. and Canada), can book you into any hotel room or villa without a fee. Hours are Monday to Saturday from 9am to 5pm.

Another option is renting a private home, villa, or condo—a great choice for families if it fits into their budget. For up-to-date availability, rates, and bookings, contact **Island Rentals and Real Estate,** P.O. Box 5915, Hilton Head Island, SC 29938 (☎ **800/845-6134** or 843/785-3813). The toll-free number operates 24 hours, but office hours are Monday to Saturday from 8:30am to 5pm (earlier closing on some Saturdays, especially in winter).

The hotels below offer free parking.

HOTELS
VERY EXPENSIVE

Hyatt Regency Hilton Head. In Palmetto Dunes Plantation (P.O. Box 6167), Hilton Head, SC 29938. ☎ **800/233-1234** or 843/785-1234. Fax 843/842-4695. 505 units, 29 suites. A/C TV TEL. $154–$315 double; $400–$975 suite. AE, DC, DISC, MC, V.

This is the island's largest hotel, set on 2 landscaped acres surrounded by the more massive acreage of Palmetto Dunes Plantation. Owned by General Electric and managed by Hyatt, it was designed in 1976 as a 10-story high-rise virtually dominating everything around it. Later, a 5-story annex was added. This hotel lacks the pizzazz of the Westin (see below); and although you might find it odd to keep riding an elevator to travel among your room, the beach, and the various hotel facilities, you'll quickly grow used to it. Rooms are smaller and less opulent than you might expect, but you'll be compensated for the unremarkable interiors by balconies that look out over the gardens or the water.

Dining: Hemingway's is one of the island's best choices (see "Dining," below). A cabaret-style dining-and-drinking club offers more diversion. Sunday brunch here is an island event.

Amenities: Room service; laundry; Camp Hyatt for children; outdoor pool and whirlpool; three 18-hole golf courses; 25 tennis courts; sailboats; health club with saunas, whirlpool, indoor pool, exercise room.

✪ **Westin Resort.** 2 Grass Lawn Ave., Hilton Head, SC 29928. ☎ **800/ 933-3102** or 843/681-4000. Fax 843/681-1087. 450 units. $130–$320 double; from $400 suite. Children under 18 stay free in parents' room. Children 4 and under eat free. AE, DC, DISC, MC, V.

Near Hilton Head's isolated northern end, on 24 acres of landscaping, the Westin is the most opulent European-style hotel in town. Its design, including cupolas and a postmodern ornamentation that looks vaguely Moorish, evokes fanciful Palm Beach hotels. If there's a drawback, it's the atmosphere of stiff formality; adults accompanied by a gaggle of children and bathers in swimsuits won't feel comfortable in the reverently hushed corridors. The midsize to spacious rooms, most with ocean views, are outfitted in Low Country plantation style, with touches of Asian art thrown in for an upscale flourish.

Dining: The Barony (see "Dining," below) is the best place for food on the island. There's also a seafood buffet restaurant.

Amenities: Room service, baby-sitting, laundry, state-of-the-art fitness center, three top-notch golf courses, Palm Beach–style racquet club with 16 tennis courts, three outdoor pools, one indoor pool, white-sand beach.

EXPENSIVE

Crystal Plaza Resort. 130 Shipyard Dr., Shipyard Plantation, Hilton Head Island, SC 29928. ☎ **800/334-1881** or 803/842-2400. Fax 803/842-9975. www.crowneplazaresort.com. E-mail: infor@crowneplazaresort.com. 340 units. A/C MINIBAR TV TEL. $129–$319 double; $250–$550 suite. AE, DC, DISC, MC, V.

The centerpiece of 800 landscaped acres, this glorified Holiday Inn now gives the Westin stiff competition. Built in a 5-story design in 1981 as a Marriott, it was renovated in 1993 (to the tune of $10 million) and today maintains the most dignified lobby (a mahogany-sheathed postmodern interpretation of Chippendale decor) of any hotel on the island. The small to midsize guest rooms are nothing special, outfitted in basic patterned fabrics and accessories. But the sheer beauty of the landscaping, the attentive service, and the well-trained staff (in nautically inspired uniforms) can go a long way toward making your stay memorable.

Dining: On the premises are two restaurants, the most glamorous of which is **Portz,** off the main lobby, open from 5:30 to 10:30pm; and cafe-style **Brella's,** open 7pm to midnight.

Amenities: The golf course was praised by the National Audubon Society for its respect of local wildlife. Room service, laundry, baby-sitting.

Disney Hilton Head Island Resort. 22 Harbourside Lane, Hilton Head, SC 29928. ☎ **800/453-4911** or 843/341-4100. Fax 843/341-4130. www. dvc-resprts.com. 31 studios, 88 villas. A/C TV TEL. Mar 28–Apr 19 $145 studio, $195 1-bedroom villa, $220 2-bedroom villa, $410 3-bedroom villa; off-season $105–$145 studio, $140–$195 1-bedroom villa, $160–$220 2-bedroom villa, $305–$410 3-bedroom villa. AE, MC, V.

Owned and operated by Disney (but devoid of the mechanized theme-park rides), this family-conscious resort occupies a 15-acre island that rises above Hilton Head's widest estuary, Broad Creek. Opened in 1996 as the only U.S.–based Disney resort outside Florida or California, it consists of about 20 woodsy buildings arranged into a compound inspired by a circa 1940s Low Country hunting-and-fishing lodge. Expect lots of pine trees and fallen pine needles, garlands of Spanish moss, families with children, and an ambience that's several notches less intense than what you'd find in a Disney theme park. Part of the fun, if you like this sort of thing, includes summer camp–style activities. The public areas sport plenty of forest green and cranberry colors, mounted game fish, and varnished pine. Conversational aids are visible in the form of frequent references to Shadow the Dog, a fictitious golden retriever who's the mascot, and Mathilda, a maternal figure who conducts cooking lessons for children. All good-size accommodations have minikitchens, suitable for feeding sandwiches and macaroni to the kids but hardly the kind of thing a gourmet chef would enjoy. Rooms are exceedingly comfortable, with excellent mattresses and state-of the-art plumbing.

   Dining: The resort has a quick-service restaurant called **Tied-Me-Over** (☎ **843/341-4156**), which is located across from the resort pool. The take-out orders range from $6 to $7 and include homemade pork sandwiches, crab cakes, and deli sandwiches made to order. It's open 7 days a week from 8am to 4pm.

   Amenities: Ecotours with Disneyesque themes for children, who are segregated into compatible age groups. Each activity lasts between $1\frac{1}{2}$ and 2 hours, giving parents a chance to be alone while juniors are on marsh tours, weenie-and-marshmallow roasts with campfire songs, arts-and-crafts lessons, boat rides that head out looking for dolphin sightings, canoeing lessons, and "unbirthday" celebrations for any adult or child who doesn't happen to be celebrating a birthday that day. Baby-sitting can be arranged for an extra fee. Two pools, one with a giant water slide, the other at the resort's beach club, about a mile from the resort's central core. The beach club includes a lunch-only snack bar, direct access to the sands of

Palmetto Cove, and options for water sports. A shuttle bus makes frequent connections from the beach club to the hotel daily from 8:30am to 4:30pm. A deli and general store sells provisions for stocking kitchens, and one of Hilton Head's most beautiful fishing piers allows easy access to whatever it is that bites underwater.

✪ **Hilton Oceanfront and Resort Hilton Head Island.** 23 Ocean Lane (P.O. Box 6165), Hilton Head, SC 29938. ☎ **800/845-8000.** Fax 843/341-8037. www.hiltonheadhilton.com. E-mail: hiltonhh@hargray.com. 353 units. A/C TV TEL. $149–$279 double; $250–$450 suite. AE, DC, DISC, MC, V.

This award-winning property was built in 1984 and benefited from a $3.5 million renovation 10 years later. Many visitors choose the Hilton because of its expansive sandy beach and hideaway position, tucked at the end of the main road through Palmetto Dunes.

Notable in its low-rise design, the Hilton has halls open to sea breezes at either end. Designed with some of the largest rooms on the island (all with kitchenettes), this hotel also has balconies angling out toward the beach that provide sea views from every unit.

Dining: Mostly Seafood is the resort's premier restaurant, though cafes and bars (even a franchise of Pizza Hut) serve less-expensive fare.

Amenities: Room service, baby-sitting, laundry, children's vacation program that's run like a summer camp and is the island's best, modest health club, whirlpool, sauna, two outdoor pools, 54-hole golf course, sundeck, tennis courts.

MODERATE

Holiday Inn Oceanfront. (P.O. Box 5728), 1 S. Forest Beach Dr., Hilton Head, SC 29938. ☎ **800/HOLIDAY** or 843/785-5126. Fax 843/785-6678. 201 units. A/C TV TEL. $130–$220 double. AE, CB, DC, DISC, MC, V.

The island's leading motor hotel, across from Colligny Plaza, this inn opens onto a quiet stretch of beach. Though it's outclassed by the other Holiday Inn affiliate, the Crystal Sands Crowne Plaza, it's better than ever after 1995 renovations. The hotel lies on the southern side of the island, near Shipyard Plantation. Don't judge the inn by its small lobby; just continue to the oceanfront restaurant or head straight for your well-furnished, spacious room, done up in tropical pastels. The rooms have comfortable king or double beds, but the balconies are generally too small for use. The upper floors have the views. Refrigerators are available for $5 per day. In summer, the hotel plans children's activities.

Residence Inn by Marriott. 12 Park Lane (in Central Park), Hilton Head, SC 29928. ☎ **843/686-5700.** Fax 843/686-3952. 156 suites. A/C TV TEL.

Apr–Sept $149–$199 suite; off-season $85–$199 suite. Rates include continental breakfast. AE, DC, DISC, MC, V.

On the eastern edge of Hilton Head's main traffic artery, midway between the Palmetto Dunes and Shipyard Plantations, this is a complex of functionally furnished but comfortable suites, each with a firm bed. Don't expect the amenities you might find in larger (and more expensive) hideaways, like the Hilton and Hyatt Regency. The limited resort facilities include a pool, a hot tub, a cluster of lighted tennis courts, and an exercise facility. Both families and business travelers on extended stays appreciate the simple cooking facilities available in each accommodation.

South Beach Marina Inn. 232 South Sea Pines Dr. (in the Sea Pines Plantation), Hilton Head, SC 29928. ☎ **843/671-6498.** 17 suites. A/C TV TEL. $109–$139 1-bedroom suite; $159–$169 2-bedroom suite. AE, DISC, MC, V.

Of the dozens of available accommodations in Sea Pines Plantation, this clapboard-sided complex of marina-front buildings is the only one that offers traditional hotel-style rooms. The compound was inspired by New England saltbox cottages, with exteriors painted red and blue. Exuding lots of charm, despite its aggressive "theme," the complex unfolds over a labyrinth of catwalks and stairways above shops, souvenir kiosks, and restaurants. Each small to midsize unit is cozy, with a kitchenette, country-style braided rugs, pinewood floors, firm beds, and a homespun decor celebrating rural 19th-century America.

INEXPENSIVE

Fairfield Inn by Marriott. 9 Marina Side Dr., Hilton Head, SC 29928. ☎ **800/228-2800** or 843/842-4800. Fax 843/842-4800. 133 units. A/C TV TEL. $46–$79 double; $59–$89 suite. Children under 18 stay free in parents' room. Rates include continental breakfast. Senior discounts and golf packages available.AE, DC, DISC, MC, V.

In Shelter Cove, this motel boasts all the special features of Marriott's budget chain, including complimentary coffee (always available in the lobby), no-smoking rooms, and same-day dry cleaning. There's also easy access to the beach, golf, tennis, marinas, and shopping. The rooms are wheelchair accessible, and, though sporting your average unremarkable modern decor, they're a good value for expensive Hilton Head, as each is well maintained and comes with a firm mattress. Families can save extra money by using one of the grills outside for a home-style barbecue, later enjoyed at one of the picnic tables. In addition, a heated pool is provided.

Hampton Inn. 1 Airport Rd., Hilton Head, SC 29926. ☎ **800/HAMPTON** or 843/681-7900. Fax 843/681-4330. 125 units (12 with kitchenettes). A/C TV TEL. $68–$124 double; $77–$124 double with kitchenette. Children under 18 stay free in parents' room. Rates include continental breakfast. AE, CB, DC, DISC, MC, V.

Though slightly edged out by its major competitor, the Fairfield Inn, this is the second most sought after motel, especially with families and business travelers. Lying 5 miles from the bridge, this motel closest to the airport offers rooms that seem like Florida condos, in pastel pinks and greens—sure, it's a cliche, but still comfortable and well maintained. Some units have refrigerators, and 12 units have kitchenettes. Local calls are free, and no-smoking units are available. The health spa features an outdoor pool, whirlpool, and exercise room. There's a coin laundry, tennis and golf can be arranged, bicycles can be rented, and there is daily dry cleaning pickup.

Quality Inn. Hwy. 278, 200 Museum St., Hilton Head, SC 29926. ☎ **800/995-3928** or 843/681-3655. Fax 843/681-3655. www.qualityinn.com. 139 units. A/C TV TEL. $68–$89 double; $109–$129 suite. AE, DC, DISC, MC, V. Free parking.

Competing neck and neck with the Red Roof Inn, this motel attracts families watching their budgets. It's acceptable and well maintained in every way. Part of the Quality Inn empire, it offers basic rooms with streamlined modern furnishings and king-size or queen-size beds. Some units are reserved for nonsmokers and travelers with disabilities. An outdoor pool is generous in size. A Shoney's chain restaurant is right next door, featuring its famous all-you-can-eat breakfast bar. Golf and tennis can be arranged nearby.

⭕ **Red Roof Inn.** 5 Regency Pkwy. (off U.S. 278 between Palmetto Dunes and Shipyard Plantation), Hilton Head, SC 29928. ☎ **800/843-7663** or 843/686-6808. Fax 843/842-3352. 112 units, 4 suites. A/C TV TEL. $43–$66 double; $100 suite. AE, CB, DC, DISC, MC, V.

Popular with families, this chain hotel is the island's budget special. Its basic and rather small motel-style rooms are well maintained and contain king-size or double beds. Local calls are free, as is daily coffee and a copy of *USA Today*. Families gather around the outdoor pool, and a nearby restaurant is open daily from 7am to 10pm. Public beaches and sports facilities are close at hand, and the hotel is wheelchair accessible.

VILLA RENTALS

Palmetto Dunes Resort. Palmetto Dunes (P.O. Box 5606), Hilton Head, SC 29938. ☎ **800/845-6130** or 843/785-1161. Fax 843/842-4482. 411 units.

A/C TV TEL. $75–$105 double; $95–$240 villa. Golf and honeymoon packages available. 2-night minimum stay. 50% deposit for reservations. AE, DC, DISC, MC, V.

This relaxed enclave of privately owned villas is on the grounds of Palmetto Dunes Plantation, 7 miles south of the bridge, part of a sprawling 1,800-acre complex. Accommodations range from rather standard hotel rooms (booked mostly by groups) to four-bedroom villas (the latter furnished according to the owners' taste). If you want to check in and out in a couple of days, consider the Hilton or the Hyatt Regency nearby. Palmetto Dunes is better for longer stays and is ideal for families who want a home away from home when traveling. The villas are fully equipped and receive housekeeping service; they're on the ocean, fairways, or lagoons. Each comes with a full kitchen, washer and dryer, living room and dining area, and balcony or patio.

Facilities include a tennis center with 25 courts, 5 golf courses, 3 miles of beach, 20 restaurants, a 10-mile lagoon ideal for canoeing, a playground, and a 200-slip marina.

✪ **Sea Pines Resort.** Sea Pines Plantation (P.O. Box 7000), Hilton Head, SC 29938. ☎ **800/SEA-PINE**S or 843/785-3333. Fax 843/842-1475. www.seapines.com. 500 villas. A/C TV TEL. Apr–Sept $762–$1,600 weekly 1-bedroom villa; $918–$2,100 weekly 2-bedroom villa; off-season $528–$1,188 weekly 1-bedroom villa; $648–$1,542 weekly 2-bedroom villa. AE, DC, DISC, MC, V.

Since 1955, this has been one of America's leading condo developments, sprawling across 5,500 acres at the southernmost tip of the island. There are 4 miles of beaches alone, 14 miles of bike trails, 3 championship golf courses, 42 tennis courts, and 25 pools; there are also 12 restaurants, various entertainment spots, two marinas, children's summer recreation programs, a small fitness center, and 600 acres of forest preserve (even a riding center).

Don't come to Sea Pines looking for a quick in-and-out overnight. The entire complex (except for the 17-room South Beach Marina Inn on the premises, reviewed above) encourages stays of at least a week. Accommodations vary, incorporating everything from one- to four-bedroom villas, as well as sometimes opulent private homes available when the owners are away. It's a popular place with golfers, since Sea Pines is the home of the MCI Classic, a major stop on the PGA tour. If you're not a guest, you can eat, shop, or enjoy its nightlife, but there's a $3 entrance fee. For full details on this varied resort/residential complex, write to the address above for a free *Sea Pines Vacation Brochure.*

CAMPING

The **Outdoor Resorts RV Resort & Yacht Club,** 43 Jenkins Rd., Hilton Head, SC 29926 (☎ **800/845-9560** or 843/681-3256), has some 200 RV sites on the Intracoastal Waterway. Amenities include two pools, saunas and whirlpools, lighted tennis courts, charter-fishing arrangements, a marina and ramp, a grocery shop, a coin laundry, and a restaurant. Rates for up to four range from $28 depending on the season.

3 Dining

All the specialties of the Low Country, along with fine European, Asian, and Mexican cuisine, are served at Hilton Head's some 150 restaurants. If you're a first-timer, opt for some of the local special-ties, like Frogmore stew, a combination of shrimp, hot sausage, po-tatoes, corn, and green beans. Other specialties are oysters roasted over an open fire until they can be easily opened with a knife and Daufuskie crab. Settings range from waterfront restaurants to hid-den dives—in fact, Hilton Head boasts more good restaurants than any competitive resort between New York and Florida.

VERY EXPENSIVE

✪ **The Barony.** 2 Grass Lawn Ave. (in the Westin Resort). ☎ **843/681-4000.** Reservations recommended. Main courses $25–$30. AE, DC, DISC, MC, V. Tues–Sat 5:30–10pm. INTERNATIONAL.

The Barony, quick to promote itself as Hilton Head's only four-star Mobil 4 Diamond AAA restaurant, has installed a decor that's a cross between a stage-set version of old Vienna and a brick-lined steak house. The lighting is suitably dim, the drinks appropriately stiff, and as you dine in your plushly upholstered alcove, you can check out what might be the largest wrought-iron chandelier in the state. Contrary to what you'd expect, the place caters to a resort-going crowd of casual diners, defining itself as "an upscale restaurant with a down-home feel." Everything arrives well prepared and in copious portions, though the kitchen isn't willing to experiment with more creative dishes. But you should be perfectly happy with solid dishes like filet mignon Wellington, prime rib, grilled rack of lamb, roast veal, pork chop or chicken, and the justifiably very popu-lar fresh "seafood in stuffed pastry."

✪ **Hemingway's.** Palmetto Dunes Resort (in the Hyatt Regency Hilton Head). ☎ **843/785-1234.** Reservations recommended. Main courses $22–$28. AE, DC, DISC, MC, V. Daily 5–11pm. SEAFOOD/AMERICAN.

This is the island's most upscale and charming hotel restaurant. Though the theme of a glamorous "Papa Hemingway as bon vivant" is hardly accurate, the dining experience offers competent and unpretentious service. The setting, which includes a view of an exposed kitchen, is appropriately nautical, and the sounds of a live pianist, vocalist, or guitarist might drift in from the late-night cocktail lounge next door. The most successful part of the menu includes your choice of fresh fish—cooked to perfection and never allowed to dry out. Other solid choices are filet mignon, bullfighter's-style paella, and charcoal-grilled poultry with lemon-thyme sauce. You might begin your meal with any of a round of upscale rums or a frothy rum-based tropical concoction flavored with coconut, banana, pineapple, and grenadine.

EXPENSIVE

Cattails. 302 Moss Creek Village. ☎ **843/837-7000.** Reservations recommended for dinner. Lunch main courses $9–$13; dinner main courses $17–$25. AE, DC, DISC, MC, V. Mon–Sat 11:30am–2pm and 6–10pm. INTERNATIONAL/MODERN AMERICAN.

The only drawback here is the location, in a shopping center 17 miles north of the resort's southern tip. Many locals, however, search the place out for its food and international zest. With high ceilings and big windows, this airy place is decorated with lace curtains and lots of hanging plants. Many of the dishes are inspired by Low Country traditions; others are more international or Californian. You'll relish such dishes as focaccia with roasted eggplant, red peppers, and mushrooms; chowder with roasted corn and crabmeat; pan-seared flounder with South Carolina pecans and white-wine butter sauce; and tempting pastas, many of them made with seafood. The owners are Iranian-born chef Mehdi Varedi and his American wife, Corinne, who directs a charming staff in the dining room.

✪ **Charlie's L'Etoile Verte.** 1000 Plantation Center. ☎ **803/785-9277.** Reservations required. Main courses $19–$28. AE, DISC, MC, V. Tues–Sat 11:30am–2pm and 6–9pm. INTERNATIONAL.

Looking like a tongue-in-cheek Parisian bistro, with lots of amusing Gallic and Low Country memorabilia, this is our favorite restaurant on the island, an opinion shared by President Clinton, who came with a large entourage during one of his island conferences. The atmosphere is unpretentious but elegant—a cauldron of energy in an otherwise sleepy shopping center. Service is attentive and polite, with an appealingly hip mix of the Old and New Worlds. The kitchen has a narrow opening, allowing you to peek inside at the controlled hysteria. Expect a sparkling lively cuisine. Begin with shrimp-stuffed ravioli and move on to a zesty grilled tuna with jalapeño beurre-blanc sauce, grilled quail with shiitake mushrooms and Merlot sauce, or veal chops in peppercorn sauce. End this rare experience with a biscotti or a sailor's trifle (sponge cake with layers of blackberry marmalade, custard, and rum). The wine list is impressive.

✪ **Starfire Contemporary Bistro.** 37 New Orleans Rd, New Orleans Plaza. ☎ **843/785-3434.** Reservations recommended. Main courses $19–$29. AE, DC, DISC, MC, V. Mon–Sat 6–9pm. AMERICAN.

Chef Keith Josefiak offers full-bodied cookery that is nonetheless light and imaginative. When he combines products and seasonings, it is like a clever joining of hands, each complementing the other without overpowering. Many of his dishes offer the finest of South Carolina's sea and farmland. The place is offbeat yet has an urban hip, and some of the most demanding palates on the island at any given time flock here to enjoy such original dishes as quesadilla with a Granny Smith salsa and cilantro cream sauce. If not that, dig into his sesame-crusted salmon for a delight to your palate. The vegetarian is also catered to here, and most dishes are cooked to order. Save room for the chef's signature dessert—a ginger peach crème brûlée. You'll be glad you did.

MODERATE

Café Europa. Harbour Town, Sea Pines Plantation. ☎ **843/671-3399.** Reservations recommended for dinner. Main courses $16–$24. AE, MC, V. Daily 10am–2:30pm and 5:30–10pm. CONTINENTAL/SEAFOOD.

This European eatery, one of Hilton Head's finest, is at the base of the much-photographed Harbour Town Lighthouse, opening onto a panoramic view of Calibogue Sound and Daufuskie Island. In a cheerfully informal atmosphere, you can order fish that's poached, grilled, or baked, not always fried. To make your taste buds revel, baked shrimp Daufuskie was inspired by local catches, stuffed with crab, green peppers, and onions. You'll also relish grilled grouper offered with a sauté of tomatoes, cucumbers, dill, and white wine. An intriguing array of specialty dishes include a country-style chicken recipe from Charleston, with honey, fresh cream, and pecans; and tournedos au poivre flambéed with brandy and simmered in a robust green-peppercorn sauce. The fluffy omelets, 14 in all, are served at breakfast (beginning at 10am) and are the island's finest. The heavenly pastries are made in-house daily. The signature dessert is Café Europa's Triple Terring, a chocolate fudge cake with three layers of chocolate mousse (white, milk, and dark) engulfed in chocolate glaze. And the bartender's bloody Mary won an award as "island best" from a *Hilton Head News* contest.

Chart House. Palmetto Bay Marina (at the end of Palmetto Bay Rd.). ☎ **843/785-9666.** Reservations recommended. Early-bird dinner (5–6pm only) $11–$13; main courses $17–$27. Sun–Thurs 5–10pm, Fri–Sat 5–11pm. AMERICAN.

Opening onto Broad Creek, this member of the Chart House chain has a panoramic location and has outdistanced its competitors in the succulent flavor and tenderness of its specialty: prime rib. But seafood lovers will find appetizers and can order the catch of the day (often grouper) as a main dish. This is one of the better Chart Houses, and we've sampled them all, ranging from California to the Virgin Islands. The staff is well trained, and dress is casual. Amazingly, the chef continues to offer unlimited servings of fresh hot bread, so delicious that it usually prevents diners from ordering any extra dishes. Mud pie is the classic dessert.

Fitzgerald's. Adventure Inn. South Beach Forest Dr. ☎ **843/785-5151.** Reservations recommended. Main courses $13–$27. AE, DC, DISC, MC, V. Mon–Sat 5:30–10pm. AMERICAN.

The larger portion of the establishment is for dining on house specialties such as grilled steak, rack of lamb, and various seafood dishes. Very fresh ingredients when possible are used in the creation of these familiar dishes. The kitchen staff has a razor-sharp technique in preparation, and most diners leave full, satisfied, and pleased. If what you desire is a drink, head to the bar just off the main dining area. The small, intimate bar with full liquor and wine lists is perfect for a leisurely drink before or after dinner.

Hudson's Seafood House on the Docks. 1 Hudson Rd. ☎ **843/681-2772.** Reservations not accepted. Main courses $13–$19. AE, DC, MC, V. Daily 11am–2:30pm and 5–10pm. Go to Skull Creek just off Square Pope Rd. (signposted from U.S. 278).

Built as a seafood processing factory in 1912, this restaurant still processes fish, clams, and oysters for local distribution, so you know that everything is fresh. If you're seated in the north dining room, you'll be in the original oyster factory. A few "drydock" courses are on the menu, but we strongly recommend the seafood, such as crab cakes, steamed shrimp, and blackened catch of the day. Local oysters (seasonal) are also a specialty, breaded and deep fried. The cookery is reasonably priced and extremely professional. Before and after dinner, stroll on the docks past shrimp boats and enjoy the view of the mainland and nearby Parris Island. The sunsets here are spectacular. Lunch is served in the Oyster Bar.

✪ **Lagniappe.** 1000 William Hilton Pkwy., Village at Wexford. ☎ **843/341-3377.** Reservations recommended. Main courses $8–$24. AE, MC, V. Tues–Sat 11:30am–4pm and 5–10pm. CONTEMPORARY AMERICAN.

The Lagniappe doubles as a restaurant and Southern folk art gallery. The atmosphere is bright, colorful, and airy. The name of the restaurant comes from an old Creole word meaning "a little something extra," and the chefs live up to the promise in the name. The word is still used in New Orleans to denote a little bonus that a friendly storekeeper might add to a purchase. At lunch the menu is trimmed down but still quite satisfying. For a change of pace, order root chips as an appetizer—thinly sliced root vegetables such as the yucca or sweet potato that are flash fried and seasoned to taste. A selection of salads, both meat (such as grilled salmon) and Caesar, is also offered, followed by a main course such as a delicious fried eggplant over tomato-basil linguine.

We prefer the place in the evening when you can order homemade crab cakes delectably presented with a green curry aioli and a roasted yellow pepper purée. Pastas are succulent, especially the curried lamb with sea scallops and shrimp pan sautéed in a yogurt curry sauce with sun-dried berries and tricolor fettuccine. Spices enliven the main dishes that range from grilled mahimahi in a toasted pecan salsa to an osso bucco, braised veal worthy of Milan where the specialty originated.

Santa Fe Café. 700 Plantation Center. ☎ **843/785-3838.** Reservations recommended. Lunch main courses $6–$8; dinner main courses $14–$26. AE, DISC, MC, V. Mon–Fri noon–2pm; daily 6–10pm. MEXICAN.

This stylish Mexican restaurant boasts a decor inspired by Taos or Santa Fe and a cuisine infusing traditional recipes with nouvelle flair. The setting is as rustic as Mexico's arid highlands. Menu items are fun and imaginative, often presented with colors as bright as the painted desert. They might include tequila shrimp, herb-roasted chicken with jalapeño cornbread stuffing and mashed potatoes laced with red chiles, grilled tenderloin of pork with smoked habañero sauce and sweet-potato fries, and recommendable burritos and chimichangas. The chiles rellenos are exceptional, stuffed with California goat cheese and sun-dried tomatoes; and the quesadilla is one of the most beautifully presented dishes you'll find anywhere in town.

INEXPENSIVE

Crazy Crab North. Hwy. 278 at Jarvis Creek. ☎ **843/681-5021.** Reservations not accepted. Main courses $13–$19. AE, DC, DISC, MC, V. Daily 5–10pm. SEAFOOD.

This is the more desirable of a pair of seafood eateries. In a low-slung modern building near the bridge connecting the island with the South Carolina mainland, it serves baked, broiled, or fried versions of stuffed flounder, seafood kebabs, oysters, catch of the day, or any combination thereof. She-crab soup and New England clam chowder are prepared fresh daily, children's menus are available, and the desserts are considered a high point by chocoholics. This is real down-home cookery prepared with gusto and flair. This is the chain's branch most likely to be patronized year-round by locals.

Hofbrauhaus. Pope Avenue Mall. ☎ **843/785-3663.** Reservations recommended. Early-bird dinner (5–6:30pm only) $13; main courses $10–$18. AE, DISC, MC, V. Daily 5–10pm. GERMAN.

A sanitized version of a Munich beer hall, this family favorite is the only German restaurant on Hilton Head. Since 1973, it has served locals and visitors specialties like grilled bratwurst, smoked Westphalian ham, Wiener schnitzel, and sauerbraten. Guests settle in and delight at this robust, rib-sticking fare, and sometimes have to loosen their belts. A specialty we like to order is roast duckling with spaetzle, red cabbage, and orange sauce. Note the stein and mug collection as you're deciding which of the large variety of German beers to order. A children's menu is available.

4 Beaches, Golf, Tennis & Other Outdoor Pursuits

You can have an active vacation here at any time of year; Hilton Head ranges in temperature from the 50s to the mid-80s in summer. And if you've had your fill of historic sights in Savannah or Charleston, don't worry—the "attractions" on Hilton Head consist mainly of nature preserves, beaches, and other places to play.

As well as featuring exhibits of biodiversity (including aquariums, seashell collections, and environmental and historical exhibits), the **Coastal Discovery Museum**, 100 William Hilton Parkway (☎ 843/689-6767) sponsors nature walks and guided tours of the island. Tours go along island beaches and explore the salt marshes, stopping at Native American sites and the ruins of old forts or long-gone plantations. Most of the emphasis is on the ecology of local plants and animals. Fees are $10 for adults, $5 for children 5 to 12, and free for children 4 and under. You can also call for information about any cruise tours being offered at the time of your visit, with prices ranging from $15 to $25 per person. For reservations, contact the museum Monday to Saturday from 10am to 5pm or Sunday from noon to 4pm (these are the museum's hours as well).

BEACHES

Travel & Leisure has ranked Hilton Head's beaches among the most beautiful in the world, and we concur. The island offers 12 miles of white-sand beaches, plus others fronting Calobogue and Port Royal sounds, all against a backdrop of natural dunes, live oaks, palmettos, and tall Carolina pines. The sands are extremely firm, providing a good surface for biking, hiking, jogging, and beach games. In summer, watch for the endangered loggerhead turtles that lumber ashore at night to bury their eggs.

At high tide, many of the beaches still remain wide for most activities, except biking, of course. At low tide, the width of the island's beaches is often enormous.

All beaches on Hilton Head are public; land bordering the beaches, however, is private property. Most beaches are safe, though there's sometimes an undertow at the northern end of the island. Lifeguards are posted at only the major beaches, and concessions are available to rent you beach chairs, umbrellas, and water-sports equipment.

There are four **public entrances** to Hilton Head's beaches. The main parking and changing areas are on Folly Field Road, off U.S. 278 (the main hwy.) and at Coligny Circle, close to the Holiday Inn. Other entrances (signposted) from U.S. 278 lead to Singleton and Bradley beaches.

The most frequently used beach is adjacent to Coligny Circle: the **North and South Forest Beach** (enter from Pope Ave. across from Lagoon Rd.). You'll have to use the parking lot opposite the Holiday Inn, paying a $4 daily fee until after 4pm. The adjacent Beach Park has toilets and a changing area, as well as showers, vending machines, and phones. It's a family favorite.

Of the beaches on the island's north, we prefer **Folly Field Beach.** Toilets, changing facilities, and parking are available.

GOLF

With 22 challenging golf courses on the island and 9 within a 30-minute drive, this is heaven for professional and novice golfers

A Walk on the Wildlife Side

Hilton Head has preserved more of its wildlife than most other East Coast resort destinations. Birds and alligators roam freely beside lagoons and streams.

Hilton Head Island **alligators** are a prosperous lot, and the S.C. Department of Wildlife and Marine Resources uses the island as a resource to repopulate state parks and preserves where alligator numbers have greatly diminished. These creatures represent no danger if given a respectful distance. However, as strange as it may seem, some unsuspecting visitors, thinking that the dead-still gators are some sort of Disney props, often approach the reptiles and hit or kick at them. Needless to say, this isn't a wise thing to do.

Many of the large **waterbirds** that regularly grace the pages of nature magazines are natives of the island as well. More than 350 species of native American birds have been sighted on the island in the past decade, including the **snowy egret,** the large **blue heron,** and the **osprey.**

And here you'll find the **white ibis** with its strange curving beak as well as the smaller **cattle egrets,** which first arrived on Hilton Head Island in 1954 from a previous South American habitat. They follow the island cows, horses, and tractors to snatch grasshoppers and other insects.

The island's Audubon Society reports around 200 species every year in its annual bird count, but beyond the bird life, Hilton Head counts **deer, bobcat, loggerhead turtles, otter, mink,** and even a few **wild boar** among its residents. The bobcats are difficult to see, lurking in the deepest recesses of the forest preserves

alike. Some of golf's most celebrated architects, including George and Tom Fazio, Robert Trent Jones, Pete Dye, and Jack Nicklaus, have designed championship courses on the island. Wide scenic fairways and rolling greens have earned Hilton Head the reputation of being the resort with the most courses on the World's Best List.

Many of Hilton Head's championship courses are open to the public, including the **George Fazio Course** at the Palmetto Dunes Resort (☎ **843/785-1130**), an 18-hole, 6,534-yard, par-70 course, named in the top 50 of *Golf Digest's* "75 Best American Resort Courses." The cost is $55 to $118 for 18 holes, and hours are daily from 7am to 6pm.

and in the undeveloped areas. The deer, however, are easier to encounter. One of the best places to watch these timid creatures is Sea Pines Plantation, on the southern end of the island. With foresight, the planners of this plantation set aside areas for deer habitat back in the 1950s when the island master plan was conceived. The endangered loggerhead turtle nests extensively along Hilton Head's 12 miles of wide, sandy beaches. Because the turtles choose the darkest hours of the night to crawl ashore and bury eggs in the soft sand, few visitors meet these 200-pound giants. To see them, you have to make a late-night visit to the beach in summer.

Ever-present is the **bottle-nosed dolphin,** usually called a porpoise by those not familiar with the island's sea life. Hilton Head Plantation and Port Royal Plantation adjacent to Port Royal Sound are good places to meet up with the playful dolphin, as are Palmetto Dunes and Forest Beach. In summer, dolphins are inclined to feed on small fish and sea creatures close to shore. Island beaches are popular with bikers, and this often offers a real point of interest for these curious fellows, who sometimes seem to swim along with the riders. Several excursion boats offer tours from the island and provide an opportunity for fellowship with dolphins. Shrimp boats are guaranteed to attract hungry dolphins.

The Sea Pines Forest Preserve, the Newhall Audubon Preserve, and the Pinckney Island Wildlife Preserve, just off the island between the bridges, are of interest to nature lovers. The Museum of Hilton Head hosts several guided nature tours and historical walks. For information, call the museum at ☎ **843/689-6767.**

The **Old South Golf Links,** 50 Buckingham Plantation Dr., Bluffton (☎ **800/257-8997** or 843/785-5353), is an 18-hole, 6,772-yard, par-72 course that's open daily from 7:30am to 7pm. It's recognized as one of the "Top 10 New Public Courses" by *Golf Digest,* which cites its panoramic views and setting, ranging from an oak forest to tidal salt marshes. Greens fees are $65 before noon; $55 after noon. The course lies on Hwy. 278, a mile before the bridge leading to Hilton Head.

The **Hilton Head National,** Hwy. 278 (☎ **843/842-5900**), is a Gary Player Signature Golf Course, including a full-service pro shop and a grill and driving range. This 18-hole, 6,779-yard, par-72 course boasts gorgeous scenery that evokes Scotland. Greens fees range from $52 to $100, and hours are daily from 7:45am to 7pm.

The **Island West Golf Club,** Hwy. 278 (☎ **843/689-6660**), was nominated by *Golf Digest* in 1992 as "Best New Course of the Year." With its backdrop of oaks, elevated tees, and rolling fairways, it's a challenging but playable 18-hole, 6,803-yard, par-72 course. Greens fees range from $35 to $65, and hours are daily from 7am to 6pm.

The **Harbour Town Golf Links,** at the Sea Pines Resort (☎ **843/363-4485**), home of the annual MCI Heritage Classic, is also outstanding. The panoramic views alone are worth the visit to this 18-hole, 6,916-yard, par-71 course. Its finishing hole fronts the waters of Calibogue Sound. Greens fees are $190, and hours are daily from 7am to 6:30pm.

Ocean Course, at the Sea Pines Resort (☎ **843/842-1894**), the island's first, is still favored as a resort classic. Its dramatic beachfront 15th hole is one of the most photographed on Hilton Head, with its views of the ocean. Renovated in 1995, the 18-hole, 6,933-yard, par-72 course is open daily from 6:45am to 6:30pm. Greens fees are $52 to $85 for 18 holes.

The **Robert Trent Jones Course** at the Palmetto Dunes Resort (☎ **843/785-1138**) is an 18-hole, 6,710-yard, par-72 course with a winding lagoon system that comes into play on 11 holes. The cost is $55 to $70 for greens fees for 18 holes, and hours are daily from 6:30am to 6pm.

TENNIS

Tennis magazine has rated Hilton Head as one of the 50 best tennis destinations in the country. No other domestic destination can boast of a greater concentration of facilities, with more than 300 courts divided among 19 tennis clubs (7 of these clubs are open to the public). Programs and clinics are available for all ability levels.

The **Sea Pines Racquet Club,** at the Sea Pines Plantation (☎ **843/563-4495**), has been ranked by *Tennis* magazine as a top-50 resort and was selected by the *Robb Report* as the best tennis resort in the United States. The club has been the site of more nationally televised tennis events than any other and is the home of the *Family Circle* Magazine Cup Women's Tennis Championships. Tennis is free to guests of the hotel; otherwise, there's a $20 charge per hour. There are 23 clay and 5 hard courts (hard courts are lit for night play), and hours daily are 8am to 7pm.

Other leading tennis courts are at the **Port Royal Racquet Club,** at the Port Royal Plantation (☎ **843/686-8803**), which offers 10 clay and 4 hard courts, plus 2 natural-grass courts with night games possible. Charges range from $6 per hour, and a 1-day reservation is recommended.

The **Hilton Head Island Beach and Tennis Resort,** 40 Folly Field Rd. (☎ **843/842-4402**), features a dozen hard, lighted courts, costing only $8 per hour. The **Palmetto Dunes Tennis Center,** at the Palmetto Dunes Resort (☎ **843/785-1152**), has 23 clay, 2 hard, and 4 artificial-grass courts (some lighted for night play). Hotel guests get a discount; otherwise, the charge is $23 per hour.

OTHER OUTDOOR ACTIVITIES

BIKING   Some beaches are firm enough to support wheels, and every year cyclists seem to delight in dodging the waves. Children on bikes often appear to be racing the fast-swimming dolphins in the nearby water. Enjoy Hilton Head's 25 miles of bicycle paths, but stay off U.S. 278, the main artery, which has far too much traffic.

Most hotels and resorts rent bikes to guests. If yours doesn't, try **Hilton Head Bicycle Co.,** off Sea Pines Circle at 11B Archer Dr. (☎ **843/686-6888**). The cost is $12 per day but only $18 for 3 days or $25 for a week. Baskets, child carriers, locks, and head gear are supplied, and the inventory includes cruisers, BMXs, mountain bikes, and tandems. Hours are Monday to Friday from 9am to 5pm and Saturday and Sunday from 9am to 5pm.

Another possibility is **South Beach Cycles,** South Beach Marina Village in Sea Pines (☎ **843/671-2453**), offering beach cruisers, tandems, child carriers, and bikes for kids. There's free delivery island-wide. The cost is $8 for a half day, $10 for a full day, $19 for 3 days, or $25 for a week. It's open Monday to Friday from 9am to 5pm, Saturday and Sunday from 9am to 6pm.

HORSEBACK RIDING   Riding through beautiful maritime forests and nature preserves is reason enough to visit Hilton Head. We like **Lawton Fields Stables,** 190 Greenwood Dr., Sea Pines (☎ **843/671-2586**), offering rides for both adults and kids through the Sea Pines Forest Preserve. (Kids ride ponies.) The cost is $30 per person for a ride lasting about 1 hour. You must reserve with a credit card, and kids must be at least 8 years old.

Happy Trails (☎ **843/842-7433**) offers 1-hour tours Monday to Saturday in the 5,000-acre Buckingham Plantation. Happy Trails departs twice daily, at 9:30 and 11am. Because they travel in small groups, they suggest that you call 1 or 2 days in advance to make reservations. The prices are $20 for adults and $15 for children 12 and under.

Lawton Stables (☎ 843/671-2586) offers trail rides Monday to Saturday in the 600-acre preserve at Sea Pines Plantation. Trail rides depart five times daily, at 8:30am, 10am, 11:30am, 4pm, and 5:30pm for anyone 8 years or older, costing $35 per hour. Riding lessons can be scheduled daily for $40, and pony rides are available for children under 8 years, from 10am to 4:30pm, for $5.

JOGGING   Our favorite place for jogging is a run through Harbour Town at Sea Pines just as the sun is going down. Later you can explore the marina and have a refreshing drink at one of the many outdoor cafes. In addition, the island offers lots of paved paths and trails that cut through scenic areas. Jogging along U.S. 278, the main artery, can be dangerous because of heavy traffic.

NATURE PRESERVES   The **Audubon–Newhall Preserve,** Palmetto Bay Road (☎ 843/785-5775), is a 50-acre preserve on the south end of the island. Here you can walk along marked trails to observe the wildlife in its native habitat. Guided tours are available when plant life is blooming. Except for public toilets, there are no amenities. It's open from sunrise to sunset and admission is free.

The second leading preserve is also in the south of the island. **Sea Pines Forest Preserve,** at the Sea Pines Plantation (☎ 843/671-6486), is a 605-acre public wilderness with marked walking trails. You can see nearly all the birds and animals known to live on Hilton Head (yes, there are alligators, but there are also less fearsome creatures, such as egrets, herons, osprey, and white-tailed deer). All trails lead to public picnic areas in the center of the forest. Maps and toilets are available. It's open from sunrise to sunset year-round, except during the Heritage Golf Classic in early April. There's a $5 fee to enter for guests not staying at the Sea Pines Resort.

WATER SPORTS

CRUISES & TOURS   To explore Hilton Head's waters, contact **Adventure Cruises,** Shelter Cove Harbour, Suite G, Harbourside III (☎ 843/785-4558). Outings include a nature cruise to Daufuskie Island (made famous by Pat Conroy's *The Water Is Wide* and the film *Conrack*), with a guided safari on a jungle bus, costing $18 for adults and $7 for children round-trip. Departures are daily at 12:15pm, with a return to Hilton Head at 4:45pm on a guided bus, costing $10 for adults and $5 for children.

Other popular cruises include a dolphin-watch cruise, 2 hours long, costing $17 for adults and $7 for children. A sunset dinner cruise aboard the vessel *Adventure* costs $29 for adults and $15 for children, including a 3-hour look at the Carolina Low Country and an all-you-can-eat buffet.

FISHING No license is needed for saltwater fishing, though fresh-water licenses are required for the island's lakes and ponds. The general season for fishing offshore is from April to October, and inland fishing is good between September and December. Crabbing is also popular; crabs are easy to catch in low water from docks or boats or right off a bank.

Off Hilton Head you can go deep-sea fishing for amberjack, barracuda, sharks, and king mackerel. Many vessels are available for rent. We've recommended only those with the best track record. Foremost is **A Fishin' Mission,** 145 Squire Pope Rd. (☎ 843/785-9177), captained by Charles Getsinger aboard his 34-foot *Sportsfish.* Ice, bait, and tackle are included. Reservations are needed 1 to 2 days in advance. The craft carries up to six, costing $315 for half a day, $475 for three-quarters of a day, and $630 for a full day.

The **Harbour Town Yacht Basin,** at the Harbour Town Marina (☎ 843/671-2704), has five boats available at various sizes and prices. *The Manatee,* a 40-foot vessel, can carry a group of 6 to 15. The rates are set for 6 passengers: $365 for 4 hours, $548 for 6 hours, and $730 for 8 hours. Each passenger over 6 costs an extra $12.50 per hour. *The Hero* and *The Echo* are 32-foot ships. Their rates for a group of 6 are $325 for 4 hours, $490 for 6 hours, and $680 for 8 hours. They also have a smaller three-passenger inshore boat that's priced at $225 for 4 hours, $340 for 6 hours, and $450 for 8 hours.

A cheaper way to go deep-sea fishing, for only $35 to $40 per person, is aboard *The Drifter* (☎ 843/671-3060), a party boat departing from the South Beach Marina Village. Ocean-bottom fishing is possible at an artificial reef 12 miles offshore.

KAYAKING **Eco-Kayak Tours,** at the Palmetto Bay Marina (☎ 843/785-7131), operates guided tours in Broad Creek. Four or five trips are offered each day; most cost $35 per person, and anyone from age 7 to 82 is welcome. The Ascatsgrin outing begins at 8am; the excursion lasts 2 hours and costs $35 for adults and $25 for children under 12. The tour explores the South Carolina Low Country environment, and you'll see local wildlife along the way.

Outside Hilton Head, both the **Plaza at Shelter Cove** (☎ 843/686-6996) and the affiliated **South Beach Marina Village** (☎ 843/671-2643) allow you to tour Low Country waterways by kayak. A 2-hour Dolphin Nature Tour, costing $35, takes you through the salt-marsh creeks of the Calibogue Sound or Pinckney Island Wildlife Refuge. Their Off-Island Day Excursion at $60 per person goes along the Carolina barrier islands and the surrounding marshlands. These trips are 6 to 8 hours long and include lunch.

PARASAILING   Para-Sail Hilton Head, Harbour Town (☎ 843/363-2628), takes you in a Sea Rocket powerboat for parasailing daily from 8am to 7pm. The cost is $39 per person for 400 feet of line or $49 for 800 feet of line, and reservations are necessary. Catamaran rides for up to six are also a feature, and sailing lessons are offered.

SAILING   Ascatsgrin Sailing Charters, 86 Helmsman Way Palmetto Bay Marina (☎ 843/785-7131), is the largest charter sailboat outfitter on Hilton Head. You can pack a picnic lunch and bring your cooler aboard for a 2-hour trip in the morning, afternoon, or at sunset. The cost is $25 per person.

Flying Circus Sailing Charters, 86 Hemsman (☎ 843/785-7131 or 843/686-2582), offers 2-hour boat trips on the island's fastest and most fun catamarans. Dolphin, sunset, and moonlight cruises are daily features. Spend the afternoon enjoying the natural and beautiful scenery. Boats are limited to six passengers, but are spacious. The cost is $25 per seat for 2 hours, an additional $60 if over 2 hours. Private charters are also available for $150. Fishing boats and parasailing crafts are rented as well.

WINDSURFING   Just outside Hilton Head, the **South Beach Marina Village** (☎ 843/671-2643) offers board rentals for $55 to $70. Windsurfing lessons are available at $45 to $75 for 3- to 6-hour courses.

OTHER WATER SPORTS   H20, Harbour Town (☎ 843/671-4386), features Yamaha WaveRunner rentals costing $39 single or $49 double by the hour. Parasailing is also a feature, costing $49 per person for either a 400-foot or 800-foot line. Waterskiing is a major summer activity. Two hours cost $150 for up to five passengers, and surfing, kneeboarding, and hydrosliding are included in the waterskiing price. The outfitter also offers 1-hour dolphin cruises costing $20 for adults and $17 for children. The center is next to the lighthouse, and hours are daily from 8am to 7pm.

5 Shopping

Hilton Head is a browsing heaven, with more than 30 shopping centers spread around the island, stocked with everything from designer clothing to island and Low Country crafts.

The major shopping areas are **Pinelawn Mall,** at Matthews Drive and U.S. 278, with more than 30 shops and half a dozen restaurants; and **Coligny Plaza,** at Coligny Circle (☎ 843/842-6050 for information), with more than 60 shops, a movie theater, food stands, and several good restaurants.

We've found some of the best bargains in the South at the **Low Country Factory Outlet Village** (☎ 843/837-4339), on Hwy. 278 at the gateway to Hilton Head. Here are more than 45 factory stores, including Laura Ashley, Brooks Brothers, and J. Crew. The hours of most shops in complexes are Monday to Saturday from 10am to 9pm and Sunday from 11am to 6pm.

ART

Hammock Company. 20 Jefferson St., City Market. ☎ **800/344-4264** or 843/686-3636.

This outlet specializes in limited-edition and original wildlife prints, each numbered and signed. There's also a catalog of prints available.

Morris & Whiteside Galleries. 807 William Hilton Pkwy., Suite 1302. ☎ **843/842-4433.**

A wide collection of 19th- and 20th-century American paintings and sculpture is offered here. The gallery is strong on Western masters and cowboy art, with still lifes, frontier landscapes, and genre scenes.

BOOKS

Book Warehouse. Festival Centre, next to Publix. ☎ **843/689-9419.**

This outlet offers new books sometimes at discounts of 50% to 90% off publisher's retail. Best-sellers, history books, children's books, cookbooks, and computer books are sold, with profits given to the Cancer Research Department at Emory University Hospital.

CRYSTAL

Crystal Gallery. 1 Mathews Court, Suite D. ☎ **843/342-2002.**

This is one of the island's most exciting new galleries. Here you'll find a collection of exquisite crystals, original art, artistic crystal jewelry, handmade dolls, pottery, sculpture, aromatherapy candles, and indoor fountains in every style and size.

Late-Night Bites

When you think of Hilton Head, a nightlife of raving parties may not come to mind, but that will change after visiting "The Bermuda Triangle" of three enjoyable watering holes at Hilton Head Shopping Plaza, Sea Pines Circle.

For those seeking a place to socialize and mingle, the place to go is **The Lodge** (☎ 843/842-8966). The decor has the atmosphere of a rustic ski lodge mixed with that of a martini-and-cigar bar. Open daily from 4pm to 2am, and charging no cover, the patrons are welcomed with antler chandeliers, four pool tables, a walk-in humidor, a full menu of single malts, a large selection of cigars, and two stone fireplaces complete with roaring fires.

For a more upbeat environment, step across the hall to Hilton Head's first state brew pub, **Hilton Head Brewing Company** (☎ 843/785-2789), where you can enjoy a full menu of appetizers, plus seafood and steak main courses, daily from 11am to 2am. The hardwood interior is enhanced with beer memorabilia and live entertainment from professional performers to the pub-goers on Friday, karaoke night. The highlight of the week is Wednesday, better known as disco night on the island. There is no cover and by midnight a hip young crowd has arrived.

For more snug surroundings, **Moneypenny's** (☎ 843/785-7878) is where you'll want to go. This underground locals bar offers live performances, a large selection of wines, and a candle-light setting full of cozy couches and modern artwork. There is no cover to enter the bar, open daily from 9pm to 4am.

GIFTS & CRAFTS

Harbour Town Crafts. Harbour Town. ☎ 843/671-3643.

In the most scenic spot on the island, this store offers dozens of gifts and decorative items along with handcrafted jewelry. The famed Low Country sweetgrass baskets are also for sale, but be warned that the prices are high.

GOLD & JEWELRY

Forsythe Jewelers. 311 Sea Pines Center. ☎ 843/671-7070.

Three generations of the Forsythe family have been selling one-of-a-kind pieces of jewelry, along with fine watches and unusual gifts, since 1927.

Goldsmith Shop. 3 Lagoon Rd. (off Pope Ave.). ☎ **843/785-2538.**

Here you'll find the exquisite work of Gary Fronczak, who crafts many of the items sold. The shop is known for its signature island charms; Gary can create a piece just for you.

PORCELAIN & CHINA

Villeroy & Boch. Low Country Factory Village, Hwy. 278. ☎ **843/837-2566.**

This is the best center for bone china, quality porcelain, and crystal. Gift items and even heirloom pieces are for sale as well.

SPORTS EQUIPMENT

Players World. The Market Place. ☎ **843/842-5100.**

The island's best-equipped sports store is a 10,000-square-foot emporium, with all sorts of tennis gear, along with beachwear and plenty of athletic footwear.

6   Hilton Head After Dark

Hilton Head doesn't have the nightlife of, say, Myrtle Beach, to the north. As a result, it doesn't attract the serious party-goers that the Grand Strand does. But there's still a lot here, centered mainly at the hotels and resorts. Casual dress (but not swimsuits) is acceptable in most clubs.

Cultural interest focuses on the **Hilton Head Playhouse,** Dunnagan's Alley, at Arrow Road (☎ 843/842-2787), which enjoys one of the best theatrical reputations in the Southeast. Shows seat 225 persons at 8pm Tuesday to Saturday. Begun almost 3 decades ago, the theater presents a wide range of musicals, contemporary comedies, and classic dramas in a renovated warehouse. A 350-seat state-of-the-art theater was completed in 1996. Adult ticket prices range from $19 to $26 for a play to $24 to $39 for a musical. Children 16 and under pay $12.

Here are some island hot spots for drinks, music, or laughs:

Jazz Corner. The Village at Wexford. ☎ **843/842-8620.** No cover.

This dinner/jazz bar offers a full night's entertainment. The intimate environment is enhanced with musical jazz performances. The Corner also pleases its guests with a full menu of appetizers and main courses such as veal marsala, filet mignon topped with crabmeat, or their signature burger, "the Corner Burger." Menu items range from $9 to $25.

Quarterdeck. Harbour Town, Sea Pines Plantation. ☎ **843/671-2222.** No cover, but you must pay $3 at the gate to Sea Pines.

Our favorite waterfront lounge is the best place on the island to watch sunsets, but you can visit at any time during the day after noon and in the evening until 2am. Bar food is available. Try to go early and grab one of the outdoor rocking chairs to prepare yourself for nature's light show. There's dancing every night to beach music and Top 40 hits.

Remy's. 28 Arrow Rd. ☎ **843/842-3800.** No cover.

This bar is ideal late at night, when many other places on Hilton Head have closed. The setting is rustic and raffish, and live music is often on tap. Got the munchies? You can devour buckets of oysters or shrimp served with the inevitable fries. Open Monday to Friday from 11am to 4pm and Saturday from 11am to 2pm.

Salty Dog Café. South Beach Marina. ☎ **843/671-2233.** No cover.

Locals used to keep this laid-back place near the beach to themselves, but now more and more visitors are showing up. Soft guitar music or tunes like Jimmy Buffett's "Margaritaville" usually provide the background. Dress is casual. Sit under one of the sycamores, enjoying your choice of food from an outdoor grill or buffet.

Signals. 130 Shipyard Dr. (in the Crystal Sands Crowne Plaza Resort). ☎ **843/842-2400.** No cover.

In this upscale resort you can enjoy live bands, often performing 1940s golden oldies, along with R&B, blues, and jazz. The dance floor is generally crowded. Bands perform Tuesday to Sunday from 11:30am to 2am, and live jazz is heard on Monday from 6 to 9:30pm. A Sunday brunch is presented from noon to 2pm at Umbrellas cafe, also on-site.

5

Savannah: The Old South with a Touch of Decadence

*I*f you have time to visit only one city in the Southeast, make it Savannah. It's that special.

Nothing has changed the face of Savannah more than the 1994 publication of John Berendt's *Midnight in the Garden of Good and Evil* and the 1997 release of the film, directed by Clint Eastwood. The impact has been unprecedented, bringing in millions in revenue as thousands flock to see the sights described in the huge best-seller. Savannah tourism has increased some 45% since publication of what's known locally as "The Book." Many locals now earn their living off The Book's fallout, hawking postcards, walking tours, T-shirts, and in some cases their own careers, as in the case of the Lady Chablis, the black drag queen depicted in The Book who played herself in the Eastwood film (see "Visitor Information" in chapter 1 for the Lady's Web sites).

Since The Book and The Film (which was, alas, not as big a hit as The Book), real-estate prices have soared in Savannah. Once nearly deserted streets in the historic district are busy and thriving again, as tour buses roll through with guides pointing out sites mentioned by Berendt, particularly where the late antiques dealer Jim Williams lived at Mercer House before killing his assistant/hustler lover, Danny Hansford.

"What's special about Savannah?" we once asked an old-timer. "Why, here we even have water fountains for dogs," he said. And that's not mentioning the members of the Married Woman's Card Club, the Lady Chablis, and all the other unique personalities and events both mentioned and not mentioned in The Book.

The free spirit, the passion, and even the decadence of Savannah resemble that of Key West or New Orleans more than the Bible Belt down-home interior of Georgia. In that sense, it's as different from Georgia as New York City is from Upper New York State. Is it any wonder that Aaron Spelling set his short-lived steamy nighttime soap here?

*If you go to Atlanta, the first question people ask is, "What's your
business?" In Macon they ask, "Where do you go to church?" In
Augusta they ask, "What's your grandmother's maiden name?" In
Savannah the first question they ask is, "What would you like to
drink?"*

—Savannah saying

Savannah—pronounce it with a drawl—conjures up the cliche
images of the Deep South: live oaks dripping with Spanish moss,
stately antebellum mansions, mint juleps sipped on the veranda,
magnolia trees, peaceful marshes, horse-drawn carriages, and even
memories of General Sherman, no one's favorite military hero.

Today the economy and much of the city's day-to-day life still
revolve around port activity. For the visitor, however, it's Old Savannah, a beautifully restored and maintained historic area, that
draws the most attention. For this we can thank seven Savannah ladies who, after watching mansion after mansion be demolished in
the name of progress, managed in 1954 to raise funds to buy the
dilapidated Isaiah Davenport house—just hours before it was slated
for demolition to make way for a parking lot. The women banded
together as the Historic Savannah Foundation, then went to work
buying up architecturally valuable buildings and reselling them to
private owners who'd promise to restore them. As a result, more
than 800 of the 1,100 historic buildings of Old Savannah have been
restored, using original paint colors—pinks and reds and blues and
greens. This living museum is the largest urban National Historic
Landmark District in the country—some $2^1/_2$ square miles, including 20 1-acre squares that still survive from Gen. James Oglethorpe's
dream of a gracious city.

A LOOK AT THE PAST

Spanish missions gained a brief foothold on St. Simons and Jekyll
islands as early as 1566, but "civilization" came to stay on this part
of the Atlantic coast on February 12, 1733, when Gen. James
Oglethorpe arrived at Yamacraw Bluff with 114 English settlers
(mostly nonconformist Protestants and former inmates of England's
debtor prisons who were looking at the New World for a new beginning). Oglethorpe's idealism encompassed a new future for the
unfortunates he'd brought along. He planned a town that would

provide space, beauty, and comfort for every resident of the colony: a settlement of houses, each with its own garden plot, laid out around town squares (there were 24 in the original plan) and with an orderly mercantile section. In this respect, Savannah was America's very first planned city.

The natural deep-water harbor soon attracted Spanish, Portuguese, German, Scottish, and Irish immigrants, and a lively sea trade brought seafarers from all over the world—along with hordes of pirates who put into port from time to time. In 1775, when Savannah got word that war had broken out at Lexington, Massachusetts, a patriot battalion was hastily formed. Savannah changed hands frequently during the Revolution. The city was named the state capital following the 1776 Declaration of Independence and remained so until 1807, when proslavers managed to have the government moved to Milledgeville.

The years between the Revolutionary and Civil wars were a period of prosperity for Savannah; many of the Classic Revival, Regency, and Georgian colonial homes you'll see restored today were built at that time. It was the era of King Cotton and great tobacco farms. Cotton "factors" (brokers) kept track of huge fortunes along River Street on what came to be known as Factors Walk. Through it all, builders, merchants, and shippers kept to Oglethorpe's master plan for the city, preserving the parks and squares in the midst of the commercial hubbub.

When secession rumblings reached fever pitch in 1861, Georgia's governor ordered state troops to seize Fort Pulaski, 15 miles east of Savannah, even though the state didn't withdraw from the Union until 16 days later. The war brought devastation to the area, since Sherman ended his march to the sea here in December 1864. Sherman entered Savannah more quietly than was his usual custom; because Confederate General Hardee had already evacuated his troops, Savannah was spared the destruction that befell Atlanta and other towns in Sherman's path.

1 Orientation

ARRIVING

Savannah International Airport is 8 miles west of downtown just off I-95. **American** (☎ 800/433-7300), **Delta** (☎ 800/221-1212), **United** (☎ 800/241/6522), and **US Airways** (☎ 800/428-4322) have flights from Atlanta and Charlotte, which are both served by many other carriers. **Limousine service** from the airport to downtown locations (☎ **912/966-5364**) costs $16 plus $5 for each additional passenger. **Taxi fare** is $18 for one person and $5 for each extra passenger; call **Yellow Cab** (☎ **912/236-1133**).

From north or south, I-95 passes 10 miles west of Savannah, with several exits to the city, and U.S. 17 runs through the city; from the west, I-16 ends in downtown Savannah and U.S. 80 also runs through the city from east to west. AAA services in Savannah are available through **AAA Auto Club South,** 712 Mall Blvd. (☎ **912/352-8222**).

The **train station** is at 2611 Seaboard Coastline Dr. (☎ **912/234-2611**), some 4 miles southwest of downtown. For **Amtrak** schedule and fare information, call ☎ **800/USA-RAIL.** Cab fare into the city is around $4.

VISITOR INFORMATION

The **Savannah Visitor Center** at 301 Martin Luther King Jr. Blvd., Savannah, GA 31401 (☎ **912/944-0455**), is open Monday to Friday from 8:30am to 5pm and Saturday and Sunday from 8:30am to 5pm. The staff is friendly and efficient. Offered here are an audiovisual presentation costing $3 for adults, $2.50 for seniors, and $1.75 for children; organized tours; and self-guided walking, driving, or bike tours with excellent maps, cassette tapes, and brochures.

Tourist information is also available from the **Savannah Area Convention & Visitors Bureau,** 222 W. Oglethorpe Ave., Savannah, GA 31401 (☎ **877/SAVANNAH** or 912/694-6401; www.savannahvisit.com). For information on current happenings, call the **Arts Line** at ☎ **912/236-7284,** ext. 456.

CITY LAYOUT

Every other street—north, south, west, and east—is punctuated by a "green lung." The grid of **21 scenic squares** was laid out by Gen. James Oglethorpe, the founder of Georgia, in 1733. The design, still in use, has been called "one of the world's most revered city plans." It has been said that if Savannah didn't have its history and its architecture, it would be worth a visit just to see the city layout.

Bull Street is the dividing line between east and west. On the south side is odd numeration of street numbers, with even street numbers falling on the north side.

NEIGHBORHOODS IN BRIEF

Historic District The real reason to visit Savannah, the Historic District takes in both the Riverfront and the City Market, described below. It's bordered by the Savannah River and Forsyth Park at Gwinett Street and Montgomery and Price streets. Within it are more than 2,350 architecturally and historically significant buildings in a 2^1/$_2$-square-mile area. About 75% of these buildings have been restored.

Riverfront   The most popular tourist district, Riverfront borders the Savannah River. In 1818, about one-half of Savannah fell under a quarantine during a yellow-fever epidemic. River Street, once lined with warehouses holding King Cotton, never fully recovered and fell into disrepair, until its rediscovery in the mid-1970s. A massive urban-renewal project turned this strip into a row of restaurants, art galleries, shops, and bars.

City Market   The market lies at Jefferson and West Julian streets, bounded by Franklin Square on its western flank and Ellis Square on its eastern. Two blocks from River Street and bordering the Savannah River, City Market was Savannah's former social and business mecca. Since the late 18th century, it has known fires and devastation, including a threatened demolition. But in a major move, the city decided to save the district. Today, once-decaying warehouses are filled with restaurants and shops, offering everything from antiques to collectibles, including many Savannah-made products. Everything from seafood and pizza to French and Italian cuisine is served here. Live music often fills the nighttime air—some of the best jazz in the city.

Victorian District   The Victorian District, south of the Historic District, holds some of the Deep South's finest examples of post–Civil War architecture. The district is bounded by Martin Luther King Jr. Boulevard, East Broad Street, and Gwinnett and Anderson streets. Houses here are characterized by gingerbread trim, stained-glass windows, and imaginative architectural details. In all, the district encompasses an area of nearly 50 blocks, spread across some 165 acres. The entire district became listed in the National Register of Historic Places in 1974. Most of the two-story homes are wood frame and were constructed in the late 1800s on brick foundations. The district, overflowing from the historic inner core of the city, became the first suburb of Savannah.

2 Getting Around

Though you can reach many points of interest outside the Historic District by bus, your own wheels will be much more convenient,

Impressions

For me, Savannah's resistance to change was its saving grace. The city looked inward, sealed off from the noises and distractions of the world at large. It grew inward, too, and in such a way that its people flourished like hothouse plants tended by an indulgent gardener. The ordinary became extraordinary. Eccentrics thrived. Every nuance and quirk of personality achieved greater brilliance in that lush enclosure than would have been possible anywhere else in the world.

—John Berendt, *Midnight in the Garden of Good and Evil (1994)*

and they're absolutely essential for sightseeing outside the city proper.

All major car-rental firms have branches in Savannah and at the airport, and it pays to shop around for those with the best rates and unlimited mileage. Try **Hertz** (☎ 800/654-3131 or 912/964-9595 at the airport); **Avis** (☎ 800/331-1212), with offices at 422 Airways Ave. (☎ 912/964-1781) and 2215 Travis Field Rd. (☎ 912/964-0234); and **Budget** (☎ 800/527-0700), with offices at 7070 Abercorn (☎ 912/966-1771).

To take the local **city buses,** you'll need exact change for the $1 fare, plus 5¢ for a transfer. For route and schedule information, call **Chatham Area Transit** (CAT) at ☎ **912/233-5767.**

The grid-shaped Historic District is best seen on foot, and, in fact, the real point of your visit is to take leisurely strolls with frequent stops in the many squares. The base rate for **taxis** is 60¢, with $1.20 extra for each mile. For 24-hour taxi service, call **Adam Cab Co.** at ☎ **912/927-7466.**

FAST FACTS: Savannah

American Express   The American Express office has closed, but cardholders can obtain assistance locally by calling ☎ **912/920-0020.**

Dentist   For complete dental care and emergencies, go to **Abercorn South Side Dental,** 11139 Abercorn St. (☎ **912/925-9190**).

Drugstore   Drugstores are scattered throughout Savannah. One with longer hours is **CVS,** 11607 Abercorn St. (☎ **912/925-5568**), open Monday to Saturday from 8am to midnight and Sunday from 10am to 8pm.

Emergencies   Dial ☎ **911** for police, ambulance, or fire emergencies.

Hospitals   There are 24-hour emergency room services at **Candler General Hospital,** 5353 Reynolds St. (☎ **912/692-6637**), and **Memorial Medical Center,** 4800 Waters Ave. (☎ **912/350-8390**).

Newspapers   The *Savannah Morning News* is a daily filled with information about local cultural and entertainment events. The *Savannah Tribune* and the *Herald of Savannah* are geared to the African-American community.

Police   Call ☎ **911** for emergencies, or ☎ **912/232-4141** to reach the local police for non-emergency matters.

Post Office   Post offices and sub–post offices are centrally located and open Monday to Friday from 7am to 6pm and Saturday from 9am to 3pm. The **main office** is at 2 N. Fahn St. (☎ **912/235-4653**).

Safety   Although it's reasonably safe to explore the Victorian and Historic Districts during the day, the situation changes at night. The clubs along the riverfront, both bars and restaurants, report very little crime. However, muggings and drug dealing are common in the poorer neighborhoods. Wander in those neighborhoods at night only with great caution.

Taxes   The city of Savannah adds a 2% local option tax to the 4% state tax.

Weather   Call ☎ **912/964-1700.**

3 Accommodations

The undisputed stars here are the small inns in the Historic District, most in restored old homes that have been renovated with modern conveniences while retaining every bit of their original charm. Book into one of these if you want to experience Savannah graciousness firsthand.

Only Charleston has more historic inns than Savannah. After a burst of hotel openings, Savannah's hotel scene seems to have quieted down. Of course, those who don't want the charm of the restored homes will find such big names as Hyatt and Marriott still going strong. The cheapest lodgings remain the chain hotels and motels on the periphery of the Historic District, though most are

---

A Note on Rates

Because many of Savannah's historic inns are in former converted residences, prices within an individual hotel can vary greatly. A very expensive hotel might have some smaller and more moderately priced rooms because of the architectural layout of the building, for instance.

---

without distinction and could be along the road of any major artery leading into any garden-variety American town.

Advance reservations are absolutely necessary in most cases, since many of the best properties are small.

ALONG THE RIVERFRONT

EXPENSIVE

Hyatt Regency Savannah. 2 W. Bay St., Savannah, GA 31401. ☎ **800/ 223-1234** or 912/238-1234. Fax 912/944-3678. www.hyatt.com. E-mail: ccharness@savrspo.hyatt.com. 347 units. A/C TV TEL. $129–$290 double; $275–$900 suite. AE, DC, DISC, MC, V. Parking $12.

You should've heard the outcry among Savannah's historic preservation movement when this place went up in 1981. Boxy and massively bulky, it stands in unpleasant contrast to the restored warehouses flanking it on either side along the legendary banks of the Savannah River. Today, it's grudgingly accepted as the biggest and flashiest hotel in town, the one best suited for corporate conventions. As in Hyatts everywhere, there's a soaring atrium as well as glass-sided elevators. The midsize rooms are comfortable, modern, and international in their feel, many with balconies overlooking the atrium. The rates vary according to the views—the units without views are quite a bargain. You'll find a stylish bar and two restaurants with a big-city feel and views over the river. Facilities include a health club, an indoor pool, and a small fitness room.

Olde Harbour Inn. 508 E. Factors Walk, Savannah, GA 31401. ☎ **800/ 553-6533** or 912/234-4100. Fax 912/233-5979. 24 units. A/C TV TEL. $129– $199 1-bedroom suite; $169–$229 2-bedroom suite. Rates include continental breakfast and wine and cheese in the afternoon. AE, DC, DISC, MC, V. Parking $5 nearby.

The neighborhood has been gentrified and the interior of this place is well furnished, but you still get a whiff of riverfront seediness as you approach from Factors Walk's eastern end. It was built in 1892 as a warehouse for oil, and its masonry bulk is camouflaged with shutters, awnings, and touches of wrought iron. Inside, a labyrinth

Savannah Accommodations

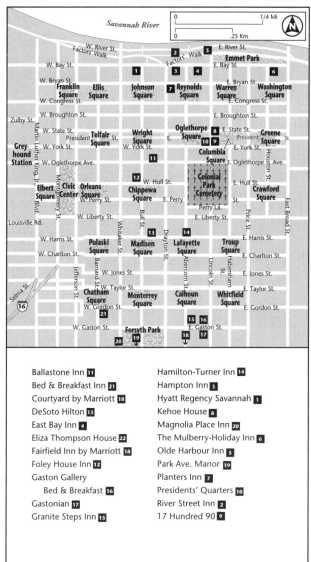

Ballastone Inn 11

Bed & Breakfast Inn 21

Courtyard by Marriott 18

DeSoto Hilton 13

East Bay Inn 4

Eliza Thompson House 22

Fairfield Inn by Marriott 18

Foley House Inn 12

Gaston Gallery
   Bed & Breakfast 16

Gastonian 17

Granite Steps Inn 15

Hamilton-Turner Inn 14

Hampton Inn 3

Hyatt Regency Savannah 1

Kehoe House 8

Magnolia Place Inn 20

The Mulberry-Holiday Inn 6

Olde Harbour Inn 5

Park Ave. Manor 19

Planters Inn 7

Presidents' Quarters 10

River Street Inn 2

17 Hundred 90 9

of passages leads to small but comfortable suites, many of which show the building's massive timbers and structural iron brackets and offer views of the river. Each unit contains its own kitchen, a useful option for anyone in town for an extended stay. Despite the overlay of chintz, you'll have a constant sense of the building's thick-walled bulk.

Savannah Marriott Riverfront Hotel. 100 General McIntosh Blvd., Savannah, GA 31401. ☎ **800/228-9290** or 912/233-7722. Fax 912/233-3765. www.marriott/marriott/savrf. 383 units. A/C TV TEL. $139–$169 double; $189–$519 suite. Children under 18 stay free in parents' room. AE, CB, DC, DISC, MC, V. Parking $7.

At least the massive modern bulk of this place lies far enough from the 19th-century restored warehouses of River Street to not clash with them aesthetically. Constructed as a Radisson in the early 1990s, it towers 8 stories, with an angular facade in orange and yellow brick. It doesn't quite succeed at being a top-rated luxury palace but nonetheless attracts corporate business and conventions. Among local hotels of this type, we prefer the Hyatt, but this would be an acceptable backup, with comfortable, midsize modern rooms, of which 19 are accessible for travelers with disabilities. The soaring atrium contains an awkwardly positioned pool loaded with children. The lobby's T.G.I. Friday's suffers from a very low ceiling and has a faux-Victorian decor with a kaleidoscope of stained-glass lamps.

MODERATE

✪ **River Street Inn.** 115 E. River St. (lobby entrance 124 E. Bay St.), Savannah, GA 31401. ☎ **800/253-4229** or 912/234-6400. Fax 912/234-1478. 86 units. A/C MINIBAR TV TEL. $129–$225 double. Children under 12 stay free in parents' room. Rates include full breakfast. AE, DC, MC, V. Parking $2.50.

When cotton was king and Liverpool-based ships were moored on the nearby river, this place stored massive amounts of cotton produced by upriver plantations. After the boll weevil decimated the cotton industry, it functioned as an icehouse, a storage area for fresh vegetables, and the headquarters of an insurance company. Its two lowest floors, built in 1817, were made of ballast stone carried in the holds of ships from faraway England; its three brick-built upper floors were added a few decades later.

In 1986, a group of investors poured millions into its development as one of the linchpins of Savannah's River District, adding a well-upholstered colonial pizzazz to the public areas and converting the warren of brick-lined storerooms into some of the most comfortable and well-maintained midsize to spacious guest rooms in town.

In 1999, the hotel completed renovating an adjoining warehouse, which added 42 units to the inn. The hotel is also in the process of redecorating common areas and meeting places. There are many pluses to staying here, including the inn's position near a slew of bars, restaurants, and nightclubs. Breakfast is served in **Huey's** (see "Dining"). There is a wine and cheese reception Monday to Saturday from 5 to 7pm.

THE HISTORIC DISTRICT
VERY EXPENSIVE

✪ **Ballastone Inn.** 14 Oglethorpe Ave., Savannah, GA 31401. ☎ **800/ 822-4553** or 912/236-1484. Fax 912/236-4626. 19 units. A/C TV TEL. $195– $315 double; $275–$315 suite. Rates include full breakfast, afternoon tea, hors d'oeuvres, brandy and chocolate at turndown. Strict 10-day cancellation policy. AE, MC, V. Free parking.

This glamorous inner-city B&B occupies a dignified 1838 building separated from the Juliette Gordon Low House (original home of Girl Scouts of America) by a well-tended formal garden; its good-size bedrooms are richly decorated with all the hardwoods, elaborate draperies, and antique furniture you'd expect. Enjoy luxury mattresses and elegant appointments at every turn. It was named for the stones carried as ballast in the holds of sailing vessels, which, when unloaded to make room for cotton crops at Savannah, were then recycled as the buildings' foundations. For a brief period (only long enough to add a hint of spiciness), the place functioned as a bordello and a branch office for the Girl Scouts organization (now next door) between bouts as an upper-class residence.

Former occupants have included at least three prominent warriors for the Confederacy, one of whom hired Boston-based architect William Gibbons Preston to rebuild and redesign the place after the end of the war. In 1987, in a real-estate swap that has become legendary for its savvy, the building was acquired by Chicago-based entrepreneur Richard Carlson and his partner, Tim Hargus.

Oddities abound: There's an elevator, unusual for Savannah B&Bs; there are no closets (they were taxed as extra rooms in the old days and therefore never added); there are many unusual furnishings noted for their comfort and dignified style. In addition, there are cachepots filled with scented potpourri and art objects that would thrill the heart of any decorator, and a full-service bar area is tucked into a corner of what was once a double parlor. The suites are in a clapboard-sided town house a 5-minute walk away; the building is staffed with its own live-in receptionists.

⚐ Family-Friendly Accommodations

The Mulberry (Holiday Inn) *(see p. 140)* Right in the heart of the Historic District, this hotel lets kids under 18 stay free if sharing a room with their parents. Children enjoy the pool, and cribs are provided free.

Foley House Inn *(see p. 138)* This is one of the few upscale B&Bs that caters to families. Kids under 12 stay free in their parents' room, and cribs are provided free.

River Street Inn *(see p. 134)* The best bet for families with children along the riverfront is a converted cotton warehouse from 1817. Large rooms make family life easier, and children under 12 stay free. There's also a game room, and many fast-food joints are just outside.

Courtyard by Marriott *(see p. 144)* One of the best bets for families who want to stay in the Historic District, this chain hotel is reasonably priced. The coin laundry will certainly come in handy, and free cribs are available for those with small children. The restaurant serves family fare at standard prices.

✪ **The Gastonian.** 220 E. Gaston St., Savannah, GA 31401. ☎ **800/ 322-6603** or 912/232-2869. Fax 912/232-0710. www.gastonian.com. 17 units. A/C TV TEL. $195–$275 double; $250 suite. Rates include full breakfast, afternoon tea, and wine. AE, DISC, MC, V. Free parking. Children under 12 aren't allowed.

This elegant place is proof of what good taste, historical antecedents, and lots of money can do. It incorporates a pair of Italianate Regency buildings constructed as private homes in 1868 by the same unknown architect. (The larger one was owned by the Champion family, proprietors of a chain of grocery stores.) Hard times began with the 1929 stock market crash, and the buildings were chopped into apartments for the payment of back taxes. In 1984, the visiting Lineberger family from California saw the places, fell in love with them, and poured $2 million into restoring their severely dignified premises.

Everything is a testimonial to Victorian taste and charm, except for a skillfully crafted serpentine bridge that connects the two buildings and curves above a verdant semitropical garden. Afternoon tea is served in a formal English-inspired drawing room where Persian carpets and a grand piano add to the luster of the good life of another era. The good-size guest rooms are appropriately plush, with everything from deluxe mattresses to elegant toiletries.

✪ **Kehoe House.** 123 Habersham St., Savannah, GA 31401. ☎ **800/ 820-1020** or 912/232-1020. Fax 912/231-0208. 15 units. A/C TV TEL. $195–$250 double; $230–$250 suite. Rates include full breakfast and afternoon tea. AE, DC, DISC, MC, V. Free parking.

Kehoe House was built in 1892 by the owners of an iron foundry as a testimonial to their wealth, and they ordered that the trim, window casements, columns, and soffits be cast in iron and bolted into place. In the 1960s, after the place had been converted into a funeral parlor, it became Savannah's most scandalous building when its owners tried to tear down the Isaiah Davenport house (see "Seeing the Sights, above") to build a parking lot. The resulting outrage led to the founding of the Historic Savannah Foundation and the salvation of most of the neighborhood's remaining old buildings.

Today, Kehoe functions as a spectacularly opulent B&B, the finest in Savannah, with a collection of fabrics and furniture in its roomy bedrooms that is almost forbiddingly valuable and tasteful. However, it lacks the warmth and welcome of the Ballastone Inn. This isn't a place for children: The ideal guest will tread softly on floors that are considered models of historic authenticity. Breakfast and afternoon tea are part of the ritual that has seduced the likes of Tom Hanks, who stayed in room no. 301 during the filming of parts of *Forrest Gump*.

Magnolia Place Inn. 503 Whitaker St., Savannah, GA 31401. ☎ **800/ 238-7674** outside Georgia, or 912/236-7674. Fax 912/236-1145. www. magnoliaplace.com. 15 units. A/C TV TEL. $135–$250 double; $180–$250 suite. Rates include full breakfast, afternoon tea and wine, and evening coffee. AE, DISC, MC, V. Free parking.

The building was begun in 1878 on a desirable plot overlooking Forsyth Square and completed 4 years later by a family who'd been forced off their upriver plantation after the Civil War for nonpayment of taxes. An ancestor had represented South Carolina at the signing of the Declaration of Independence, and so the Second Empire ("steamboat Gothic") house was designed to be as grand and accommodating as funds would allow. The result includes the most endearing front steps in town, front verandas worthy of a Mississippi steamer, and an oval skylight (an "oculus") that illuminates a graceful staircase ascending to the dignified rooms. New owners acquired the place in 1994 and have molded it into their own vision. About half the good-size and luxuriously appointed rooms contain whirlpool baths, and 11 have fireplaces.

EXPENSIVE

DeSoto Hilton. 15 E. Liberty St. (P.O. Box 8207), Savannah, GA 31412.
☎ **800/426-8483** or 912/232-9000. Fax 912/232-6018. www.hilton.com.
246 units. A/C TV TEL. $109–$209 double. AE, DC, MC, V. Parking $7.

Built in 1890 in what was the showcase commercial neighborhood,
this hotel functioned for many generations as the city's grandest.
Thousands of wedding receptions, Kiwanis meetings, and debutante
parties later, the building was demolished and rebuilt in a bland
modern format in 1967 and has since grasped at the vestiges of antique glamour its name still manages to evoke. It's a well-managed
commercial hotel, fully renovated by new owners in 1995. The
cookie-cutter midsize rooms are conservatively modern and reached
after registering in a stone-sheathed lobby. Each is comfortably furnished and well appointed, with excellent mattresses and restored
plumbing. Despite the absence of antique charm, many guests like
the place for its polite efficiency. On the premises are the Lion's Den
bar (formerly a famous club known as Mercers), Knickerbocker's
coffee shop, and the more formal Pavillion.

Foley House Inn. 14 W. Hull St., Savannah, GA 31401. ☎ **800/647-3708**
or 912/232-6622. Fax 912/231-1218. www.foleyinn.com. E-mail:
foleyinn@aol.com. 19 units. A/C TV TEL. $175–$300 double. Children under 12
stay free in parents' room. Rates include full breakfast, hors d'oeuvres, tea, and
cordials. AE, DC, DISC, MC, V. Meter parking off-street; weekend parking free.

Small scale and decorated with all the care of a private home, this
B&B opened in 1982 in a 5-story brick house built in 1896. Two
years later, its size was doubled when the owners managed to acquire
the simpler white-fronted house next door, whose pedigree predates
its neighbors by half a century. The staff will regale you with tales
of the original residents of both houses: the older one functioned as
a dentist's office for many years, and the other was the site of one
of Savannah's most notorious turn-of-the-century suicides.

Each of the rooms has its own fireplace or wood-burning stove,
four-poster beds, elaborate wall coverings, and enough antiques to
evoke the graciousness of old-time Savannah. Those on the ground
floor are more rustic, with exposed brick and ceiling beams, and in
most cases, quick access to one of at least two verdant, formally designed courtyards. Your hosts are Mark Moore and his gracious
Danish-born wife Inge Svennson, who together have entertained or
housed many of the diplomats, especially the Danish ones, who visit
Savannah from, among others, Copenhagen and Washington, D.C.
Breakfast and afternoon hors d'oeuvres, tea, and cordials are served

in a large verdant space formed by the connected expanse of the two houses' original gardens.

Granite Steps Inn. 126 E. Gaston St., Savannah, GA 31401. ☎ **912/ 233-5380.** Fax 912/236-3116. www.granitesteps.com. 5 units. A/C TV TEL. $250 double; $350 suite. AE, MC, V.

This inn is glossier, larger, more opulent, and contains fewer accommodations than most of its other competitors within Savannah. Originally built in 1881 as a showy Italianate residence for a successful cotton merchant, it later belonged to celebrity decorator Jim Williams (the alleged murderer of Danny Hansford in The Book) just before his death. In May 1998, it was lavishly restored by a team of hardworking entrepreneurs associated with Georgia's premier spa, the Château Élan, outside Atlanta. Consequently, you'll find more emphasis on hot tubs (most rooms contain one) and somewhat fussy pampering than at any other B&B in town. None of this is lost on clients who have included Hollywood producer Nora Ephron (Sleepless in Seattle; You've Got Mail) and other West Coast clients who appreciate the inn's striking mixture of gilded-age glamour, gilded Japanese screens, and free-form modern art that decorates the public areas. The midsize to spacious bedrooms are endlessly tasteful and very upscale. If you opt for a stay here, don't expect down-home Southern folksiness, as the setting is simply too urbane, too discreet, too restrained, and too linked to the European spa motif for hushpuppy, cornpone regionalisms to surface, let alone survive. The very charming co-owner and manager Donna Sparks will greet you on arrival and almost certainly provide you with whatever you need during your stay.

Hamilton-Turner Inn. 330 Abercorn St., Savannah, GA 31401. ☎ **912/ 233-1833** or 888/448-8849. www.hamilton-turnerinn.com. 16 units. A/C TV TEL. $160–$275 double. AE, DC, MC, V.

Few other B&Bs in Savannah have as close and intimate a relationship to the events in The Book as this one. It was built in 1873 in the then intensely fashionable French Second Empire style by the founder of the Hamilton Watch company (and the then mayor of Savannah). During the events that followed the murder of Danny Hansford and the trial of Jim Williams, it was owned by Mandy, the torchlit *femme fatale* who cohosted some of Savannah's most notorious parties within this building. After years of legal wrangling to determine the rightful owners, it was acquired by natives Charlie and Sue Strickland, who cleaned up the building's image, poured millions of dollars into the site, and transformed the place into an inn that's not at all shy about publicizing its murky past. A rather jarringly modern breakfast kitchen was added to one of the ground-floor parlors, and a series of appealingly and somewhat quirky antiques were hauled into each of the bedrooms.

Today, the place is staffed with young locals, some of them barely out of college. Although they're not always dripping with magnolia charm, most of them seem to get their jobs done efficiently. Frankly, this is not the most overwhelmingly charming, or the most appealing, B&B in Savannah, but it carries the benefit of very comfortable mid-size rooms that contain all the amenities—including phones and VCRs—of a modern high-rise hotel. There's one additional benefit associated with this place: Mandy, always a controversial figure, still occupies a ground-floor apartment here, an arrangement that was part of the real-estate transfer that brought the building under the control of the new owners. Consequently, for whatever it's worth, you might actually see one of The Book's now-celebrity characters coming and going from the premises of this hotel.

✪ **The Mulberry (Holiday Inn).** 601 E. Bay St., Savannah 31401. ☎ **800/ 465-4329** or 912/238-1200. Fax 912/236-2184. www.savannahhotel.com. 155 units. A/C TV TEL. $129–$189 double; $189–$229 suite. Children under 18 stay free in parents' room. AE, DC, DISC, MC, V. Parking $5.

Locals point with pride to the Mulberry as a sophisticated transfor-mation of what might've been a derelict building into a suprisingly elegant hotel. Built in 1868 as a stable and cotton warehouse, it was converted in the early 1900s into a bottling plant for Coca-Cola. In 1982, it was reconverted into a simple hotel; and in the 1990s, it received a radical upgrade and a gloss of decorator-inspired Chippen-dale glamour. Today, its lobby looks like that of a grand hotel in London, and its rooms, though small, have a formal decor (think English country house with a Southern accent) and are exceedingly comfortable. The brick-covered patio, with its fountains, trailing ivy, and wrought-iron furniture, evokes New Orleans. On the premises is Sergeant Jasper's Lounge and two restaurants, the Café for break-fast and dinner and the Mulberry for more formal dinners. A pool provides a cool dip on a hot day, and you get access to a nearby health club.

Presidents' Quarters. 255 E. President St., Savannah, GA 31401. ☎ **800/ 233-1776** or 912/233-1600. Fax 912/238-0849. www.presidentsquarters.com. 19 units. A/C TV TEL. $137–$185 double; $195–$225 suite. Rates include con-tinental breakfast and afternoon tea. AE, DC, DISC, MC, V. Free parking.

There are many unique aspects to this hotel, particularly rooms that are among the largest and most comfortable in Savannah. It manages to combine the charm of a B&B with the efficiency of a much larger hotel and does it in a family atmosphere. Until its restoration in 1986, the 1855 building was a derelict ruin, used as a backdrop for the filming of one of the scenes in the TV epic *Roots*. Its savior was Mrs. Muril Broy who, with two intelligent daughters, whipped the property into an appealing small inn. Each room is named after a U.S. president who visited Savannah during his term, with memorabilia and framed testimonials to his accomplishments. Facilities include an outdoor whirlpool, a brick-covered patio where continental breakfasts and afternoon teas are served, and a parking lot (rare in the historic heart of Savannah).

MODERATE

East Bay Inn. 225 E. Bay St., Savannah, GA 31401. ☎ **800/500-1225** or 912/238-1225. Fax 912/232-2709. www.eastbayinn.com. 28 units. A/C TV TEL. $99–$169 double. AE, DC, DISC, MC, V. Parking $5 for 48 hours.

The inn lies beside the busiest (and least attractive) expanse of Bay Street, but though the views from the windows are uninspired, its location is convenient to the bars and attractions of the nearby riverfront. It was built of brown brick in 1853 as a cotton warehouse. Now green awnings and potted geraniums disguise the once-utilitarian design. The cozy lobby contains Chippendale furnishings and elaborate moldings, and the midsize rooms have queen-size four-poster beds, reproductions of antiques, and coffeemakers. Note that the hotel frequently houses tour groups from Europe and South America. In the cellar is **Schyler's** (☎ **912/232-3955**), an independently managed restaurant specializing in European and Asian cuisine.

Eliza Thompson House. 5 W. Jones St., Savannah, GA 31401. ☎ **800/348-9378** or 912/236-3620. Fax 912/238-1920. www.elizathompsonhouse.com. E-mail: elizath@aol.com. 25 units. A/C TV TEL. $99–$230 double. Rates include full breakfast. MC, V. Free parking.

About half the rooms of this stately home are in the 1847 core, and the others are in a gracefully converted carriage house. Both were the domain of socially conscious Eliza Thompson, whose cotton merchant husband died shortly after the foundations were laid in 1846. It was bought in 1997 by Steve and Carol Day, who have completely redecorated, using original Savannah colors, beautiful antiques, and oriental carpets. The heart-of-pine floors were restored to their original luster, and linens were replaced; comfortable cotton robes and turndown service are provided. The inn is graced with one of the most beautiful and largest courtyards in the city, featuring three large fountains, sago palms, and camellias. The guest rooms are comfortable and elegant.

Breakfast is usually a lavish affair, featuring sausage casserole, assortments of muffins, and croissants. During nice weather, it's usually served on the brick terrace of the garden patio separating the two components of this historic inn.

Forsyth Park Inn. 102 W. Hall St., Savannah, GA 31401. ☎ **912/233-6800.** 9 units, 1 cottage. A/C TV. $110–$195 double; $195 cottage. AE, DC, DISC, MC, V. Free parking.

One of the grandest houses on the western flank of Forsyth Park is this yellow-frame place built in the 1890s by a sea captain (Aaron Flynt, aka Rudder Churchill) who became a hero at 16. You'll discover a paneled vestibule where a richly detailed staircase winds upstairs, a robin's-egg blue salon whose Queen Anne decor extends through the rest of the house, and guest rooms whose oak paneling and oversize doors are testimonials to the craftsmanship of the turn of the century. The more expensive rooms, including one placed in what used to be the dining room, are among the largest in town. Home-baked breads and pastries are a staple of the breakfasts. Don't expect frivolity here: The inn is serious and dignified and just a bit staid.

Gaston Gallery Bed & Breakfast. 211 E. Gaston St., Savannah, GA 31401. ☎ **800/671-0716** or 912/238-3294. Fax 912/238-4960. www.gastongallery. com. 15 units. A/C TV. Jan–Feb 10 and June–Aug $120–$185 double; Sept–Dec and Feb 11–May $135–$210 double. AE, DISC, MC, V. Free parking.

Savannah's newest major investment in period restoration was built as two separate homes united by a shared Italianate facade. After a lengthy stint as an antiques store, a partnership of Alabama-based entrepreneurs embarked in 1997 on a lavish reunification of the two houses into a well-conceived whole. Today, the building bears the distinction of having the city's longest and most stately front porch (in Savannah, they refer to it as a gallery) and inner ceilings that are almost dizzyingly high. Bedrooms are spacious, cozy, and comfortable, each like visiting a favorite aunt in the Deep South. The articulate manager, Amelia Dodd, presides with tact and charm over breakfasts that are social events, each featuring a different dish, like curried eggs or Southern grits casserole. Wine and cheese are served daily at 5pm or on your arrival, according to your wishes.

Hampton Inn. 201 E. Bay St., Savannah, GA. ☎ **800/576-4945** or 912/231-0440. www.hotelsavannah.com. 144 units. A/C TV TEL. Sun–Thurs $109–$159 double; Fri–Sat $119–$165 double. Rates include continental breakfast. AE, DC, MC, V. Parking $5.

This is in some ways the most appealing of the city's middle-bracket large-scale hotels. Opened in 1997, it was built on the site of a dilapidated parking lot and rises 7 redbrick stories above busy Bay Street, across from Savannah's Riverwalk and some of the city's most animated nightclubs. Its big-windowed lobby was designed to mimic an 18th-century Savannah salon, thanks to the recycling of heart-of-pine flooring from an old sawmill and the use of antique bricks discovered during the excavation of the foundation and garage. Comfortably formal seating arrangements, a blazing fireplace, and an antique bar add cozy touches. The midsize rooms are simple and comfortable, with wall-to-wall carpeting, tiled baths, excellent mattresses, and flowered upholstery. On the roof is a small pool and sundeck that's supplemented with an exercise room on the seventh floor. There's no restaurant, but many eateries are a short walk away.

✪ **Park Avenue Manor.** 107–109 W. Park Ave., Savannah, GA 31401. ☎ **912/233-0352.** www.bbonline.com/ga/parkavenue/. E-mail: pkavemanor. com. 5 units. A/C TV TEL. $85–$110 double; $140 suite. AE, MC, V. Free parking.

Charming, historic, and cozy, this is Savannah's premier gay-friendly guest house, outshining its more discreet competitors. Its politicized presentation includes a rainbow flag draped from the upstairs balcony and the highly visible ownership of Jonathan Santarsiero, who also owns one of Savannah's most popular gay bars, Faces (see "Savannah After Dark"). On the southern edge of Forsyth Park, the place was created after an extensive 1997 renovation, when a pair of 1879 houses were connected into this tastefully appointed guest house. Each small to standard room contains a gas-burning fireplace, an exposed brick chimney that shows the mason's craft to its best advantage, and (in most cases) soothingly dark colors. Our favorite is the Robert E. Lee room, where a four-poster bed is complemented with tones of blue and sunlight from a large bay window. Though many of the guests are male couples, the presence of a competent (mostly female) staff ensures that women will feel comfortable and welcome.

Planters Inn. 29 Abercorn St., Savannah, GA 31401. ☎ **800/554-1187** or 912/232-5678. Fax 912/232-8893. www.plantersinnsavannah.com. E-mail: plantinn@aol.com. 56 units. A/C TV TEL. $110–$165 double. Rates include continental breakfast and afternoon wine. AE, DC, MC, V. Parking $5.75.

This European-style inn is more businesslike than the average Savannah B&B. Built adjacent to Reynolds Square in 1912 as a brown brick tower, it boasts a lobby with some of the most elaborate millwork of any commercial building in town, a scattering of Chippendale reproductions, and an honor bar (sign for whatever drink you consume). The midsize to spacious rooms are dignified and formal, comfortably outfitted with four-poster beds and flowery fabrics. The Planters Inn isn't associated with the well-recommended Planters' Restaurant next door.

17 Hundred 90. 307 E. President St., Savannah, GA 31401. ☎ **800/ 497-1790** or 912/236-7122. Fax 912/236-7123. 14 units. A/C TV TEL. $119– $189 double. Rates include continental breakfast. AE, MC, V. Free parking.

A severely dignified brick-and-clapboard house, this place will remind you of the low-ceilinged houses you'd expect along an 18th-century New England street. It's Savannah's oldest inn, filled with conversation and laughter from the basement bar and restaurant (see "Dining") and also with the legends of the ghosts who haunt the place (see below). Accessible via cramped halls, the rooms are small but charming and comfortably furnished, with the colonial trappings appropriate for an inn of this age and stature. About a dozen contain fireplaces and small refrigerators.

INEXPENSIVE

Bed and Breakfast Inn. 117 W. Gordon St. (at Chatham Square), Savannah, GA 31401. ☎ **912/238-0518.** Fax 912/233-2537. 15 units. A/C TV TEL. $90– $110 double. Rates include full breakfast and afternoon tea. AE, DISC, MC, V. Free parking.

In the oldest part of historic Savannah, this is a dignified stone-fronted town house built in 1853. You climb a gracefully curved front stoop to reach the cool high-ceilinged interior, which is outfitted with a combination of antique and reproduction furniture. Some rooms contain refrigerators, and all are comfortably furnished but a bit small, each with a firm bed. There's no smoking and no pets.

Courtyard by Marriott. 6703 Abercorn St., Savannah, GA 31405. ☎ **800/ 321-2211** or 912/354-7878. Fax 912/354-1432. 156 units. A/C TV TEL. Sun– Thurs $94 double, Fri–Sat $88 double; $99–$129 suite all week. Children under stay 16 free in parents' room. Senior discounts available. AE, DC, DISC, MC, V. Free parking. From I-16, take exit 34A to I-516 East and turn right on Abercorn St.

Built around a landscaped courtyard, this is one of the more recommendable motels bordering the Historic District. Many Savannah

A Ghost Tale

Tales are plentiful about spirits who roam the halls of 17 Hundred 90. The most famous concerns the daughter of the building's first owner, young Anna, whose love for a seafaring German ultimately sealed her fate. Legend has it that one day Anna was standing on the third-floor balcony, tearfully bidding farewell to her love, who was setting sail down the Savannah River to the Atlantic. She watched and waved frantically until the sails were out of sight, then, distraught, hurled herself over the balcony to her death on the brick walk below.

motels, though cheap, are quite tacky, but this one has renovated and good-sized rooms with separate seating areas, oversize work desks, and private patios or balconies. Family-friendly, it offers a coin laundry and free cribs, and the hotel has a pool and a whirlpool. The restaurant serves an à la carte and a buffet breakfast. Exercise equipment includes weights and bicycles.

Fairfield Inn by Marriott. 2 Lee Blvd. (at Abercorn Rd.), Savannah, GA 31405. ☎ **800/228-2800** or 912/353-7100. Fax 912/353-7100. 135 units. A/C TV TEL. $60 double. Children under 18 stay free in parents' room. AE, DC, DISC, MC, V. Free parking. From I-16, take exit 34A to I-516 East, then turn right on Abercorn St. and go right again onto Lee Blvd.

Not quite as good as Marriott's other recommended motel (above), this reliable budget hotel offers standard but comfortable rooms, with in-room movies, firm mattresses, and a large, well-lit work desk. The big attraction of this 3-story motel is the outdoor pool. Health-club privileges are available nearby, as are several good and moderately priced restaurants.

4 Dining

Only 18 miles from the ocean, Savannah is known throughout the South for the excellence of its seafood restaurants. They're among the best in Georgia, rivaled only by those in Atlanta. The best dining is in the Historic District, along River Street, bordering the water. However, locals also like to escape the city and head for the seafood places on Tybee and other offshore islands.

Some of Savannah's restaurants are ranked among the finest in the entire South. And others, like Mrs. Wilkes' Dining Room, are places to go for real Southern fare—from collard greens and fried okra to fried chicken, cornbread, and hot biscuits. Amazingly, while the dining scene in Atlanta changes radically every year, the scene in Savannah has seen no serious changes since 1995.

ALONG THE WATERFRONT
EXPENSIVE

Chart House. 202 W. Bay St. ☎ **912/234-6686.** Reservations recommended. Main courses $13–$25. AE, DC, DISC, MC, V. Sun–Thurs 5–10pm, Fri–Sat 5–10:30pm. STEAK/SEAFOOD/PRIME RIB.

Overlooking the Savannah River and Riverfront Plaza, "the home of the mud pie" is part of a nationwide chain—and one of the better ones. It's housed in a building that predates 1790, reputed to be the oldest masonry structure in Georgia and once a sugar-and-cotton warehouse. You can enjoy a view of passing ships on the outside deck, perhaps ordering an appetizer and apéritif while you're there. The bar is one of the most atmospheric on the riverfront. As in all Chart Houses, the succulent prime rib is slow roasted and served au jus. The tender steaks from corn-fed beef are aged and hand-cut on the premises before being charcoal grilled. However, you might prefer one of the fresh catches of the day.

✪ **Jean Louise.** 321 Jefferson St. ☎ **912/234-3211.** Reservations required. Fixed-price 7-course dinner $48. AE, DISC, MC, V. Tues–Sat 7–9pm. AMERICAN/FRENCH.

Set within a brick-and-wrought-iron building erected in 1879, and which you might have imagined on a back alley of New Orleans, this restaurant shot into civic prominence about 6 years ago. Then, David Jawbone moved from Atlantic City, where he had prepared many meals for Donald Trump and his entourage, to Savannah, and named his new restaurant after his daughter. Since then, it's been favored by such visiting celebrities as Robert Redford and many of the scions of Hollywood who happen to be passing through the city. Within a burgundy-and-forest-green decor that seats only 32, at tables accented with huge, almost overly large, wine glasses, you'll enjoy the night's elegant fare as composed into seven-course culinary extravaganzas. Depending on his mood and the venue that night, your spectacular feast might include Caribbean lobster salad with sautéed duck breast and a tropical vinaigrette, a heavenly braised grouper with white-bean cassoulet and Napa valley cabbage, and a combination platter of roasted tenderloin of beef with a mushroom

Savannah Dining

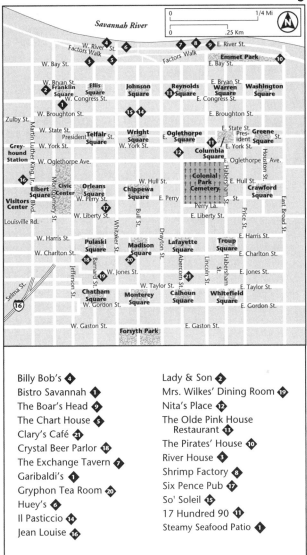

Billy Bob's ④

Bistro Savannah ①

The Boar's Head ⑨

The Chart House ⑤

Clary's Café ㉑

Crystal Beer Parlor ⑱

The Exchange Tavern ⑦

Garibaldi's ①

Gryphon Tea Room ⑳

Huey's ⑥

Il Pasticcio ⑭

Jean Louise ⑯

Lady & Son ②

Mrs. Wilkes' Dining Room ⑲

Nita's Place ⑫

The Olde Pink House
  Restaurant ⑬

The Pirates' House ⑩

River House ③

Shrimp Factory ⑧

Six Pence Pub ⑰

So' Soleil ⑮

17 Hundred 90 ⑪

Steamy Seafood Patio ①

demiglace and sliced loin of veal with green peppercorns. Between courses, a barrage of carefully orchestrated, somewhat fussy service rituals will be conducted, including presentations of hot towels between some of the courses and a sometimes obsessive emphasis on porcelain, crystal, and table settings.

MODERATE

Boar's Head. 1 N. Lincoln St. (at River St.). ☎ **912/651-9660.** Reservations recommended. Lunch main courses $8–$13; dinner main courses $12–$25. AE, DISC, MC, V. Mon–Thurs 11am–10pm, Fri–Sun 11am–11pm. CONTINENTAL/AMERICAN.

One of the most popular waterfront eateries since the 1960s, this restaurant places its tables to take advantage of the view of the Savannah River. The spot, said to be the oldest restaurant on River Street, was a cotton warehouse some 250 years ago. The stone walls, original brick, and wooden ceiling beams are intact, and the effect is that of a faux-medieval pub. Hanging baskets of greenery and soft candlelight create an intimate mood. You've probably dined on more fabulous fare, but what you get here isn't bad. There's the usual array of seafood, beef, chicken, lamb, and veal, which is the daily special. The restaurant's signature dish is crab soup served with delectable crab cakes, and dessert is white-chocolate cheesecake with a Jack Daniels glaze. The restaurant also houses a full range of liquors and wines.

✪ Huey's. 115 E. River St. (in the River Street Inn). ☎ **912/234-7385.** Reservations recommended. Brunch $6; lunch sandwiches $6–8; dinner main courses $11–$17. AE, DISC, MC, V. Mon–Thurs 7am–10pm, Fri–Sat 8am–11pm, Sun 8am–10pm. CAJUN/CREOLE.

At this casual eatery overlooking the Savannah River, there's not much to make it look different from the other restored warehouses. But you'll discover that it's special when you taste the food. The place is often packed, doing the highest turnover on this bustling street. Your breakfast may be a Creole omelet; midday might find you munching on an oyster po'boy. But the kitchen really shines at dinner, turning out dishes like jambalaya with andouille sausage; a fantastic crawfish étoufée; and crab-and-shrimp au gratin, made with Louisiana crabmeat and Georgia shrimp. The soups are homemade and the appetizers distinctive. A jazz brunch is featured on Saturday and Sunday from 8am to 3pm. The bar next door offers live entertainment.

River House. 125 W. River St. ☎ **912/234-1900.** Reservations recommended. Lunch main courses $10–$13; dinner main courses $20–$28. AE, MC, V. Sun–Thurs 11am–10pm, Fri–Sat 11am–11pm. SEAFOOD.

At the point where the S.S. *Savannah* set sail on its maiden voyage across the Atlantic in 1819, this converted riverfront cotton warehouse excels in fresh seafood, the menu depending on the catch of the day. Overlooking River Street with its boat traffic, this is one of the best dining choices on the river. Appetizers include seafood strudel made with shrimp, crabmeat, and feta cheese, as well as creamed spinach, baked in phyllo. Main courses range from deviled crab to charbroiled swordfish. Steaks, chops, chicken, and even pizzas appear on the menu, all served with Caesar salad and baked sourdough bread. Pastry chef Sam Harris prepares cookies, pastries, and sourdough French bread in a bakery inside the restaurant. Georgia pecan pie is a house specialty.

INEXPENSIVE

Billy Bob's. 21 E. River St. ☎ **912/234-5588.** Reservations not necessary. Main courses $6–$22. AE, DISC, MC, V. Sun–Thurs 11am–10pm, Fri–Sat 11am–11pm. BARBECUE.

Its decor was modeled after a barn on the Texas panhandle, with an emphasis on indestructibility (stainless-steel tabletops and thick timbers). The recorded music reminds you of the country-western tunes they play at this place's namesake (Billy Bob's) in Houston. The barbecued food is succulent and tender, having been slowly marinated and spicily flavored. Examples are baby-back ribs, chicken, shrimp, and beefsteaks. Appetizers feature warm crab-and-artichoke dip, and steaks and seafood include grilled swordfish, battered shrimp platters, and at least five kinds of Angus beef.

Exchange Tavern. 201 E. River St. (east of Bull St.). ☎ **912/232-7088.** Main courses $6–$25; child's plate $4–$6. AE, DC, MC, V. Sun–Thurs 11am–11pm, Fri–Sat 11am–1am. SEAFOOD/LOW COUNTRY.

This 1790s cotton warehouse has been turned into a much-frequented place east of Bull Street, opening onto the riverfront. The chefs make no pretense about their food: Everything is hale and hearty rather than gourmet. Your best bet is the fresh seafood, served grilled, broiled, or fried. Hand-cut grilled rib-eye steaks are a specialty, along with Buffalo-style wings, shrimp, oysters, and well-stuffed sandwiches. Since 1971, this place has been dispensing its wares, including shish kebabs, fresh salads, and homemade soups. It's also the best place for a Bloody Mary.

Gryphon Tea Room. 337 Bull St. ☎ **912/525-5880.** Reservations not necessary. Deli sandwiches $4–$8; pot of tea for two $5. No credit cards. DELI SANDWICHES/TEAROOM.

This is the closest thing to an upscale Italian cafe in all of Savannah, and as such, it combines elements of art nouveau Milan with Old Savannah. Owned and maintained by the Savannah College of Art and Design, it occupies what originally functioned as a pharmacy before the Civil War, and which later evolved into a Savannah institution, Solomon's Drug Store. (Look for the initial "S" inlaid into the floor of the entrance vestibule in colored tiles; according to legend, it was famously associated with a plot to poison General Sherman during his occupation of Savannah.) No one will mind if you order just a cuppa—the menu lists 14 kinds of tea, a dozen kinds of coffee, and lots of fresh-baked pastries to go with it. But if you're hungry, there are salads, well-garnished sandwiches, soups, and platters of the day, most of them priced from $7 to $8 each. Monday to Saturday, between 4 and 6pm, the entire site is devoted exclusively to the tea ritual.

Shrimp Factory. 313 E. River St. (2 blocks east of the Hyatt). ☎ **912/236-4229.** Reservations not accepted. Lunch main courses $12–$15; dinner main courses $17–$25. AE, DC, DISC, MC, V. Mon–Thurs 11am–10pm, Fri–Sat 11am–11pm, Sun noon–10pm. SEAFOOD.

In an 1850 cotton warehouse, the exposed brick and wooden plank floors form a setting for a harbor-view dining venue. Lots of folks drop in before dinner to watch the boats pass by, perhaps enjoying a Chatham Artillery punch in a souvenir snifter. Yes, the place is touristy, never more so than when it welcomes tour buses. A salad bar rests next to a miniature shrimp boat, and fresh seafood comes from local waters. Over a period of a year, 24 varieties of fish are offered. A specialty, pine bark stew, is served in a little iron pot with a bottle of sherry on the side; it's a potage of five seafoods simmered with fresh herbs, but minus the pine bark today. Other excellent dishes include peeled shrimp, shucked oysters, live Maine lobsters, various fish fillets, and sirloin steaks.

THE HISTORIC DISTRICT
VERY EXPENSIVE

✪ **45 South.** 20 E. Broad St. ☎ **912/233-1881.** Reservations required. Jacket advised. Main courses $20–$32. AE, MC, V. Mon–Sat 6–10pm. INTERNATIONAL.

Elegant and ritzy, recommended by such magazines as *Food & Wine, Southern Living,* and even *Playboy,* 45 South is next door to the more famous Pirates' House, to which it's infinitely superior. Moved to the site in the Pirates' House complex in 1988, this former south-side restaurant is done in the "decadent" tones of mauve and green so evocative of Savannah. This is perhaps the most expensive restaurant in town, softly lit with elegantly set tables and a cozy bar and boasting impeccable service. The ever-changing gourmet Southern menu is likely to feature smoked North Carolina trout, rack of lamb flavored with crushed sesame seeds (our favorite), grilled venison with sweet-potato gratin, chicken breast with truffled pâté, or sliced pheasant breast with foie gras. Appetizers might include everything from South Carolina quail to crab cakes.

EXPENSIVE

✪ **Olde Pink House Restaurant.** 23 Abercorn St. ☎ **912/232-4286.** Reservations recommended. Main courses $15–$25. AE, MC, V. Daily 5:30–10:30pm. SEAFOOD/AMERICAN.

This place literally glows pink (its antique bricks show through the covering of stucco). This venerable house has functioned as a private home, a bank, a tearoom, and headquarters for one of Sherman's generals. Today, its interior is outfitted with a severe kind of dignity, with stiff-backed chairs, bare wooden floors, and an 18th-century aura reminiscent of Williamsburg. (According to local legend, many of the guests who dined here in the early 1770s plotted the overthrow of the British government in what were at the time the American colonies.)

Today, the cuisine is richly steeped in age-old Low Country traditions and includes crispy scored flounder with apricot sauce, steak au poivre, a heavenly black grouper stuffed with blue crab and drenched in Vidalia onion sauce, and grilled tenderloin of pork crusted with almonds and molasses. You can have your meal in the candlelit dining rooms or the basement-level piano bar (see "Savannah After Dark," below), with a large selection of wines.

Pirates' House. At the corner of E. Broad and Bay sts. ☎ **912/233-5757.** Reservations recommended. Lunch buffet $9; Sun brunch $17; dinner main courses $17–$21. AE, DC, MC, V. Mon–Sat 11:30am–2:30pm, Sun 11am–3pm; daily 5:30–9pm. SEAFOOD/LOW COUNTRY.

This is Georgia's most famous restaurant and is certainly a Savannah legend. A labyrinth of low-ceilinged dining rooms, the Treasure Island bar, a gift shop, and a small museum share this 1754 Bay Street inn, once a rendezvous for pirates and sailors. Robert Louis Stevenson used the place as a setting in *Treasure Island,* and it's listed as an authentic house museum by the American Museum Society. You'll want to explore all its dining rooms.

We used to veer way out of our way on drives between New York and Florida just to dine here. But, sadly, that's not the case anymore. The restaurant has become touristy, and the food is often bland— not at all what it used to be. Some dishes are better than others, though, including the sautéed shrimp with herb Creole sauce and honey-pecan fried chicken. But a recent sampling of the okra gumbo and a small plate of the Low Country jambalaya proved disappointing. Bring the kids, though. They may love the place, unless they're a future Julia Child or James Beard.

17 Hundred 90. 307 E. President St. ☎ **912/236-7122.** Reservations recommended. Lunch main courses $7–$11; dinner main courses $18–$24. AE, MC, V. Mon–Fri ll:30am–2pm; daily 6–10pm. INTERNATIONAL.

In the brick-lined cellar of Savannah's oldest inn, this place evokes a seafaring tavern along the coast of New England. Many visitors opt for a drink at the woodsy-looking bar in a separate room in back, before heading down the slightly claustrophobic corridor to the nautically inspired dining room. Students of paranormal psychology remain alert to the ghost that's rumored to wander through this place, site of a famous suicide (see "A Ghost Tale" under "Accommodations").

Lunch might include a simple array of the quiche of the day with salad, Southern-style blue crab cakes, and a choice of salads and sandwiches. Dinners are more formal, featuring crab bisque, snapper Parmesan, steaks, and bourbon-flavored chicken. The cookery is of a high standard.

MODERATE

Il Pasticcio. 2 E. Broughton St. (at the corner of Bull and Broughton sts.). ☎ **912/231-8888.** Reservations recommended. Pastas $7–$10; main courses $11–$25. AE, DC, V. Mon–Thurs 5:30–10:30pm, Fri–Sun 5:30–2am. ITALIAN.

This restaurant/bakery/gourmet market is one of the city's most popular dining spots. In a postmodern style, with big windows and a high ceiling, it has a definite big-city style. A rotisserie turns out succulent specialties. Adjacent to the dining room is a market showcasing Italian specialties, including cold cuts, breads, and deli sandwiches. Many locals come here just for the pastas, all homemade and served with savory sauces. Begin with carpaccio (thinly sliced beef tenderloin) or a tricolor salad of radicchio, endive, and arugula. Main dishes are likely to feature a mixed grilled seafood platter or grilled fish steak with tricolor sweet roasted peppers. The Sunday brunch buffet features live jazz.

✪ **So'Soleil.** 1 W. Broughton St. Reservations recommended. ☎ **912/ 234-1212.** Main courses $16–$26. AE, DC, MC, V. Mon–Thurs 5–10pm, Fri–Sat 5–11pm, Sun 5–9pm. FRENCH/MEDITERRANEAN.

In 1998, Ian Winslade, a veteran employee of some of the most glamorous restaurants in Europe and North America, established an upscale bistro within the former premises of a Depression-era department store (McCrory's). Almost immediately, it took off as the most urbane and hip restaurant in town, soon after surpassing better established dining spots such as Elizabeth's on 37th. The venue might remind you of something in New York's Soho or London's Chelsea district, thanks to an airy, big-windowed decor, a staff composed largely of graduate students at Savannah's Academy of Art and Design, and clients who have already included Michelle Pfeiffer, Kim Basinger, and Robert Redford. Made from quality ingredients, menu items derive from throughout the Mediteranean, particularly the south of France. Examples include lime-marinated black bass with black truffles and celery juice; terrine of foie gras with asparagus salad and spring leek vinaigrette; seared grouper and steamed clams over fettuccine with Vidalia onion and asparagus; and herbed, marinated loin of lamb with Yukon gold potatoes, bacon, English peas, and herb-flavored vinaigrette. The wine list is particularly extensive, a testimonial to the chef's long-ranging experience in the great kitchens of the world.

INEXPENSIVE

✪ **Clary's Café.** 404 Abercorn St. (at Jones St.). ☎ **912/233-0402.** Breakfast specials $5–$8; main courses $7–$11. AE, DC, DISC, MC, V. Mon–Fri 7am–4pm, Sat–Sun 8am–4pm. AMERICAN.

Clary's Café has been a Savannah tradition since 1903, though the ambience today, under the devilish direction of Michael Faber, is decidedly 1950s. The place was famous long before it was featured in *Midnight in the Garden of Good and Evil* in its former role as Clary's drugstore, where regulars like the eccentric flea-collar inventor Luther Driggers breakfasted and lunched. John Berendt is still a frequent patron, as is the fabled Lady Chablis, who was featured in the novel and costarred in the film. Begin your day with the classic Hoppel Poppel (scrambled eggs with chunks of kosher salami, potatoes, onions, and green peppers) and go on from there. Breakfast is served all day on Saturday and Sunday. Fresh salads, New York–style sandwiches, and stir-fries, along with Grandmother's homemade chicken soup and flame-broiled burgers, are served throughout the day, giving way to specials of the evening, likely to include chicken pot pie and seafood quesadilla.

Crystal Beer Parlor. 301 W. Jones St. ☎ **921/232-1153.** Reservations not necessary. Burgers and salads $6–$9; platters $10–$16. AE, DISC, MC, V. Daily 11am–9pm. AMERICAN.

The aura of this all-American, quirkily charming place hasn't changed very much since it was established in 1933. Set in a quiet backwater of the city's historic core, within a low-slung, brick-sided building whose oldest section might remind you of a 19th-century prison in the American Southwest, it's outfitted with scarlet naugahyde banquettes and the same battered wooden tables that have fed and nurtured countless thousands of barbecue lovers.

The menu here might remind you of an old-fashioned Southern diner—almost everything seems to be high in calories, cholesterol, and salt, and usually tastes absolutely delicious. There's a short list of meal-size salads (chicken, shrimp and pecan, and Caesar) that taste good on a hot day, but especially popular are fried shrimp, rib-eye steaks, fried oysters and scallops, and barbecued pork. Burgers can be accompanied with chili and cheese, if you want, and either iced tea, lemonade, or beer. Bring your appetite, and your sense of history, since photos of Old Savannah are placed strategically near one of the entrances.

✪ **Mrs. Wilkes' Dining Room.** 107 W. Jones St. (west of Bull St.). ☎ **912/232-5997.** Reservations not accepted. Breakfast $5; lunch $10. No credit cards. Mon–Fri 8–9am and 11am–3pm. SOUTHERN.

Remember the days of boardinghouses, where everybody sat together and belly-busting food was served in big dishes in the center of the table? Mrs. Selma Wilkes has been serving locals and travelers in just that manner since the 1940s, though no one remembers when they last rented rooms. Bruce Willis, Demi Moore, and Clint Eastwood are among the long list of celebrities who've dined here. You won't find a sign ("It would look so commercial, not at all like home," according to Mrs. Wilkes), but you probably will find a long line of people patiently waiting for a seat at one of the long tables in the basement dining room of an 1870 gray brick house with curving steps and cast-iron trim. Mrs. Wilkes believes in freshness and plans her menu around the seasons. Your food will be a reflection of the cuisine Savannah residents have enjoyed for generations—fried or barbecued chicken, red rice and sausage, black-eyed peas, corn-on-the-cob, squash, yams, okra, cornbread, and collard greens.

Nita's Place. 140 Abercorn St. ☎ **912/238-8233.** Lunch $10. DISC, MC, V. Mon–Sat 11:30am–3pm. SOUTHERN.

In its way, Nita's is one of the most popular restaurants in town, an institution favored by a broad cross section of diners. With Formica-clad tables and chairs that look straight out of a bowling alley lounge, it occupies no-frills cramped quarters about a block from Oglethorpe Square, in a building dominated by the black community's most visible Mama, Nita Dixon. Survivor of such earlier jobs as a chef at Burger King and veteran of years of cooking for teams of construction workers, she established her stake in the early 1990s with a $2,000 inheritance left to her by her father.

You'll be greeted with a broad smile from Nita or her designated representative (any of a squadron of loyal friends); then follow in line to a steam table where simmering portions of Southern food wait delectably. It will include crab cakes, crab balls, meat loaf, fried chicken, collards, pork or beef ribs, several preparations of okra, butter beans, yams, and hoecakes (many recipes were handed down from generation to generation through Nita's long line of maternal forebears). Past guests have included Meg Ryan and former *People's Court* justice Judge Wapner.

Six Pence Pub. 245 Bull St. ☎ **912/233-3156.** Reservations not necessary. Main courses $5–$7. AE, DISC, MC, V. Mon–Thurs 11am–midnight, Fri–Sat 11am–1am, Sun 12:30–10pm. ENGLISH.

Despite the heat and the Southern drawls, this is the closest approximation of an English pub in Savannah. There's a scarlet-colored London phone booth outside its entranceway, a half-paneled interior where you might suspect that a lot of beer has been swilled and spilled, and a short list of Americanized pub grub that focuses on platters of the day, salads, and sandwiches. The dishes include beef, Guinness, and mushroom pie; shepherd's pie with a garden salad; and more predictable items such as BLTs, club sandwiches, and shrimp or tuna salads. Beers derived from England and North America cost from $2.50 to $4.25 a pint.

THE CITY MARKET AREA
MODERATE

Bistro Savannah. 309 W. Congress St. ☎ **912/233-6266.** Reservations recommended. Main courses $15–$22. AE, MC, V. Sun–Thurs 5:30–10:30pm, Fri–Sat 5:30–11pm. INTERNATIONAL/LOW COUNTRY.

Near the City Market, this self-consciously artsy restaurant boasts a staff dressed in the style of a Lyonnais bistro in long aprons and white shirts and a selection of paintings on exhibit from local art galleries. The decor includes long, uninterrupted expanses of reddish gray Savannah brick, a reminder of the space's days as a commercial building in the late 1800s. (The staff isn't shy about telling you about the place's former role as a bordello.)

Menu items feature an eclectic mix of Low Country and international cuisine and may include barbecue local black grouper with chutney, garlic sautéed with mussels and asparagus, or crispy scored flounder in apricot glaze.

Garibaldi's. 315 W. Congress St. ☎ **912/232-7118.** Reservations recommended. Main courses $10–$24. AE, MC, V. Sun–Thurs 5:30–10:30pm, Fri–Sat 5:30pm–midnight. ITALIAN.

Many of the city's art-conscious students appreciate this Italian cafe because of the fanciful murals adorning its walls. (Painted by the owner's daughter, their theme is defined as the "Jungles of Italy.") If you're looking for a quiet, contemplative evening, we advise you to go elsewhere—the setting is loud and convivial in the early evening and even louder as the night wears on. Designed as a fire station in 1871, it boasts the original pressed-tin ceiling, whose ornate design seems to reverberate the sound around the room.

Dishes show flair and technique. Menu items include roasted red peppers with goat-cheese croutons on a bed of wild lettuces, crispy calamari, artichoke hearts with aioli, about a dozen kinds of pasta, and a repertoire of Italian-inspired chicken, veal, and seafood dishes. Daily specials change frequently but sometimes include king-crab fettuccine, and lusciously fattening desserts.

✪ **Lady and Sons.** 311 W. Congress St. ☎ **912/233-2600.** Reservations recommended for dinner. Lunch main courses $5–$10; dinner main courses $7–$23. All-you-can-eat buffet lunch $9, dinner $13, Sunday brunch, $10. AE, DISC, MC, V. Mon–Sat 11:30am–3pm, Sun 11am–5pm; Mon–Thurs 5–9pm, Fri–Sat 5–10pm. SOUTHERN.

Owner Paula Deen started this restaurant in 1989 with her sons, $200, and a 1910 structure. Today, she runs one of the most celebrated restaurants in Savannah. Her cookbook, *Lady and Sons Savannah Country Cookbook* (1998, Random House) is in its second printing. John Berendt wrote the introduction to the cookbook. One taste of the food, and you'll understand the roots of her success. Menu items such as crab cakes (one Maryland visitor claimed they were the best he had ever eaten), crab burgers, and several different creative varieties of shrimp best exhibit her style in the kitchen. The locals love her buffets, which are very Southern. Usually consisting of fried chicken, meat loaf, collard greens, beef stew, "creamed" potatoes, and macaroni and cheese, this buffet is aptly described as more than you can eat.

Lunches are busy with a loyal following who won't skip a meal; dinners are casual and inventive. The aphrodisiac dish has to be the oyster shooters—a half-dozen raw oysters, each served in a shot glass filled with tequila and vodka ("it's like killing two birds with one stone").

INEXPENSIVE

Steamy Seafood Patio. 319 W. Congress St. ☎ **912/233-2887.** Main courses $5–$15. AE, MC, V. Mon–Wed 11am–10pm, Thurs–Sat 11am–11pm, Sun noon–10pm. SEAFOOD.

This reigns without competition as the most eclectic, offbeat, irreverent, and good-natured restaurant in Savannah, the almost aggressively whimsical creation of former flower child Sandi Baumer, owner and muralist. A "hater of plain white walls," she combined carloads of 1950s kitsch with pink leopard skin and tongue-in-cheek testimonials to the proud but passé days of psychedelic rock.

Scion of a New Jersey family of pizza parlor magnates and survivor of several years' residency in a bus surrounded by an organic farm in Montana, she arrived in Savannah in the mid-1980s with a baby daughter, a beat-up car, and little money, determined to survive in the restaurant trade. Good food and drinks are served by Cyndi Lauper look-alikes in short crinoline skirts, and live music is usually featured on a side terrace outfitted like a New Orleans courtyard as viewed through a purple haze. Seafood dishes are steamed or boiled.

THE VICTORIAN DISTRICT
VERY EXPENSIVE

✪ **Elizabeth on 37th.** 105 E. 37th St. ☎ **912/236-5547.** Reservations required. Main courses $25–$30. AE, DC, DISC, MC, V. Sun–Thurs 6–9:30pm, Fri–Sat 6–10pm. MODERN SOUTHERN.

This reigns as the place most frequented by business and media moguls from Atlanta, Los Angeles, and New York. It's the most glamorous and upscale choice, housed in a palatial building reminiscent of a neoclassical villa in Monaco and ringed with semitropical landscaping and cascades of Spanish moss. It was built in 1900 as a copy of a house the original owner, a cotton broker, had admired in Boston.

Since 1980, it has been run by Savannah's most successful culinary team, Elizabeth Terry and her husband, ex-attorney Michael, the chef and wine steward, respectively. The menu items change frequently and seasonally and manage to retain their gutsy originality despite their elegant presentation. Examples are roast quail with mustard-and-pepper sauce and apricot-pecan chutney, herb-seasoned rack of lamb, and broiled salmon with mustard-garlic glaze. You might begin with the popular grilled eggplant soup. There's also an impressive wine list, and on Thursday all wines are sold by the glass. They're proud that Clint Eastwood made this his favorite restaurant while directing *Midnight in the Garden of Good and Evil.*

NEARBY

Bryan's Pink Pig. Hwy. 170-A, Levy, S.C. ☎ **843/784-3635.** Reservations not necessary, but a phone call for directions is advisable. Barbecue platters $5–$9. No credit cards. Tues–Wed 11am–7pm, Thurs–Sat 11am–8pm. BARBECUE.

It's so eccentric that despite its location 5 miles northeast of town (across the South Carolina border, en route to Hilton Head), many Savannahians head here for informal and often raucous dinners. It's hard to miss. What makes it different from other greasy spoons scattered across the state? It's painted in pinks and Day-Glo purples that range from soothing to lurid, and scattered throughout are tongue-in-cheek depictions of pigs, swine, hogs, and piglets, all playing and cavorting like cherubs across a trompe-l'oeil ceiling from the Renaissance. The genteel owners, extended members of the Bryan family, used land their forebears farmed as the site of a tidy cinder-block building they designed and erected themselves.

And what do you get as a reward for your trek out to pigland? A friendly greeting from one of the hippest and most charming staffs of any barbecue joint in the Southeast—and oak- and hickory-smoked barbecue that's positively sublime, made according to recipes perfected by many generations of barbecue gourmands. Everyone's favorite seems to be the chopped pork sandwiches, though Brunswick stew, coleslaw, ribs, chicken, burgers, onion rings, and homemade ice cream are also popular. No liquor is sold, but most locals compensate by bringing in large jugs of tequila or beer.

Savannah is a beautiful woman with a dirty face.
—Lady Nancy *Astor (1946)*

Johnny Harris Restaurant. 1651 Victory Dr. (Hwy. 80). ☎ **912/354-7810.**
Reservations recommended. Jacket required Sat night in main dining room.
Lunch main courses $6–$9; dinner main courses $10–$21. AE, DC, DISC, MC,
V. Mon–Thurs 11:30am–10:30pm, Fri–Sat 11:30am–midnight. AMERICAN.

Started as a roadside diner in 1924, Johnny Harris is Savannah's oldest continuously operated restaurant. The place has a lingering aura
of the 1950s and features all that great food so beloved back in the
days of Elvis and Marilyn: barbecues, charbroiled steaks, and seafood. The barbecued pork is especially savory and the prime rib is
tender. Colonel Sanders never came anywhere close to equaling the
fried chicken here. You can dine in the "kitchen" or the main dining room and dance under the "stars" in the main dining room on
Friday and Saturday nights, when live entertainment is provided.
This place will make you nostalgic.

River's End. 3122 River Dr. ☎ **912/354-2973.** Reservations required Fri–Sat.
Full dinners $13–$25. AE, DC, MC, V. Mon–Thurs 5–10pm, Fri–Sat 5–11pm. Go
5¹/₂ miles east on U.S. 80 to Victory Dr., then ¹/₂ mile south on River Dr.
SEAFOOD.

At Tassie's Pier next door to the Thunderbolt Marina on the Intracoastal Waterway, this is the preferred place to relax and watch
shrimp boat and pleasure boat traffic. To the sounds of grand piano
music, you can begin with oysters Rockefeller or Savannah she-crab
soup, each prepared with a solid, time-tested technique. Charbroiled
seafood items include salmon, swordfish, grouper, mahimahi, and
tuna. Specials of the day are recited by the waiter. Fish isn't the only
item served. You can try chicken Alfredo, charbroiled steaks, succulent lamb, and duck à l'orange. The desserts range from fresh key-
lime pie to Georgia bourbon pecan pie.

5 Seeing the Sights

Most likely, the first sights that you'll want to see in Savannah are
those mentioned in *Midnight in the Garden of Good and Evil.* So if
that's your wish, go directly to the special walking tour below. But,

of course, there are many other draws in this lovely old city, as you'll quickly find out.

WALKING TOUR—
Midnight in the Garden of Good & Evil

Start: Mercer House.
Finish: Whitefield Square.
Time: 2¹/₂ hours.
Best Times: Any day from 9am to 5pm, when there's less traffic.
Worst Times: Between 5 and 6:30pm, when shops and stores are closing and traffic is heavier, or after dark.

At press time, John Berendt's *Midnight in the Garden of Good and Evil* has reached 1.5 million in hardcover sales alone, and the release of the film, directed by Clint Eastwood, has spurred renewed interest in The Book, as it's called in Savannah. The tour below assumes that you've read the book and/or seen the film and are somewhat familiar with the principal characters. *Midnight* is to Savannah what *Gone With the Wind* was (and is) to Atlanta.

You might as well begin at the center of all the excitement, at the "scene of the crime," which stands on the southeast corner of Monterey Square:

1. **Mercer House,** 429 Bull St., a splendid circa 1860 Italianate red-brick mansion. It was here in May 1981 that wealthy antiques dealer Jim Williams, about 50, fatally shot his lover/assistant, blond "walking streak of sex" Danny Hansford, age 21. Williams claimed that he'd shot Danny in self-defense because Danny was waving a gun around and taking shots. Williams was tried three times in Savannah. He was found guilty twice, though each conviction was overturned; the third time was declared a mistrial because of a hung jury. He finally was acquitted at a fourth trial, held in Augusta, far removed from the intrigues of the Savannah swamps. As a result, Jim Williams became the first person in Georgia to be tried four times for murder.

Mercer House is also where each year Williams gave his legendary Christmas parties—Friday night for the cream of society and Saturday night "for gentlemen only." Note the lavender interior shutters on the second story's right-hand window. They shield from the sun what Williams called his "playroom," site of trompe-l'oeil baroque-style frescoes and one of Savannah's most valuable pipe organs. The shooting occurred (as you face the house) in Williams's study, illuminated by the ground floor's right-hand window.

In January 1990, Jim Williams died of a heart attack at 59. As recounted in the book, a strange little coincidence occurred at this time: Williams died in the room where he'd killed Hansford, and his body was found behind his desk in the exact spot where his body would've been found in 1981 if Hansford had shot at him and not missed.

Though Jacqueline Kennedy Onassis reportedly once offered Williams $2 million for Mercer House, it's today inhabited by Williams's sister, Dorothy Williams Kingery, who allowed Clint Eastwood's film crew complete access—all for a price, mind you, despite her condemnation of the "circus atmosphere" surrounding her brother's trials and the publication of The Book.

And, no, Johnny Mercer never lived in this house, though it was built by his great-grandfather.

Monterey Square itself is one of the most interesting in Savannah. However, the statue seen in The Movie was a plywood, Styrofoam, and plastic copy of the statue of Casimir Pulaski, the gallant Polish military officer of Revolutionary War fame. He looks back archly over his shoulder at Mercer House. The real-life statue of Pulaski was removed for restoration several years ago and hasn't been replaced. In its place is an empty stone plinth (the Eastwood replica has long since been removed, too).

Head from Mercer House directly across Monterey Square to see:

2. **Congregation Mickve Israel.** The oldest congregation of Reform Judaism in America, this synagogue was established in 1733. In 1979, on what he called "Flag Day," Williams shocked Savannah by draping a Nazi banner over a balcony at Mercer House, sending ripples of outrage through the city and especially this synagogue. The action wasn't an anti-Semitic act: A film crew was in town shooting a TV movie, *The Trial of Dr. Mudd,* and wanted to use Monterey Square and Mercer House as a backdrop. The people who lived around the square weren't consulted and weren't pleased with the mess and inconvenience, so they asked Williams to intercede. When the producer didn't respond appropriately, Williams decided to ruin their shot (they managed to get the shot anyway).

Williams said that he didn't intend any disrespect to the synagogue: By spoiling the camera's views, he claimed, he had intended merely to teach a lesson to a film crew who, like latter-day carpetbaggers, were trampling on the sensitivities of his beloved Savannah. However, he had no such scruples years later—after his third trial but before his fourth—when a crew came to town to film scenes for *Glory*. He not only didn't interfere with filming but actually opened Mercer House and let the crew use it.

Walk directly east across the square to Bull Street. On your right, across the side street from Mercer House, is:

3. Lee Adler's house, 425 Bull St. This half of a double town house is the home of Williams's nemesis, antagonistic Lee Adler and his wife, Emma. Though they seemed to always be at odds, the major animosity between Adler and Williams started when Williams (then president of the Telfair museum's board of directors) set about getting Adler kicked off the board. It's said that Williams used to play his thunderous organ to counter Adler's howling dogs. Facing West Wayne Street, this house is where Adler runs his business of restoring historic properties—and where he used binoculars to spy on one of the all-male Christmas parties of his "decadent" neighbor.

Now walk immediately south to Mercer House again. In back of the house still stands the building that housed:

4. Williams's Antiques Shop, 430 Whitaker St. In Mercer House's detached carriage house, Williams offered for sale some of the Deep South's finest antiques, lovely pieces that he'd discovered and restored. He even managed to run this business while he was in jail following his second trial. No longer an antiques store, the property is now a private residence, its occupants long used to rubberneckers who come around to stare at the building.

Proceed to the intersection of West Gordon Street and Bull Street, directly to the southeast of Monterey Square. Here you'll find:

5. Serena Dawes's house, 17 W. Gordon St., the former home of Helen Drexel, whose pseudonym was Serena Dawes. Known as one of the world's most beautiful women, she was Willliams's flamboyant neighbor—called "the soul of pampered self-absorption." On most days, she received guests in her boudoir, where she drank pink ladies or martinis, gossiping indiscreetly and planning her appearances at various parties in the evening. One of her most frequent gentleman callers—to borrow an expression from Tennessee Williams (no relation to Jim)—was Luther Driggers, the inventor of the flea collar, who was said to possess a poison so powerful that it could wipe out the entire city of Savannah.

Walking Tour—*Midnight in the Garden of Good and Evil*

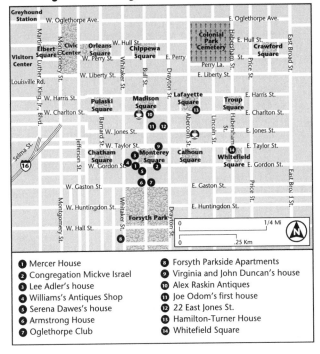

1. Mercer House
2. Congregation Mickve Israel
3. Lee Adler's house
4. Williams's Antiques Shop
5. Serena Dawes's house
6. Armstrong House
7. Oglethorpe Club
8. Forsyth Parkside Apartments
9. Virginia and John Duncan's house
10. Alex Raskin Antiques
11. Joe Odom's first house
12. 22 East Jones St.
13. Hamilton-Turner House
14. Whitefield Square

Continue along Bull Street until you reach:

6. **Armstrong House,** 447 Bull St., an Italian Renaissance palazzo that, after its construction in 1917, was Savannah's largest and most expensive home. Once owned by Williams, who faithfully restored the building, it housed the collector's antiques business for a year until he sold it to the law firm of Bouhan, Williams and Levy. Frank "Sonny" Seiler, the colorful attorney who represented Williams in his last three trials, is a partner in this firm. The house, as depicted in The Book, sits with a curvy colonnade that reaches "out like a giant paw as if to swat the Oglethorpe Club off its high horse across the street."

Legend has it that George Armstrong built the house to dwarf the Oglethorpe to retaliate for his being blackballed from the exclusive club. It was here that Berendt met Simon Glover, an 86-year-old singer working as a porter for the law firm. Glover told the author that he earned $10 extra every week by walking a former law partner's deceased dog, Patrick, up and down Bull Street. Though the dog was long buried, many passersby always commented on the good health of the dog and asked about his welfare.

Across from Armstrong House is the:

7. **Oglethorpe Club,** 450 Bull St., the most exclusive club in Savannah and the oldest gentlemen's club in Georgia. The club, which Berendt used to visit, attracts the cream of Savannah's blue bloods. Ladies are admitted only if wearing a dress; pant suits are forbidden.

Lying south of Armstrong House, at the far southwestern corner of Forsyth Park, is the:

8. **Forsyth Parkside Apartments.** It was here, in his second Savannah apartment, that Berendt wrote most of *Midnight*. It was here also that he met the Grand Empress of Savannah, the Lady Chablis. She had just emerged from Dr. Myra Bishop's office across the street where she'd received her latest estrogen shots to make her "body smooth all over." Berendt soon became her "chauffeur" and witnessed several of her scenes, the most outrageous of which was gate-crashing the black debutante ball.

Return to Monterey Square to the north and walk to the far northeast corner, where you'll come to:

9. **Virginia and John Duncan's house,** 12 E. Taylor St., between Bull and Drayton. Owned by John Duncan, professor of local history, and his charming wife, Virginia, this stucco-fronted house was built in 1869, with embellishments added in the 1890s. Long known for the parties given here, this was the setting where Berendt picked up stories and heard local gossip that he later included in the book. Virginia plays a minor role: It was she who, while walking her dog, was the first to detect the swastika banner waving from Jim Williams's balcony at Mercer House.

At the building's street level is **V&J Duncan Antique Maps, Prints, and Books** (☎ 912/232-0338), where antique maps from around the world, as well as from the lowlands around Savannah are sold. The house's upper floors contain the bed (acquired after her death) where Serena Dawes used to hold court.

Continue north along Bull Street to the next square, Madison Square. Here's an ideal place to stop for refreshments.

☕ **TAKE A BREAK**   Run by the Savannah College of Art and Design, the **Gryphon Tea Room,** 37 Bull St. (☎ 912/238-2481), serves beverages, lunch specials, soups, baked goods, and salads throughout the day. For the "flavors of the day." It was on this site that Robert E. Lee filled his last medical prescription—it was Solomon's Drug Store back then. That building is gone, and the present structure dates from 1913, though SOLOMON is still spelled out in mosaic tiles on the floor of the entrance vestibule.

The adjacent building is the site of:

10. Alex Raskin Antiques, 441 Bull St. (☎ **912/232-8205**). Williams often came to this stately building, constructed in stages between 1860 and 1870 and known as the Noble Hardee Mansion, to shop for antiques. With a shrewd eye for taste and value, he often made purchases from the present owner, Alex Raskin, who's loath to discuss the notoriety surrounding his friend. "He was a neighbor," is about all Raskin has to say on the subject.

After a visit, head south from Madison Square along Bull Street, taking a left turn to reach East Jones Street. Along this street lived the author when he first arrived in Savannah as well as some of the characters associated with The Book.

Heading east, you'll reach:

11. Joe Odom's first house, 16 E. Jones St. This was the temporary home of the notorious Joe Odom (tax lawyer, real estate broker, and piano player) when Berendt moved to Savannah. Berendt first came here in the company of Mandy Nichols, Odom's "fourth wife-in-waiting." Odom had an open-door policy: Though this "sentimental gentleman from Georgia" was constantly broke and almost never paid rent anywhere (except for a bounced check or two), a party was always going on day or night. He was known for living as an uninvited guest in uninhabited residences, and Odom once operated the piano jazz bar Sweet Georgia Brown's until it went bankrupt, though it's now immortalized in The Book.

Proceed until you reach:

12. 22 E. Jones St., the carriage house where Berendt first lived in Savannah. It was here that he began to gather information that after 7 years, he'd publish in his best-seller. In 1992, however, his first agent (whose name the author graciously won't reveal) turned the manuscript back, claiming that she didn't think she could interest a publisher in "taking a chance on a book of this kind." She believed the book was "too local."

Continue along East Jones Street, heading east until you reach Abercorn Street. This is the site of:

🌀 **TAKE A BREAK**   **Clary's Café,** 404 Abercorn St., at Jones Street (☎ **912/233-0402**). Savannah has been enjoying great food and lively conversation here since 1903. Today, along with flame-broiled burgers, owner Michael Faber—self-styled as "Savannah's own rascal"—hawks souvenirs of The Book, not only T-shirts but also postcards of the Lady Chablis herself. Both Chablis ("My mama took my name from a wine bottle") and multimillionaire Berendt have frequently visited the place for its good-tasting food. When we last encountered her ladyship here, she informed us that all this "fuss about The Book is helping [her] save up the big ones for [her] retirement one day."

Continue north along Abercorn Street to Lafayette Square and the site of:

13. Hamilton–Turner House, 330 Abercorn St. (☎ **912/233-4800**). In The Book, this was Joe Odom's fourth and grandest residence, built in 1873 in the Second Empire style. The exterior remains intact, though the interior has been subdivided into apartments. One apartment is occupied by Mandy Nichols (real name, Nancy Hillis). Once voted Miss Big Beautiful Woman, she was involved with Joe Odom until she kicked him out. She used to sing at Sweet Georgia Brown's. Nancy has done more than most to capitalize on the fame brought by The Book, including making a video about the sites in The Book, operating a gift shop on the premises, and even leading tour groups around Savannah and around the antiques-filled first floor of this house. If you want to view the interior, see the entry under "Historic Homes."

From Lafayette Square, head east along East Charlton, cutting right along Habersham. This will lead to:

14. Whitefield Square. One of Savannah's lovely though overlooked squares, Whitefield was the turf of hustler Danny Hansford. Fiercely territorial, Danny guarded this square as if he owned it. Once when another hustler moved in on his territory, he beat him up so badly that the competition nearly ended up in the hospital. This idyllic-looking verdant square, centered around a gazebo, was named after the Rev. George Whitefield, who in 1738 succeeded John Wesley as the Church of England's minister to the Georgia colony.

At the edge of the square is the redbrick bulk of the **Rose of Sharon,** a retirement home/hospital. Run by the Catholic Sisters of Mercy, it was here that a penniless Joe Odom, suffering from

AIDS, came to die, at age 44. It's fitting to end the tour on Danny's once ferociously guarded turf because it's often forgotten that without him there would've been no murder, no four trials, no book, no millions in royalties and film rights. And Savannah itself would be poorer by some $100 million (the estimate to date of how much tourism revenue the city has generated from his murder and The Book). Not bad for a young man who used to sell himself for $30 a night.

WALKING TOUR—
Historic Savannah

Start: River Street.
Finish: Chippewa Square.
Time: 2¹/₂ hours.
Best Times: Monday to Saturday from 9am to 5pm, when most of the stores and attractions are open. On the first Saturday of each month there's a River Street festival.
Worst Times: Monday to Saturday after 5pm, when traffic is heavy. On Sunday, there's little life except on the riverfront.

Begin your walk almost where Savannah began, at the port opening onto:

1. **River Street,** which runs along the Savannah River. (Ramps lead down from Bay St.) The cobblestones came from ballast left behind by early sailing ships coming up the Savannah River. In the mid–19th century, the present brick buildings were most often warehouses holding King Cotton.

   On your left is **John P. Rousakis Plaza.** A multimillion-dollar restoration has revived the riverfront, now a 9-block area ideal for strolling and watching ships. Some 80 boutiques, galleries, restaurants, pubs, and artists' studios line the riverfront. All the old cotton warehouses have been restored to a rustic beauty. If you happen to be here on the first Saturday of any month, you'll be swept up in a River Street festival, with entertainment, street vendors, and sidewalk artists and craftspeople hustling their achievements.

   Near the end of the walk you'll reach Morrell Park, the site of the:

2. **Waving Girl statue,** a tribute to Florence Martus (1869–1943), at the foot of the East Broad Street ramp. The statue depicts a young girl waving toward the ships in the harbor. It's said that

Florence fell in love with a sailor and she promised to greet every ship until he returned to marry her. For 44 years, she waved a white cloth by day and a lantern by night to every ship entering the harbor past the Elba Island Light, where she lived with her brother. Greatly loved and looked for eagerly by seamen, she never missed an arriving ship (she said that she could "feel" them approaching) and assisted in at least one heroic rescue. Her own sailor never returned.

At the end of the eastern end of the park, take a sharp right and begin your stroll along:

3. **Factors Walk,** lying between River and Bay streets. In the 19th century, Factors Walk was named for the factors (brokers) who graded the cotton for its quality. Now restored, the walk is filled with specialty shops, often selling antiques. Buildings rise two or three floors above the bluff. The lower floors were cotton and naval warehouses. Connecting bridges lead to upper-level offices opening onto Bay Street.

After refueling, climb the brick stairs up to Bay Street, exiting at the River Street Inn. You'll be at Old City Exchange Hill, site of the:

Savannah Cotton Exchange, which now houses the Solomon's Lodge Number 1 of the Free Masons. When it was built in 1887, it was the major center for cotton trading. An example of the Romantic Revival period, it became one of the first buildings in America to use "air rights" and was erected completely over a public street. Its wrought-iron railing honors famous writers and politicians.

🌐 **TAKE A BREAK**   **Wet Willie's,** 101 E. River St. (☎ 912/ 233-5650), which offers an array of frozen alcoholic beverages. Hamburgers, quesadillas, and chicken fingers are featured.

Continue to walk down the street, heading west until you reach:

5. **City Hall,** dating from 1905. The stone bench to the left commemorates the landing of Gen. James Oglethorpe, founder of Georgia, on February 12, 1733. The two floors of this building open onto the spot where, on May 22, 1819, the S.S. *Savannah* set sail. It became the first steamship to cross the Atlantic.

Continue along Bay Street, going left onto Whitaker. Go down Whitaker until you reach Congress Street, then turn right, passing:

Walking Tour—Historic Savannah

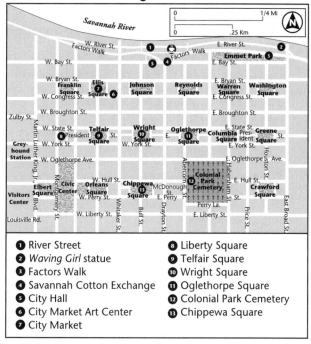

- **1** River Street
- **2** *Waving Girl* statue
- **3** Factors Walk
- **4** Savannah Cotton Exchange
- **5** City Hall
- **6** City Market Art Center
- **7** City Market
- **8** Liberty Square
- **9** Telfair Square
- **10** Wright Square
- **11** Oglethorpe Square
- **12** Colonial Park Cemetery
- **13** Chippewa Square

6. **City Market Art Center** on your right. This complex in a restored feed-and-seed warehouse houses the working studios of three dozen of Savannah's finest artists, including photographers, stained-glass designers, sculptors, painters, wood-carvers, and fiber artists.

Congress Street opens onto Ellis Square, site of the:

7. **City Market,** occupying 4 blocks in the Historic District. Renovated to capture the atmosphere of the past, it's filled with specialty shops, restaurants, bars, and open-air jazz clubs, along with many theme shops, particularly those selling crafts, accessories, and gifts.

When you reach the end of the City Market at Franklin Square, turn left onto Montgomery Street and walk down to:

8. **Liberty Square,** lying between York and State streets. It was laid out in May 1799 and named to honor the Sons of Liberty, who fought against the British during the Revolutionary War.

From Liberty Square, cut east along President Street to:

9. Telfair Square, between York and State streets. Originally it was called St. James's Square, but it was renamed for the Telfair family in 1883. Modern federal buildings are on two sides of the square, and it's also home to the **Telfair Mansion and Art Museum,** which was the site of the Royal Governor's residence from 1760 until the end of the Revolutionary War. Today it's a museum of the arts.

Continue east along President Street until you come to:

10. Wright Square, named for Sir James Wright, the third and last colonial governor of Georgia. A large boulder marks the grave of Tomochichi, the Yamacraw Indian chief who befriended Oglethorpe's colonists. A monument here honors William Washington Gordon I, early Georgia financier and founder of the Central Georgia Railway.

Going east from the square (still on President St.) takes you to:

11. Oglethorpe Square, between State and York streets. Mapped out in 1742, it, of course, honors Gen. James Oglethorpe, founder of Georgia.

From Oglethorpe Square, head south along Abercorn until you reach:

12. Colonial Park Cemetery, on your left, which was opened to burial from 1750 to 1850. It became the second public burial ground of Old Savannah, and many famous Georgians were buried here, including Button Gwinnett, a signer of the Declaration of Independence, and Edward Green Malbone, the famous miniature painter. You can wander the grounds from dawn to dusk, exploring the inscriptions on the old tombstones.

From the cemetery, go west this time along East McDonough Street until you reach:

13. Chippewa Square along Bull Street, between Perry and Hull streets. The bronze figure in the square immortalized General Oglethorpe and is by Daniel Chester French, dean of American sculptors. The square is visited today by hordes not wanting to see Georgia's founder but to sit on the bench where Tom Hanks sat in *Forrest Gump.* The movie bench isn't here, since it was only a prop, but plop yourself down somewhere on the square anyway and have a few minutes of relaxation.

HISTORIC HOMES

Andrew Low House. 329 Abercorn St. ☎ **912/233-6854.** Admission $7 adults, $4.50 students and children 6–12, free for children 5 and under.

Mon–Wed and Fri–Sat 10:30am–4pm, Sun noon–4pm. Last tour 3:30pm. Closed major holidays.

After her marriage, Juliette Low (see above) lived in this house built in 1848, and it was here that she actually founded the Girl Scouts. She died here in 1927. The classic mid-19th-century house is of stucco over brick with elaborate ironwork, shuttered piazzas, carved woodwork, and crystal chandeliers. William Makepeace Thackeray visited here twice (the desk at which he worked is in one bedroom), and Robert E. Lee was entertained at a gala reception in the double parlors in 1870. It faces Lafayette Square.

✪ **Davenport House Museum.** 324 E. State St. (on Columbia Sq.). ☎ **912/236-8097.** Admission $6 adults, $3 children 6–18, free for children 5 and under. Mon–Sat 10am–4pm, Sun 1–4pm. Closed major holidays.

This is where seven determined women started the whole Savannah restoration movement in 1954. They raised $22,500, a tidy sum back then, and purchased the house, saving it from demolition and a future as a parking lot. They established the Historic Savannah Foundation, and the city was spared. Constructed between 1815 and 1820 by master builder Isaiah Davenport, this is one of the truly great Federal-style houses in this country, with delicate ironwork and a handsome elliptical stairway.

Green-Meldrim Home. 14 W. Macon St. (on Madison Sq.). ☎ **912/ 233-3845.** Admission $3 adults, $2 children and students. Tues and Thurs–Fri 10am–3:30pm, Sat 10am–1pm.

This impressive house was built for cotton merchant Charleston Green, but its moment in history came when it became the Savannah headquarters of Maj. Gen. William Tecumseh Sherman at the end of his 1864 March to the Sea. It was from this Gothic-style house that the general sent his now infamous (at least in Savannah) Christmas telegram to President Lincoln, offering him the city as a Christmas gift (see "Impressions", below). Now the Parish House for St. John's Episcopal Church, the building is open to the public. The former kitchen, servants' quarters, and stable are used as a rectory for the church.

Hamilton-Turner House & Ghost House. 330 Abercorn St. ☎ **912/ 233-4800.** Admission $5. Tours daily 10am–4:30pm.

Constructed by a former mayor of Savannah, this is the only Victorian house open to the public, and it's said to be haunted. Featured in *Midnight in the Garden of Good and Evil*, it was once described as "the finest furnished home in the South." *A Field Guide to American Houses*, published by Knopf, cites it as a prime example of the Second Empire style, popular in America from 1855 to 1885. The ground floor of the house, once a setting for countless cotillions, debuts, receptions, and weddings, is furnished with museum-quality antiques from the 17th and 18th centuries.

Juliette Gordon Low's Birthplace. 10 E. Oglethorpe Ave. ☎ **912/ 233-4501.** Admission $6 adults, $5 children 6–18, free for children under 6. Mon–Tues and Fri–Sat 10am–4pm, Sun 12:30–4:30pm. Closed some Sun in Dec–Jan and major holidays.

The founder of the Girl Scouts lived in this Regency-style house that's now maintained both as a memorial to her and as a National Program Center. The Victorian additions to the 1818–1821 house were made in 1886, just before Juliette Gordon married William Mackay Low.

Owen Thomas House Museum and Shop. 124 Abercorn St. ☎ **912/ 233-9743.** Admission $7 adults, $4 students, $2 children 6–12, free for children 5 and under. Tues–Sat 10am–5pm, Sun 2–5pm, Mon noon–5pm.

Famed as the place where Lafayette spent the night in 1825, this jewel box evokes the heyday of Savannah's golden age. It was designed in 1816 by English architect William Jay, who captured the grace of Georgian Bath in England's county of Avon and the splendor of Regency London. You can visit not only the bedchambers and kitchen but also the garden and the drawing and dining rooms where gilded entertainment once occurred. Lafayette addressed the people from a balcony on the side of the building.

✪ **Telfair Mansion and Art Museum.** 1212 Bernard St. ☎ **912/ 232-1177.** Admission $6 adults, $2 students, $1 children 6–12, free for children 5 and under. Free admission Sun. Tues–Sat 10am–5pm, Sun 2–5pm, Mon noon–6pm.

The oldest public art museum in the South, housing a collection of both American and European paintings, was designed and built by William Jay in 1818. He was a young English architect noted for introducing the Regency style to America. The house was built for Alexander Telfair, son of Edward Telfair, the governor of Georgia. A sculpture gallery and rotunda were added in 1883, and Jefferson Davis, former president of the Confederacy, attended the formal opening in 1886. William Jay's period rooms have been restored, and the Octagon Room and Dining Room are particularly outstanding. A new celebrity and famous attraction at the museum is Bird Girl, the bronze funerary cover girl of *Midnight in the Garden of Good and Evil.* The statue was recently placed in the museum for safekeeping, where attendance has doubled since her arrival. Adapted from the original slave quarters and stable, the Carriage House Visitors' Center opened in 1995.

NEARBY FORTS

About 2¹/₂ miles east of the center of Savannah via Islands Expressway stands **Old Fort Jackson,** 1 Fort Jackson Rd. (☎ **912/232-3945**), Georgia's oldest standing fort, with a 9-foot-deep tidal moat around its brick walls. In 1775, an earthen battery was built on the future site of Fort Jackson. The original brick fort was begun in 1808 and was manned during the War of 1812. The fort was enlarged and strengthened between 1845 and 1860 and saw its greatest use as the headquarters for the Confederate river defenses during the Civil War. Sherman arrived to conquer it in 1864. Its arched rooms, designed to support the weight of heavy cannons mounted above, hold 13 exhibit areas. The fort is open daily from 9am to 5pm and charges $3 for adults and $2.50 for seniors and children 6 to 18 (children 5 and under are free).

Fort McAllister, Richmond Hill, 10 miles east of U.S. 17 (☎ **912/727-2339**), on the banks of the Great Ogeechee River, was a Confederate earthwork fortification. Constructed from 1861 to 1862, it withstood nearly 2 years of almost constant bombardment from the sea before it finally fell on December 13, 1864, in a bayonet charge that culminated General Sherman's infamous March to the Sea across Georgia. Sherman remarked that the taking of Fort McAllister was "the handsomest thing [he had] seen in this war." There's a visitors' center with historic exhibits and also walking trails and campsites. Hours are Monday to Saturday from 9am to 5pm and Sunday from 2 to 5:30pm. Admission is $2 for adults and $1 for children.

Fort Pulaski (☎ **912/786-5787**), a national monument, is 15 miles east of Savannah off U.S. 80 on Cockspur and McQueen islands at the mouth of the Savannah River. It cost $1 million and took 25 tons of brick and 18 years of toil to finish. Yet it was

---

Impressions

To His Excellency President Lincoln Washington, D.C. I beg to present you as a Christmas gift the city of Savannah, with one hundred and fifty heavy guns and plenty of ammunition, also about twenty-five thousand bales of cotton.

—Maj. Gen. William Tecumseh Sherman (December 22, 1864)

captured in just 30 hours by Union forces. Completed in 1847 with walls 7¹/₂ feet thick, the fort was taken by Georgia forces at the beginning of the war. However, on April 11, 1862, defense strategy changed worldwide when Union cannon, firing from more than a mile away on Tybee Island, overcame a masonry fortification. The effectiveness of rifled artillery (firing a bullet-shaped projectile with great accuracy at long range) was clearly demonstrated. The new Union weapon marked the end of the era of masonry fortifications. The fort was pentagonally shaped, with casemate galleries and drawbridges crossing the moat. You can still see shells from the 1862 battle embedded in the walls. There are exhibits of the fort's history in the visitors' center. The fort is open daily during summer from 9am to 7pm and during winter from 9am to 5pm (closed Dec 25). Admission is $2 for adults and free to those 16 and under, with a $4 maximum per car.

LITERARY LANDMARKS

Long before *Midnight in the Garden of Good and Evil* was written, there were other writers who were associated with Savannah.

Chief of these was **Flannery O'Connor** (1925–64), author of such novels as the 1952 *Wise Blood* and the 1960 *The Violent Bear It Away.* She was also known for her short stories, including the collection *A Good Man Is Hard to Find* (1955). She won the O. Henry Award three times for best short story, and her portraits of the South have earned her much acclaim. Between October and May, an association dedicated to her holds readings, films, and lectures about her and other Southern writers. You can visit the **Flannery O'Connor Childhood Home** at 207 E. Charlton St. (☎ **912/ 233-6014**). From June to August, the house is open only Saturday and Sunday from 1 to 4pm; the rest of the year, it's open Friday to Sunday from 1 to 4pm. Admission is free.

Conrad Aiken (1889–1973), the American poet, critic, writer, and Pulitzer Prize winner, was also born in Savannah. He lived at 228 and also at 230 E. Oglethorpe Ave. The first home helped launch the revitalization of Savannah's Historic District. No. 228 was Aiken's home for the first 11 years of his life. He lived at no. 230 for the last 11 years of his life. In *Midnight in the Garden of Good and Evil,* Mary Hardy and its author sipped martinis at Aiken's bench-shaped tombstone in Bonaventure Cemetery (see the box Martinis in the Cemetary," below).

Mercer House, 429 Bull St., is one of the most fabled and scandalous homes in town, though not open to the public. It's been

Downtown Savannah Attractions

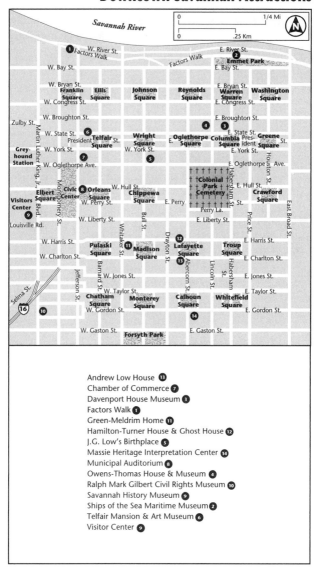

Andrew Low House ⑬
Chamber of Commerce ⑦
Davenport House Museum ③
Factors Walk ①
Green-Meldrim Home ⑪
Hamilton-Turner House & Ghost House ⑫
J.G. Low's Birthplace ⑤
Massie Heritage Interpretation Center ⑭
Municipal Auditorium ⑧
Owens-Thomas House & Museum ④
Ralph Mark Gilbert Civil Rights Museum ⑩
Savannah History Museum ⑨
Ships of the Sea Maritime Museum ②
Telfair Mansion & Art Museum ⑥
Visitor Center ⑨

called "the envy of Savannah," and thousands of visitors stop by to photograph it. For more details on the house and the events that took place in it, see the first walking tour in this chapter.

MUSEUMS

✪ **Savannah History Museum.** 303 Martin Luther King Jr. Blvd. ☎ **912/ 238-1779.** Admission $3 adults, $2 students and children. Daily 9am–5pm.

Housed in the restored train shed of the old Central of Georgia Railway station, behind the visitors' center at Liberty Street and Martin Luther King Jr. Boulevard, this museum is a good introduction to the city. In the theater, the Siege of Savannah is replayed. In addition to the theatrics, there's an exhibition hall displaying memorabilia from every era of Savannah's history.

Ships of the Sea Maritime Museum. 41 Martin Luther King Jr. Blvd. ☎ **912/232-1511.** Admission $5 adults, $4 children 7–12, free for children 6 and under. Tues–Sun 10am–5pm. Closed major holidays.

In a renovated waterfront building, this museum has intricately constructed models of seagoing vessels from Viking warships right up to today's nuclear-powered ships. In models ranging from the size of your fist to 8 feet in length, you can see such famous ships as the *Mayflower* and the S.S. *Savannah,* the first steamship to cross the Atlantic. There are more than 75 ships in the Ship-in-a-Bottle collection, most of them constructed by Peter Barlow, a retired British royal naval commander.

ESPECIALLY FOR KIDS

Massie Heritage Interpretation Center. 207 E. Gordon St. ☎ **912/ 651-7022.** Admission $2. Mon–Fri 9am–4pm.

Here's a stop in the Historic District for the kids. Geared to school-age children, the center features various exhibits about Savannah, including such subjects as the city's Greek, Roman, and Gothic architecture; the Victorian era; and the history of public education. Other exhibits include a period-costume work room and a 19th-century classroom, where children can experience a classroom environment from days gone by.

BLACK HISTORY SIGHTS

Savannah boasts the First African Baptist Church in North America. It's the **First African Baptist Church,** 23 Montgomery St. (☎ 912/233-6597), with sunday worship at 11:30am. It was established by George Leile, a slave whose master allowed him to preach to other slaves when they visited plantations along the Savannah

River. Leile was granted his freedom in 1777 and later raised some $1,500 to purchase the present church from a white congregation relocating to Chippewa Square. The black congregation rebuilt the church brick by brick, and it became the first brick building in Georgia to be owned by African Americans. The church also houses the oldest pipe organ in Georgia, dating from 1888. The pews on either side of the organ are the work of African slaves.

The **Ralph Mark Gilbert Civil Rights Museum,** 460 Martin Luther King Jr. Blvd. (☎ **912/231-8900**), close to the Savannah Visitors' Center, opened in 1996. It's dedicated to the life and service of African Americans and the civil rights movements in Savannah. The museum is a catalyst for educating the public on the rich heritage of African Americans here. Dr. Gilbert died in 1956 but was a leader in early efforts to gain educational, social, and political equality for blacks in Savannah. Hours are Monday to Saturday from 9am to 5pm. Admission is $4 for adults, $3 for seniors, and $2 for children and students.

6 Organized Tours

A delightful way to see Savannah is by horse-drawn carriage. An authentic antique carriage carries you over cobblestone streets as the coachman spins a tale of the town's history. The 1-hour tour ($17 adults, $8 children) covers 15 of the 20 squares. Reservations are required, so contact **Carriage Tours of Savannah** (☎ **912/236-6756**).

The **Old Town Trolley** (☎ **912/233-0083**) operates tours of the Historic District, with pickups at most downtown inns and hotels ($20 adults, $8 children under 12), as well as a 1-hour Haunted History tour detailing Savannah's ghostly past (and present). Call to reserve for all tours. Trolley tours are available every 30 minutes daily from 9am to 4:30pm.

Gray Line Savannah Tours (☎ **912/236-9604**) has joined forces with **Historic Savannah Foundation Tours** (☎ **912/234-TOUR**) to feature narrated bus tours ($18 adults, $7 children under 12) of museums, squares, parks, and homes. Reservations must be made for all tours, and most have starting points at the visitors' center and pickup points at various hotels and motels.

The **Negro Heritage Trail Tour,** 502 E. Harris St. (☎ **912/234-8000**), offers organized tours ($15 adults, $9 children) from an African-American perspective. The trail is sponsored by the King–Tinsdell Cottage Foundation. Tours start daily at 1 and 3pm.

Martinis in the Cemetery

All fans of *Midnight in the Garden of Good and Evil* must pay a visit to the now world-famous **Bonaventure Cemetery,** filled with obelisks and columns and dense shrubbery and moss-draped trees. Bonaventure is open daily from 8am to 5pm. You get there by taking Wheaton Street east out of downtown to Bonaventure Road. (You don't want to approach it by boat like Minerva, the "voodoo priestess," and John Berendt did—and certainly not anywhere near midnight.)

Regrettably, the statue of the little Bird Girl that appears on the cover of the book was removed for safekeeping and no longer graces the cemetery; however, you can see it in the Telfair Museum.

Savannah Riverboat Cruises are offered aboard the *Savannah River Queen* operated by River Street Riverboat Co., 9 E. River St. (☎ **800/786-6404** or 912/232-6404). You get a glimpse of Savannah the way Oglethorpe saw it back in 1733, as you sit back and listen to a narration of the river's history. You'll see the historic cotton warehouses lining River Street and the statue of the Waving Girl the way the huge modern freighters see it today as they arrive at Savannah's port daily. Lunch and bar service are available. Adults pay $14 and children under 12 are $9. Daily dinner cruises are available. Adults pay $35 and children $22.

Ghost Talk Ghost Walk takes you through colonial Savannah on a journey filled with stories and legends based on Margaret Debolt's *Savannah Spectres and Other Strange Tales.* Guides will unfold stories of hauntings, howlings, and habitations. If you're not a believer at the beginning of the tour, perhaps you will be at the end. The tour ($10 adults, $5 children under 12) begins at Reynolds Square. For information, call Jack Richards at **New Forest Studios,** 127 E. Congress St. (☎ **912/233-3896**). Hours for tour departures can vary.

Tours by BJ, departing from Madison Square (☎ **912/ 233-2335**), cover sights mentioned in *Midnight in the Garden of Good and Evil* every Sunday (call for reservations and times). The cost is $12.50 per person. You can also join a storyteller for a 90-minute "Spirited Stroll" daily, lasting 1^1/$_2$ hours and costing $12.50. That tour departs at twilight from Madison Square, and reservations are necessary.

Low Country River Excursions (☎ **912/898-9222**), a narrated nature cruise, is available at Bull River Marina, 8005 Old Tybee Rd. (Hwy. 80 East). You're taken on a 1993 38-foot pontoon boat, *Nature's Way*, for an encounter with the friendly bottlenose dolphin. Both scenery and wildlife unfold during the 90-minute cruise down the Bull River. Trips ($15 adults, $12 seniors, $10 children under 12) are possible daily at noon, 2pm, and 6pm during summer, weather permitting. September through October trips are available Monday to Thursday at 2 and 6pm, Friday and Saturday at 2, 4, and 6pm. There's a 30-passenger limit.

7 Outdoor Pursuits

A 10-minute drive across the river from downtown Savannah delivers you to the wild, even though you can see the city's industrial and port complexes in the background. The **Savannah National Wildlife Refuge,** which overflows into South Carolina, is a wide expanse of woodland and marsh, ideal for a scenic drive, a canoe ride, a picnic, and most definitely a look at a variety of animals.

From Savannah, get on U.S. 17A, crossing the Talmadge Bridge. It's about 8 miles to the intersection of Hwys. 17 and 17A, where you turn left in the direction of the airport. You'll see the refuge entrance, marked Laurel Hill Wildlife Drive, after going some 2 miles.

The refuge draws naturalists, botanists, canoeists, birders, and just plain visitors—it's like visiting a zoo without the cages. Inside the gate to the refuge is a visitors' center, distributing maps and leaflets.

Laurel Hill Wildlife Drive goes on for 4 miles or so. It's also possible to bike this trail. Mainly people come here to spy on the alligators; spottings are almost guaranteed. However, other creatures in the wild abound, including bald eagles and otters. Hikers can veer off the drive and go along Cistern Trail leading to Recess Island. As the trail is marked, there's little danger of getting lost.

Nearly 40 miles of dikes are open to birders and backpacking hikers, among others. Canoeists float along tidal creeks that are "fingers" of the Savannah River. Fishing and hunting are allowed in special conditions and in the right seasons. Deer and squirrel are commonplace. Rarer is the feral hog known along coastal Georgia and South Carolina. The refuge was the site of rice plantations in the 1800s.

Visits are possible daily sunrise to sunset. For more information, contact the Savannah National Wildlife Refuge, U.S. Fish & Wildlife Service, Savannah Coastal Refuges, P.O. Box 8487, Savannah, GA 31412 (☎ **912/652-4415**).

BIKING   Of course, it's always dangerous to ride bikes in any city, but Savannah doesn't usually have a lot of heavy traffic except during rush hours. Therefore, you can bicycle up and down the streets of the Historic District, visiting as many of the green squares as you wish. There's no greater city bicycle ride in all of the state of Georgia.

Bicycle Link, 22 W. Broughton St. (☎ **912/233-9401),** provides a map and tips on the city's most scenic routes with single-speed rentals costing $20 per day. It's open Monday to Saturday from 10am to 6pm.

DIVING   The **Diving Locker-Ski Chalet,** 74 W. Montgomery Cross Rd. (☎ **912/927-6604),** offers a wide selection of equipment and services for various water sports. Scuba classes cost $230 for a series of weekday evening lessons and $245 for a series of lessons that run from Friday evening to Sunday. A full scuba package, including buoyancy-control device, tank, and wet suit, goes for $13 to $27. It's open Monday to Friday from 10am to 6pm and Saturday from 10am to 5pm.

FISHING   **Amicks Deep Sea Fishing,** 6902 Sand Nettles Dr. (☎ **912/897-6759),** offers daily charters featuring a 41-foot 1993 custom-built boat. The rate is $75 per person and includes rod, reel, bait, and tackle. Bring your own lunch and beverages. Reservations are recommended, but if you show up 30 minutes before scheduled departure, there may be space available. Daily departures from Bull River Marina on Hwy. 80 are at 7am, with returns at 6pm.

Another possibility is **Bull River Marina,** Wilmington Island (☎ **912/897-7300).** Options include inland, near coastal, snapper banks, Gulf Stream, and deep-sea fishing, as well as sightseeing runs. Bull River offers half-day and full-day offshore charters costing $75 per person to $650 per group of six. Rates include rod, reel, and tackle, but you must supply your own food and beverages. Call for reservations and charter times.

GOLF   **Bacon Park,** 1 Shorty Cooper Drive (☎ **912/354-2625),** is a 27-hole course with greens fees costing $24 to $26 for an 18-hole round, cart fee included. Golf facilities include a lighted driving range, putting greens, and a pro shop. It's open daily year-round from dawn to dusk.

Henderson Golf Club, 1 Henderson Dr. (☎ **912/920-4653),** includes an 18-hole championship course, a lighted driving range, a PGA professional staff, and golf instruction and schools. The greens fees are $35 Monday to Friday and $40 Saturday and Sunday. It's open daily from 7:30am to 10pm. *Note:* Dress policy says no denim clothing.

Another option is the 9-hole **Mary Calder,** West Congress Street (☎ **912/238-7100**), where the greens fees are $9 per day Monday to Friday and $10 per day Saturday and Sunday. Carts rent for $4 for a 9-hole round. It's open daily from 7:30am to 7pm (until 5:30pm in winter).

IN-LINE SKATING   At the **Diving Locker-Ski Chalet** (see "Diving," above), 4-hour skate rentals cost $12 and full-day rentals are $20, with a Friday-to-Monday rental going for $35. All prices include protective gear except helmet.

JET SKIING   At the **Bull River Marina,** 8005 Old Tybee Rd., Hwy. 80 East (☎ **912/898-9222**), you can rent one-, two-, and three-seater jet skis. Prices, regardless of how many seats, rent for $30 per half an hour or $50 per hour. It's open daily from 9am to 6pm. Reservations are recommended. Jet skis are not provided.

JOGGING   "The most beautiful city to jog in"—that's how the president of the Savannah Striders Club characterizes Savannah, and he's correct. The historic avenues provide an exceptional setting for your run. The Convention and Visitors Bureau can provide you with a map outlining three of the Striders Club's routes: **Heart of Savannah YMCA Course,** 3.1 miles; **Symphony Race Course,** 5 miles; and **Children's Run Course,** 5 miles.

NATURE WATCHES   Explore the wetlands with **Palmetto Coast Charters,** Lazaretto Creek Marina, Tybee Island (☎ **912/786-5403**). Charters include trips to the Barrier Islands for shell collecting and watches for otter, mink, birds, and other wildlife. The captain is a naturalist and a professor, so he can answer your questions. Palmetto also features a dolphin watch usually conducted daily, when the shrimp boats come in with dolphins following behind. Times of the charters depend on the weather and the tides; you must call ahead for an appointment. A minimum of 2 hours is required, costing $100 for up to six people and $50 for each extra hour.

RECREATIONAL PARKS   **Bacon Park** (see "Golf," above, and "Tennis," below) includes 1,021 acres with archery, golf, tennis, and baseball fields. **Daffin Park,** 1500 E. Victory Dr. (☎ **912/351-3851**), features playgrounds, soccer, tennis, basketball, baseball, a pool, a lake pavilion, and picnic grounds. Both of these parks are open daily: May to September from 8am to 11pm and October to April from 8am to 10pm.

Located at Montgomery Cross Road and Sallie Mood Drive, **Lake Mayer Park** (☎ 912/652-6780) consists of 75 acres featuring a multitude of activities, such as public fishing and boating, lighted jogging and bicycle trails, and a playground. Open daily from 8am to 11pm.

The public school system operates **Oatland Island Education Center,** 1711 Sandtown Rd. (☎ 912/897-3773), set on 175 acres with a marsh walkway, observatories, compass trails, a marine monitoring station, and trails to 10 animal habitats. Admission is a minimum $2 donation per person. Open May to August and October to March, Monday to Friday from 8:30am to 5pm and every Saturday year-round from 10am to 5pm.

SAILING   Sail Harbor, 618 Wilmington Island Rd. (☎ 912/897-2896), features the *Precision 21* boat, costing $100 per half a day and $140 to $500 per day, with an extra day costing $100 to $240. A Saturday and Sunday outing goes for $240 to $1,000. It's open Tuesday to Saturday from 10am to 6pm and Sunday from 1 to 5pm.

TENNIS   Bacon Park (see "Golf," above; ☎ 912/351-3850) offers 16 lighted courts with operating hours of Monday to Thursday from 9am to 9:30pm, Friday from 9am to 4:30pm, and Saturday from 9am to 1pm. **Forsyth Park,** at Drayton and Gaston streets (☎ 912/351-3852), has four courts that are open Monday to Thursday from 9am to 9pm, Friday from 9am to 4pm, and summer Saturdays and Sundays from 9am to 2pm. Both parks charge $1.75 per hour during the day and $2.25 per hour after 5pm. The use of the eight lighted courts at **Lake Mayer Park,** at Montgomery Cross Road (see "Recreational Parks," above), costs nothing. Courts are open daily from 8am to 11pm.

8 Shopping

River Street is a shopper's delight, with some 9 blocks (including Riverfront Plaza) of interesting shops, offering everything from crafts to clothing to souvenirs. The **City Market,** between Ellis and Franklin squares on West St. Julian Street, has art galleries, boutiques, and sidewalk cafes along with a horse-and-carriage ride. Bookstores, boutiques, and antiques shops are located between Wright Square and Forsyth Park.

Oglethorpe Mall, at 7804 Abercorn St., has more than 100 specialty shops and four major department stores, as well as restaurants and fast-food outlets. The **Savannah Mall,** 14045 Abercorn St., is Savannah's newest shopping center, offering two floors of shopping. Included on the premises is a food court with its own carousel. The anchor stores include J. B. White, Montgomery Ward, Parisian, and Belk. In general, stores are open 10am to 9pm Monday through Saturday, and 10am to 5pm Sunday.

Thirty manufacturer-owned factory-direct stores offer savings up to 70% at the **Savannah Festival Factory Stores,** Abercorn Street at I-95 (☎ **912/925-3089**). Shops feature national brand names of shoes, luggage, gifts, cosmetics, household items, toys, and clothing, including T-Shirts Plus and the Duckhead Outlet.

ANTIQUES

Alex Raskin Antiques. 441 Bull St. (in the Noble Hardee Mansion), Monterey Sq. ☎ **912/232-8205.**

This shop offers a wide array of antiques of varying ages. The selection includes everything from accessories to furniture, rugs, and paintings.

J. D. Weed & Co. 102 W. Victory Dr. ☎ **912/234-8540.**

This shop prides itself on providing "that wonderful treasure that combines history and personal satisfaction with rarity and value." If you're looking for a particular item, just let the staff know and they'll try to find it for you. There's another outlet at 137 Bull St. (☎ **912/233-0997**).

Memory Lane. 230 W. Bay St. ☎ **912/232-0975.**

More than 8,000 square feet of collectibles can be found here. The specialty of the house is a collection of German sleds and wagons. You'll also find glassware, furniture, and pottery. Closed Wednesday.

V. & J. Duncan. 12 E. Taylor St. ☎ **912/232-0338.**

Small-scale, charming, and loaded with gentility and style, this shop contains the densest concentration of antique maps and engravings in Savannah, as well as a collection of semiantique, semischolarly tomes that are weighty enough for a law firm. Set at the northeast corner of Monterey Square, on the ground floor of a gracious private home, it's generous with facts, figures, information, and discreetly genteel information about local lore and scandal. Except for sales of **The Book,** which are brisk and highly commercial, some aspects of this place might remind you of a charming old-fashioned antiques store.

ART & SCULPTURE

Gallery 209. 209 E. River St. ☎ **912/236-4583.**

Housed in an 1820s cotton warehouse, this gallery displays two floors of original paintings by local artists, sculpture, woodworking, fiber art, gold and silver jewelry, enamels, photography, batiks, pottery, and stained glass. You'll also find a wide selection of limited-edition reproductions and note cards of local scenes.

Greek Festival. 143 Bull St. ☎ **912/234-8984.**

Many of the clients of this unusual store consider it a valuable resource for the creation of stage or movie sets, fashion displays, or dramatic living spaces. Co-owner Kelli Johnson acquires the molds for pieces of ancient Greek and Roman sculpture, baroque or Victorian wall brackets, carved animals, and fanciful coffee tables (everything from Chinese Foo dogs to giant tortoises bearing tufted cushions for use as coffee tables). The selection is delightful, and the fact that everything is cast in reinforced plaster or concrete makes the price a fraction of what it would've been if the objects had been carved individually. The store can arrange shipping to virtually anywhere, and if what you want isn't in stock, you can order from a voluminous catalog.

John Tucker Gallery. 5 W. Charlton St. ☎ **800/350-1401** or 912/231-8161.

This gallery offers museum-quality pieces by local artists as well as those from around the world, including Haitian and Mexican craftspeople. In a restored 1800s home, the gallery features 19th- and 20th-century landscapes, marine-art painting, portraits, folk art, and still lifes.

Morning Star Gallery. 8 E. Liberty St. ☎ **912/233-4307.**

This gallery features the works of more than 80 artists. Pieces include hand-thrown pottery, metalwork, paintings, prints, woodworks, jewelry, and glass (handblown and leaded).

Village Craftsmen. 223 W. River St. ☎ **912/236-7280.**

This collection of artisans offers a wide array of handmade crafts, including handblown glass, needlework, folk art, limited-edition prints, restored photographs, and hand-thrown pottery.

BOOKS

E. Shaver, Bookseller. 326 Bull St. ☎ **912/234-7257.**

Book aficionados will love this shop. Housed on the ground floor of a Greek Revival mansion, E. Shaver features 12 rooms of tomes. Specialties are architecture, decorative arts, regional history, and children's books, as well as 17th-, 18th-, and 19th-century maps.

CANDY & OTHER FOOD

River Street Sweets. 13 E. River St. ☎ **800/SWEETS-6** or 912/234-4608.

Begun more than 20 years ago as part of the River Street restoration project, this store offers a wide selection of candies, including pralines, fudge, and chocolates. Included among the specialties are more than 30 flavors of taffy made on a machine dating from the early 1900s. Top-quality ingredients go into this candy, with no preservatives, most of which is made on the premises.

Plantation Sweet Vidalia Onions. Route 2, Cobtown. ☎ **800/541-2272.**

On the way to Savannah, check out the Vidalia onion specialties offered by the Collins family for more than 50 years. Try one of the relishes, dressings, and gift items, as well as the world-famous sweet onions. Call for directions.

Savannah's Candy Kitchen. 225 E. River St. ☎ **800/242-7919** or 912/233-8411.

Chocolate-dipped Oreos, glazed pecans, pralines, and fudge are only a few of the delectables to be found at this confectionery. While enjoying one of the candies or ice creams, you can watch the taffy machine in action. Staff members are so sure that you'll be delighted with their offerings that they offer a full money-back guarantee if you're not satisfied.

CANDLES

Candlesticks. 117 E. River St. ☎ **912/231-9041.**

Kalten Bach owns this candle-making shop. You can watch a candle being made from beginning to end in about 15 minutes at demonstrations held throughout the day. All the personnel train for roughly 1 year before they can create their own pieces.

FASHION

Bottom Dollar Kidswear. 5 W. Broughton Rd. ☎ **912/233-4354.**

Specializing in clothes for children up to age 16, this store sells national name brands with discounts up to 50% off department store

---

A Flea Market

With more than 400 booths, **Keller's Flea Market,** 5901 Ogeechee Rd. (☎ 912/927-4848), is touted as "the largest flea market in the coastal empire." You'll see a 1920 Fairbanks and Morse diesel engine, antique farm equipment, a cane mill, and a syrup cooker. Included on the property is Janie Arkwright's Kitchen and Snack Bar, serving dishes like barbecue, popped pork pellets, corn dogs, and burgers. Open Saturday and Sunday only from 8am to 5:30pm.

---

prices. The selection includes more than 25,000 items for infants, girls, and boys.

Land & Sea Wear. 209 W. River St. ☎ **912/232-9829.**

Billed as "casual wear with a nautical flair," the inventory here covers everything you'll need for a day at sea. Offerings include T-shirts, souvenir sweatshirts, sportswear from PCH, and some of the hippest boating attire around.

Punch and Judy. 4511 Habersham St. ☎ **912/352-0906.**

Specializing in children's clothes since the mid-1940s, this store carries a large selection of brand-name clothing, in sizes for newborns up to preteen girls and to boys size 20. Other items offered are for the nursery, from furniture to accessories.

FURNITURE

Marco Polo Trading Company. 38 Bernard St. ☎ **912/234-4164.**

This shop prides itself on being the most eclectic store in downtown Savannah. The specialty is unique wooden furniture handpicked from around the world. The selection continues with an assortment of gifts and women's designer clothing.

GIFTS

Brass Crab. 205 E. River St. ☎ **912/233-3485.**

This shop is one of the oldest on River Street. The selection varies from magnolias and cookbooks to lamps, candles, scented lotions, and charms.

Checkered Moon. 422 Whitaker St. ☎ **912/233-5132.**

Located in the Historic District, this shop features more than 40 artists from throughout the Southeast. You'll find wall hangings, pottery, jewelry, clothing, furniture, and sculptures.

Graham on West Charlton. 17 W. Charlton St. ☎ **912/238-0094.**

You'll find an array of gifts and memorabilia in this shop. The selection includes unique garden items, quality jewelry and scarves, Bellamy Murphy artwork, photo images by John Gordon Anderson, and a variety of easy listening instrumental tapes. For children, there are porcelain dolls and educational CD Roms.

HAMMOCKS

Hammock Company. 20 Jefferson St. (at the City Market). ☎ **800/344-4264.**

Here you can learn about the history and tradition of the more than century-old world-famous Pawleys Island Rope Hammock. Other featured items are plantation rockers, Audubon guides, wind chimes, garden supplies, and a multitude of other nature gifts.

JEWELRY

Levy Jewelers. 4711 Waters Ave. ☎ **912/238-2125.**

Located downtown, this boutique deals mainly in antique jewelry. It offers a large selection of gold, silver, gems, and watches. Among its other offerings are crystal, china, and gift items.

SILVER

Simply Silver. 14-A Bishop's Court. ☎ **912/238-3652.**

The specialty here is sterling flatware, from today's designs to discontinued items from yesteryear. The inventory includes new and estate pieces along with a wide array of gift items.

WINES

Harvest Moon Down Home Gifts. 213 W. River St. ☎ **912/233-7487.**

This shop specializes in Georgia wines. The selection also includes wine condiments made of brass, copper, and pottery.

9 Savannah After Dark

River Street, along the Savannah River, is the major venue. Many night owls stroll the riverfront until they hear the sound of music they like, then they go inside.

In summer, concerts of jazz, big band, and Dixieland music fill downtown **Johnson Square** with lots of foot-tapping sounds that thrill both locals and visitors. Some of Savannah's finest musicians perform regularly on this historic site.

Take a Dinner Cruise

The *Savannah River Queen,* a replica of the boats that once operated on the Savannah River, is a 350-passenger vessel that departs from Savannah's River Street, behind City Hall; it's operated by *River Street Riverboat Co., 9 E. River St.* (☎ **912/232-6404**). It offers a 2-hour nightly cruise with a prime rib or fish dinner and live entertainment. Reservations are necessary. The fare is $33 for adults and $22 for children under 12. Departures are daily at 7pm, lasting to 9pm.

THE PERFORMING ARTS

The **Savannah Symphony Orchestra** has city-sponsored concerts in addition to its regular ticketed events. To spread a blanket in Forsyth Park and listen to the symphony perform beneath the stars or to be on River Street on July 4, when the group sends rousing strains echoing across the river, is to be transported.

The orchestra is one of two fully professional orchestras in the state of Georgia, and its regular nine-concert masterworks series is presented in the Savannah Civic Center's **Johnny Mercer Theater** at Orleans Square, which is also home to ballet, musicals, and Broadway shows. Call ☎ **800/537-7894** or 912/236-9536 to find out what's being presented when you visit. Tickets range from $17.50 to $48.50.

The **Savannah Theater,** Chippewa Square (☎ **912/233-7764**), presents contemporary plays, drama, and comedy. Tickets are usually $12 to $20 for regular admission and $9 to $17 for seniors and students.

September brings the 5-day **Savannah Jazz Festival,** with nationally known musicians appearing at various venues around the city. For more information, call the tourist office.

JAZZ CLUBS

✪ **Hannah's East.** 20 E. Broad St. (in the Pirates' House). ☎ **912/233-2225.** Cover $5 Fri–Sat after 9pm.

This club, the most popular in Savannah, is the showcase for jazz great Ben Tucker and also for Emma Kelly, "The Lady of 6,000 Songs," as Johnny Mercer called her. Of course, Emma was a character in *Midnight in the Garden of Good and Evil. Gourmet* magazine hailed the club as offering "the best music in the South." Emma holds forth Tuesday to Saturday from 6 to 9pm, and Ben Tucker and his friends entertain with toe-tapping classical jazz Friday and

Saturday. Ben has recorded with such stars as Duke Ellington. The club opens Tuesday to Saturday at 6pm, but closing times vary—11pm most nights but likely to be 3am on Friday and Saturday.

✪ **Planters Tavern.** 23 Abercorn St. (in the Olde Pink House). ☎ **912/232-4286.** No cover.

This is Savannah's most beloved tavern, graced with a sprawling and convivial bar area and a pair of symmetrically positioned fireplaces that cast a welcome glow over a decor of antique bricks and polished and darkened hardwoods. Because it's in the cellar of the Olde Pink House Restaurant (see "Dining," above), many folks ask for their platters of food to be served at a table in the tavern. Otherwise, you can sit, drink in hand, listening to the melodies emanating from the sadder-but-wiser pianist who warbles away the evening with remembered nostalgia. Foremost among the divas who perform is the endearingly elegant Gail Thurmond, one of Savannah's most legendary songstresses. The tavern is open nightly from 5:30pm to at least 11:30pm, though food service is likely to stop at 10:30pm.

The Zoo. 121 W. Congress St. ☎ **912/236-6266.** Cover $5, 21 and over; $10 under 21.

The Zoo is actually three clubs in one. The three dance floors offer Top 40, alternative bands, and acid rock. The 25-screen video wall is one of the largest in the Southeast. It's open Monday to Saturday from 9pm to 3am.

BARS & PUBS

Churchill's Pub. 9 Drayton St. ☎ **912/232-8501.** No cover.

If you like a cigar with your martini (the pub has a large selection), this is the place for you, 1 block south of Bay Street. It's Savannah's oldest bar, having been built in England in 1860. It was dismantled and shipped to Savannah in the 1920s and has been going strong ever since. On tap are such imported beers as John Courage, Guinness, Dry Blackthorn, and Bass Ale. You can also order pub grub like fish-and-chips, homemade bangers (English sausage), and shepherd's pie. It's open Monday to Saturday from 11:30am to 2am and Sunday from 5pm to 2am. Dinner is served until 10pm.

✪ **Crystal Beer Parlor.** 301 W. Jones St. ☎ **912/232-1153.** No cover.

This historic haunt west of Bull Street opened in the Depression days of 1933 and sold huge sandwiches for a dime. Prices have gone up since then, but local affection for this unpretentious place has diminished not one whit. You can order draft beer in a frosted mug, and owner Conrad Thomson still serves up fried oysters, shrimp salad sandwiches, crab stew, and chili (see "Dining," above). It's open Monday to Saturday from 11am to 9pm.

Kevin Barry's Irish Pub. 117 W. River St. ☎ **912/233-9626.** No cover.

The place to be on St. Patrick's Day, this waterfront pub rocks all year. Irish folk music will entertain you as you choose from a menu featuring such Irish fare as beef stew, shepherd's pie, and corned beef and cabbage. Seafood and sandwich platters are also sold. Many folks come here just to drink, often making a night of it in the convivial atmosphere. It's open Monday to Friday from 4pm to 3am and Saturday and Sunday from noon to 3am.

The Rail. 405 W. Congress St. ☎ **912/238-1311.** No cover.

Opened in 1995, this place isn't as aggressively noisy as Club One (below); but with an enviable grace and ease, it manages to be as sophisticated and welcoming of diverse lifestyles. Its name is an acknowledgment of the 19th-century day laborers who, for many decades, congregated near the site every morning in hopes of being hired that day by the foremen of the railway crews. Today, you can "work the rail" in much more comfort, positioning yourself in the brick-lined confines of a warm watering hole patronized by some of Savannah's most engaging writers, eccentrics, and artists. Tavern meisters Trina Marie Brown (from Los Angeles) and Melissa Swanson (from Connecticut) serve snacks (black-bean salsa, cold pistachio-pasta salad, pesto pizzas, and chili), but most people come just to drink and chat. It's open Monday to Saturday from 4pm to 3am.

Six Pence Pub. 245 Bull St. ☎ **912/233-3156.** No cover.

This is the most authentic-looking English pub in Savannah. You can drop in for a selection of pub grub (see "Dining," above). Drinks are discounted during happy hour Monday to Friday from 5 to 7pm. On Friday and Saturday live music is offered, ranging from beach music to contemporary to jazz. It's open Monday to Thursday from 11:30am to midnight, Friday and Saturday from 11:30am to 2am, and Sunday from 12:30 to 10pm.

Wet Willie's. 101 E. River St. ☎ **912/233-5650.** No cover.

There's a branch of this bar in Florida, but it can't be more popular than its Savannah cousin. The sign behind the bar suggests "Attitude Improvement," whereas another says they'll call a taxi when it's time to go home. Wet Willie's is like a Dairy Queen with liquor on tap. The specialty drinks are tasty and colorful—sorts of rum and sherbet in a glass. Among the ever-changing favorites are Bahama Mama, Blue Hawaiian, Jungle Juice, Monkey Shine, and Sex on the Beach. It's open Monday to Thursday from 11am to 1am, Friday and Saturday from 11am to 2am.

GAY & LESBIAN BARS

✪ **Club One.** 1 Jefferson St. ☎ **912/232-0200.** Cover (after 9:30pm only) $10 for those 18–20; $5 for those 21 and older.

It defines itself as the premier gay bar in a town that prides itself on a level of decadence that falls somewhere between that of New Orleans and Key West. But no one in Savannah pays much mind to facile definitions of sexuality, and so this is the hottest, hippest, and most amusing nightspot in town. You might meet a coterie of lesbians and gays from the coastal islands; visiting urbanites from Atlanta, New York, and Los Angeles (including such celebs as Demi Moore and Bruce Willis); and cast and crew members of whatever film is being shot in Savannah at the time. There's also likely to be a healthy dose of voyeuristic *Midnight* readers, including local suburbanites who come to see the stage where the Lady Chablis still occasionally reasserts her status as Savannah's top diva.

You pay your admission at the door, showing ID if the attendant asks for it. Then you wander through the street-level dance bar, trek down to the basement-level video bar for a change of (less noisy) venue, and (if your timing is right) climb one floor above street level for a view of the drag shows. There a bevy of artists lip-synch the hits of such oft-emulated stars as Tina Turner, Gladys Knight, and Marilyn Monroe. It's open Monday to Saturday from 5pm to 3am and Sunday from 5pm to 2am.

Faces. 17 Lincoln St. ☎ **912/233-3520.** No cover.

This place fulfills so many of the gay community's needs for a neighborhood bar that its regulars sometimes refer to it as the (gay) *Cheers* of Savannah. There's a pool table in back, plus a deliberately unstudied decor that includes battered ceiling beams, semirusted license plates, and an utter lack of concern about decorative fashion. Its provenance goes back to 1817, when the site originated as a tavern. If you detect that the dialogues here might be a bit more insightful than the norm, part of it might be due to the site's ownership by a licensed psychologist. It's open Monday to Sunday from 1pm to 3am.

10 A Side Trip to Tybee Island

For more than 150 years, **Tybee Island** has lured Savannahians who wanted to go swimming, sailing, fishing, and picnicking. Pronounced Tie-*bee,* an Euchee Indian word for "salt," the island offers 5 miles of unspoiled sandy beaches, just 14 miles east of Savannah. From Savannah, take Hwy. 80 until you reach the ocean.

The **Tybee Island Visitors' Center** (☎ 800/868-BEACH or 912/786-5444) provides complete information if you're planning to spend some time on the island, as opposed to making a day trip from Savannah.

If you're interested in daily or weekly rentals of a bedroom condo or beach house (one or two bedrooms), call ☎ **800/755-8562** or 912/786-8805, or write to **Tybee Beach Rentals,** P.O. Box 1440, Tybee Island, GA 31328.

Consisting of 5 square miles, Tybee was once called the "Playground of the Southeast," hosting millions of beach-loving visitors from across the country. In the 1880s, it was a popular dueling spot for the gentlemen of South Carolina. In the early part of the 1900s, Tybrisa Pavilion on the island's south end became one of the South's major summer entertainment pavilions. In its time it attracted some of the best-known bands, like Benny Goodman, Guy Lombardo, Tommy Dorsey, and Cab Callaway. It burned down in 1967 and was never rebuilt.

Over Tybee's salt marshes and sand dunes have flown the flags of pirates and Spaniards, the English and the French, and the Confederate States of America. A path on the island leads to a clear pasture where John Wesley, founder of the Methodist church in the colonies, knelt and declared his faith in the new land.

Fort Screven on the northern strip of the island began as a coastal artillery station and evolved into a training camp for countless troops in both world wars. You can still see remnants of the wartime installations all over Fort Screven.

Also in the area of this fort is the **Tybee Museum,** housed in what was one of the fort's batteries. On display is a collection of photographs, memorabilia, artwork, and dioramas depicting Tybee from the time the Native Americans inhabited the island through World War II. Across the street is the **Tybee Lighthouse,** built in 1742 and the third-oldest lighthouse in America. It's 154 feet high, and if you're fit, you can climb 178 steps to the top. From the panoramic deck you get a sense of "the length and breadth of the marshes," as captured in the Sidney Lanier poem, "The Marshes of Glynn."

For information about the museum and lighthouse, call ☎ **912/786-5801.** The museum and the lighthouse are open April to September, Wednesday to Saturday from 9am to 6pm; off-season, Monday and Wednesday to Sunday from 9am to 4pm. Admission is $4 for adults, $3 for seniors 62 and older, $3 for children 6 to 12, and free for children 5 and under. There are picnic tables at the lighthouse, and there's easy access to a beach.

The **Tybee Marine Center,** in the 14th Street parking lot (☎ **912/786-5917**), has aquariums with species indigenous to the coast of southern Georgia. Also on display are the usual cast of marina mammals, sharks, and other creatures. From April to October it's open Monday to Saturday from 9am to 4pm, Sunday from 1 to 4pm; hours from November to March are Monday to Friday from 9am to 4pm. Admission is free, but donations are accepted.

ACCOMMODATIONS

Fort Screven Inn Bed-and-Breakfast. 24 Van Horne St. (P.O. Box 2742), Tybee Island, GA 31328. ☎ **912/786-9255.** 3 units. A/C TV TEL. $95–$160 double. Rates include breakfast and a tour of the local museum. DISC, MC, V.

At the northernmost tip of the island, Fort Screven was built in 1897 as a bulwark against the hostilities that led to the Spanish-American War. When it was decommissioned in 1945, its cluster of officers' quarters, hospitals, and gun embankments were parceled off to homeowners, one of whom, Gary Smith, maintains his as a B&B, offering well-furnished bedrooms. Set in the southern annex of what used to be a hospital, the building has heart-of-pine floors, a large porch, and an atmosphere permeated with respect for the military traditions of both the North and the South. Many guests hail from Atlanta and share an interest in the nearby beaches with an avid devotion and respect for army and maritime history of the surrounding forts and military strongholds.

DINING

Crab Shack at Chimney Creek. 40 Estill Hammock Rd., Tybee Island. ☎ **912/786-9857.** Main courses $8–$13. MC, V. Mon–Thurs 11am–10pm, Fri–Sun 11am–11:30pm. SEAFOOD.

This place advertises itself as "where the elite eat in their bare feet." At least they're right about the bare feet part. Even if you're wearing shoes, the down-home cookery is likely to be good. Your lunch or dinner might've arrived just off the boat, having been swimming happily in the sea only an hour or so ago. Fat crab is naturally the specialty. It's most often preferred in cakes, or it can be blended with cheese and seasonings; boiled shrimp is another popular item. A Low Country boil (a medley of seafood) is a family favorite, and the jukebox brings back the 1950s.

MacElwee's Seafood Restaurant. 101 Lovell Ave. (off Hwy. 80), Tybee Island. ☎ **912/786-4259.** Main courses $7–$20. AE, DISC, MC, V. Mon–Fri 4–9pm, Sat 3–10:30pm. SEAFOOD.

This is the oldest and best seafood restaurant on Tybee Island with a casual atmosphere that makes it a family favorite. The restaurant is justifiably famous for its beer-batter shrimp, raw and steamed oysters, grilled chicken, and succulent steaks. The specials vary each week, including stuffed flounder cooked to order. The restaurant also has a full bar, take-out services, and a children's menu.

Index

HILTON HEAD